Gertrude Hoyt Memorial

BUSINESS PLANNING
for an uncertain future

Pergamon Titles of Related Interest

Dewar INDUSTRY VITALIZATION
Godet THE CRISIS IN FORECASTING AND THE EMERGENCE OF THE "PERSPECTIVE" APPROACH
Hussey CORPORATE PLANNING, Second Edition
Lundstedt/Colglazier MANAGING INNOVATION
Taylor/Hussey THE REALITIES OF PLANNING, Second Edition
Taylor/Redwood BRITISH PLANNING DATABOOK (special issue of Long Range Planning)

Related Journals*

LONG RANGE PLANNING
MANAGEMENT & MARKETING ABSTRACTS
OMEGA
SOCIO-ECONOMIC PLANNING SCIENCES

*Free specimen copies available upon request.

BUSINESS PLANNING
for an uncertain future
scenarios & strategies

Roy Amara • Andrew J. Lipinski
Institute for the Future

Pergamon Press
New York   Oxford   Toronto   Sydney   Paris   Frankfurt

79295

Pergamon Press Offices:

U.S.A.   Pergamon Press Inc., Maxwell House, Fairview Park,
                  Elmsford, New York 10523, U.S.A.

U.K.   Pergamon Press Ltd., Headington Hill Hall,
                  Oxford OX3 0BW, England

CANADA   Pergamon Press Canada Ltd., Suite 104, 150 Consumers Road,
                  Willowdale, Ontario M2J 1P9, Canada

AUSTRALIA   Pergamon Press (Aust.) Pty. Ltd., P.O. Box 544,
                  Potts Point, NSW 2011, Australia

FRANCE   Pergamon Press SARL, 24 rue des Ecoles,
                  75240 Paris, Cedex 05, France

FEDERAL REPUBLIC   Pergamon Press GmbH, Hammerweg 6,
OF GERMANY   D-6242 Kronberg-Taunus, Federal Republic of Germany

Copyright © 1983 Pergamon Press Inc.
Second printing, 1984.
Library of Congress Cataloging in Publication Data

Amara, Roy.

   Business planning for an uncertain future.

   Includes bibliographical references and index.
   1. Corporate planning. I. Lipinski, Andrew J.
II. Title
HD30.28.A42   1983   658.4′012   82-18136
ISBN 0-08-027545-1

Printed in the United States of America

To our families

CONTENTS

PREFACE

Unknowingly, collaboration on this book began about 20 years ago. In the early 1960s, while at SRI International, we were first introduced to the concepts of decision analysis by Ronald Howard of Stanford University. At the time, we were attracted by the explicitness and elegance of the analytical techniques for evaluating options and candidate strategies but troubled by the inadequate treatment of the external environment.

In the early 1970s, our collaboration continued at the Institute for the Future, focusing almost exclusively on the development and application of tools for characterizing alternative futures. The points of departure here were the forecasting methods (e.g., Delphi) developed by Olaf Helmer and Norman Dalkey at Rand. Gradually, the techniques for eliciting and aggregating group judgments were extended and tied more closely to the Bayesian statistical decision theory of Ronald Howard, Howard Raiffa, Ward Edwards, and others. In the late 1970s, a synthesis of approaches was begun by drawing together into a single planning framework the perspectives of a variety of actors — including both professional planners/analysts and operational decision makers.

Our intent is not simply to make another addition to the rapidly growing collection of publications on strategic planning, nor is our purpose to generate a comprehensive treatise on the methodology of planning or on organizational planning processes. Our primary objective is to describe and draw together — from a fresh perspective — three key elements of strategic business planning: the characterization of the external environment (uncontrollables); the generation of options or candidate strategies (controllables); and the evaluation of the interplay between environmental scenarios and candidate strategies (models). These three elements serve two important functions. They provide the methodological "handles" for our approach to business planning; and they serve as simple organizational indicators of the "state of planning" describable by the number of scenarios generated, the number of options evaluated, and the types of models used.

The continuum of planning stages extends from "little or no formal strategic planning" to "scenario-driven planning." Within this continuum, strategic management takes on new meaning: It is the continuing matching of planning to the operational needs of the enterprise. The "goodness" of match — and, therefore, a measure of the effectiveness of strategic management — depends critically on the degree of uncertainty in the external environment, the uniqueness of product or service niche, and the dominant management style.

The eleven chapters of the book may be viewed in three parts. The first three chapters lay the groundwork for our proposed planning framework. In chapters 4 through 8 the three key elements of our planning framework — scenarios, candidate strategies, and corporate models — are described in detail, and a number of examples are provided for the use and application of the tools introduced. Finally, chapters 9 through 11 address three softer but equally important aspects of strategic planning — value models, the politics of planning, and the changing nature of the management function. Summary descriptions of each chapter follow.

Chapter 1. Rationale for the Book. This book is about strategic planning in an uncertain environment. It extends the state of the art by providing the manager with new tools, approaches, and understanding for describing an uncertain environment, generating a broad range of candidate strategies, and evaluating the performance of such candidate strategies.

Chapter 2. Strategic Planning: Definitions and Examples. Starting from the simplest definition of planning — thought before action — a new and more useful definition of strategic planning is developed. Ten real-world examples are outlined that illustrate corporate strategies that have been developed or are being considered.

Chapter 3. Development of Our Strategic Planning Framework. A comprehensive framework for strategic planning is developed that defines the major stages of planning. Also provided is a descripton of how this framework is viewed by the principal corporate actors and planning practitioners.

Chapter 4. Scenarios — Shorthand Descriptions of the Future. A step-by-step process is described for generating internally consistent environmental scenarios and metascenarios from component sets of events and trends. Included are the simplest, static, tree-like scenarios as well as complex, dynamic scenarios generated by the use of structural models.

Chapter 5. Candidate Strategies. A candidate strategy is defined by a set of options and their timing. Described here are the processes for generating candidate strategies and the ways such strategies are structured from integrated sets of options affecting human, physical, and financial resources.

Chapter 6. The Corporate (Strategic) Model. The corporate model is the centerpiece of the strategic planning framework. Described are the main components of a corporate model, the way they are interrelated, and how they function.

Chapter 7. Using the Corporate Strategic Model. An operational description is provided for how a strategic model would be "flown" by an actual user. Included are the running of test programs and the description of a number of ways in which new candidate strategies may be generated and evaluated.

Chapter 8. Applications and Examples. Five examples are described that illustrate how the planning tools introduced have been applied in a variety of situations. The examples have been selected to cover the entire range of strategic planning stages from "little or no formal planning" to the full interplay of multiple scenarios and candidate strategies.

Chapter 9. Value Models. Almost everyone agrees that value models are key elements of any planning framework, yet very little guidance exists in the literature on how such models are constructed and when and how corporate objectives should be revised. Described are the processes for setting objectives, comparing them with consequences of simulation, and revising them when appropriate.

Chapter 10. The Politics of Planning. Planning is a complex amalgam of art and science. Scenarios, candidate strategies, and corporate models provide only one — and often not the most important — input to changing perceptions and behavior. Some practical implications for those who translate thoughts to action are identified and examined.

Chapter 11. The Future of Management: Ten Shapers of Management in the 1980s. The important economic, technological, and social forces shaping the management function in the next decade are identified. A key aspect of this transformation is the role of the manager as strategic planner.

ACKNOWLEDGMENTS

This book would not have been possible without the continuing support of the Institute for the Future. IFTF provided both the working environment and the resources for pursuing the substantive and methodological research that forms the basis of much of our work.

Many present and former IFTF staff members have contributed directly and indirectly to the ideas developed. Chief among them are Hubert Lipinski, Gregory Schmid, Michael Palmer, Olaf Helmer, and Paul Baran. Special thanks are due to Ellen Margaret Silva, designer/illustrator, for her patience and diligence in turning illegible chicken scrawls into useful figures and diagrams; and to Patricia Stern, who not only demonstrated incredible word processing skills in converting the original document to machine-readable form, but who also kept us on schedule, orchestrated the production of the manuscript, and helped us preserve some semblance of sanity as "book and work" priorities were smoothly balanced.

CHAPTER 1
RATIONALE FOR THE BOOK

BACKGROUND AND PURPOSE

The environment that corporations face today — and will face increasingly in the future — is markedly different from the past. The most important difference is the much higher levels of uncertainty at which they operate. Corporate managers are now confronted with a much wider variety of economic, social, regulatory, and competitive factors influencing performance. At the same time, the level of understanding of how these factors — singly and jointly — influence achievement of corporate objectives is not keeping pace with management needs.

To deal with distinctly more uncertain external environments, managers must consider broader ranges of choices for meeting corporate objectives. Choices based on historical experience or simple extrapolations, choices that are merely products of an obsolescent corporate culture, or choices that are designed primarily "not to rock the boat" are now almost certain to lead to difficulties. There must be an "opening up" of the choice generation process to mirror — or be responsive to — the sharp increase in the uncertainties of the operating environment.

But a more uncertain external environment and a wider range of choices are only the "what if" and "do what" prologues for the "so what" questions. The interplay of the external environment and corporate choices can now result in far more volatile performance outputs such as sales growth, profit, return on investment (ROI), and so forth.

Such dramatically changed circumstances — a more uncertain external environment, a wider range of candidate choices, and less stable performance — are redefining the whole concept of "what constitutes management" (Mintzberg 1973) and what constitutes strategic planning (Amara 1979). Management must quickly learn to deal effectively with soft (social, political) inputs over a broader range of circumstances where changes can occur more rapidly and unexpectedly than ever before. In these inherently riskier circumstances, strategic planning is no longer a luxury to be indulged only as time permits.

We wish we could make the claim that those who plan well strategically will always fare better than those who do not. We cannot, anymore than we can say that, for any given decision, the rational use of all available information will inevitably result in a desirable outcome. Just as good decisions can lead to poor outcomes, so too, because of the uncertainty of the future, good planning can lead to poor outcomes. *But* — and this is very important — statistically, we expect that good planning or good decisions will lead to favorable outcomes more often than will either poor or no planning, or poor decisions, or decisions reached by default. In a sense, this is the statement of faith on which all rational approaches to human affairs are based.

This book is about strategic planning in an uncertain environment. It addresses precisely those planning and management problems that have just been identified and that all corporate executives will continue to face in the future. The book unifies and extends the state of the art of strategic planning by providing the manager with new tools, approaches, and understanding for describing an uncertain environment, generating a broad range of candidate strategies, and evaluating the performance of such candidate strategies vis-à-vis a set of environmental scenarios.

A PLANNING FRAMEWORK

The simplest planning framework for thinking about these relationships is outlined in figure 1.1.

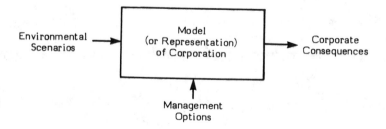

Fig. 1.1. Simplest Planning Framework

We can view this representation in at least two principal ways. One is to think of it (from left to right) in terms of three basic questions:

- What *if?* (scenarios)

- *Do* what? (options)

- *So* what? (consequences)

Another is to view the representation in reverse (from right to left) in terms of a companion set of equivalent questions:

- What do we *want?* (consequences)

- What can we *do?* (options)

- What do we *know?* (scenarios)

In either case, the basic representation is identical. For our present purposes, the framework needs to be expanded further. A more complete representation is found in figure 1.2.

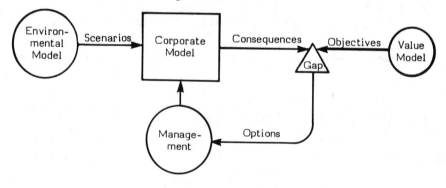

Fig. 1.2. Expanded Planning Framework

Several additions have been made. First, the external environment has been shown in two parts: an environmental model representing key trends and events in the form of environmental scenarios; and a value model representing the objectives of the principal corporate stakeholders (shareholders, employees, regulatory agencies, management, etc.). Second, a feedback loop has been included that emphasizes the iterative nature of the planning process. At each stage, consequences derived from the operation of the corporate model are compared with performance objectives. Based on the mismatches between such consequences and objectives, new options are generated by management and evaluated. In principle, this process continues until a satisfactory match is obtained and an input is then provided to management for actual resource allocation.

The last statement indicates that we have drawn only "half" of the planning framework. And indeed we have, describing only the thinking or analyzing half. In fact, the half we have described so far is the mirror image of the acting or implementing half that is normally considered the "real" (physical) world. Each element of our mirror image is, in fact, a representation of a corresponding element in the physical world where the correspondences are:

Acting/Implementing	Thinking/Analyzing
Environment ◄────────►	Environmental Model
Trends/Events ◄────────►	Scenarios
Corporation ◄────────►	Corporate Model
Decisions ◄────────►	Options
Results ◄────────►	Consequences
Goals ◄────────►	Objectives
Stakeholders ◄────────►	Value Model

The complete representation is shown in figure 1.3 together with a glossary of all terms used in table 1.1. For the moment, we will focus only on the top half, outlining the basic approaches to be developed in succeeding chapters.

"WHAT IF" ◄──► "SO WHAT"

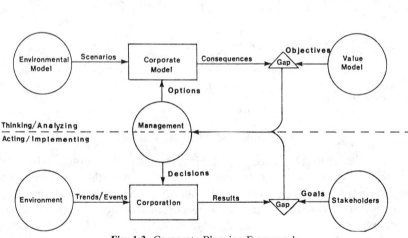

Fig. 1.3. Corporate Planning Framework

SCENARIOS

To outline the approach we will develop in this book, let's look more closely at different parts of the total system. A good place to begin is with the genera-

Table 1.1. Glossary of Terms

Candidate Strategy: An orchestrated set of options over time designed to achieve specified goals and objectives.

Consequence: Outcome of the evaluation of a particular option or candidate strategy.

Corporate Model: Representation of basic relationships among decision variables, key external factors, and performance measures (i.e., results) that are significant in managing a business.

Corporation: Human, physical, and financial assets to be managed for specified objectives and goals.

Decision: Allocation of resources.

Environment: External environment affecting performance of a business and including economic, demographic, labor force, regulatory, competitive, and technological factors.

Environmental Model: Representation of basic relationships governing interaction of key trends/events affecting an organization.

Goal: A measure of some point or milestone (along the way toward an objective) to be attained, typically but not always, in budgetary or financial terms.

Objective: An end or "destination" to be attained.

Option (or Choice):   Candidate decision to be evaluated.

Result: Outcome of a particular decision or strategy.

Scenario: Representation of an interconnected sequence of trends/events describing an internally consistent alternative future.

Stakeholders: All groups having a stake in an organization (or business) including owners, employees, customers, suppliers, lenders, management, government, the community, and society at large. As a stakeholder group, management is responsible for achieving results that satisfy the legitimate interests of each group.

Strategy: An orchestrated set of decisions over time designed to achieve specified goals and objectives.

Trends/Events: External developments or factors — usually but not always uncontrollable — affecting operating results.

Value Model: Representation of priorities, as well as time and risk preferences, of stakeholders of an organization in a form in which comparisons may be made to specified objectives.

tion of scenarios capturing the essential elements of the external environment, as shown in figure 1.4.

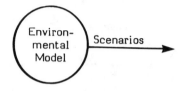

Fig. 1.4. Representation of External Environment

A relevant description of the external environment in which the corporation is likely to operate has become essential for two primary reasons. As already noted, the environment has become more complex and uncertain; and such an environment must become an increasingly major factor in forcing an "opening up" of candidate decisions and strategies a corporation must consider in order to thrive. The principal dimensions of the external corporate environment are:

- Economic/Resource, including macro indicators on the state of the economy and natural resource supply and demand factors;
- Consumer/Demographic, including changes in demographic characteristics, life-styles, and values affecting consumer demand and government at all levels as a consumer in its own right;
- Labor force/Work place, including developments affecting labor force characteristics and objectives;
- Regulatory/Political, including all factors affecting the government/private sector interface;
- Competitive/Institutional, including descriptors of organizational, market, and competitive developments and changes;
- Technology/Capital, including descriptors of technological advances and the climate for capital investment.

Each major dimension may be aggregated geographically into international, domestic, and even regional or state bases.

A key consideration in the description of the external environment is *selectivity*. Which external factors are most relevant or important to a corporation, and how do we shape the selection of factors in accordance with such judgments? In the broadest terms, we try to identify those factors that are most likely to influence achievement of corporate objectives or "goodness" (the success or failure) of corporate options. More specifically, the identification of such factors must be done by top management supplemented by inputs from outside the corporation to guard against "blinders" imposed by the internal corporate culture. And a number of direct and indirect methods for eliciting information for developing a profile of key external factors have been developed. These are based on management interviews that rely on "soft" as well as quantitative responses to structured sets of questions.

The identification of such factors is the starting point for the preparation of individual forecasts for each principal factor or variable. For time horizons of five to ten years or longer, the generation of such forecasts must necessarily rely heavily on judgmental inputs. Here, questions of the number and type of "experts" as well as the focus of elicitation and the methods for aggregation of individual judgments are key. Increasingly, quantitative methods using subjective probabilities are being used effectively to capture the full range of uncertainty in the perceptions of groups of knowledgeable individuals. The individual forecasts, in turn, provide a point of departure for structuring interrelationships among the key factors identified. Premodeling or structural modeling methods that may be used look for both qualitative and simple quantitative relationships. The most useful are either tree-like or matrix structures that can describe simple probabilistic and time-varying relationships.

The outputs of such structural models can lead directly to the generation of scenarios. Or, alternatively, scenarios may be generated by less direct means using the knowledge of intervariable relationships as a general guide. Usually, scenarios are chosen to span or bound a range of preassigned probabilities (such as from the lowest to the topmost decile), although often three scenarios may be used to provide "upper" and "lower" bounds around a "central" scenario. Scenarios normally include both quantitative and qualitative descriptions in a form that permits subsequent evaluation of corporate options. We shall return to this point shortly. In our planning framework representation, we may now expand the "environmental model" element in the fashion shown in figure 1.5.

OPTIONS

One of the most demanding aspects of a manager's job is the generation and evaluation of options prior to commitment to a particular course of action. Because of the closely intermingled nature of option generation and resource allocation, both "ends" of the management process need to be examined. Thus, in figure 1.6, although our primary interest is in the "option" half (above the dashed line), we need to look at the "decision" portion as well.

In a very real sense, management decision making is synonymous with resource allocation. Such corporate resources may be basically of three kinds: financial, physical, and human. Financial resources are derived from equity capital, debt instruments, or retained earnings. Physical resources include

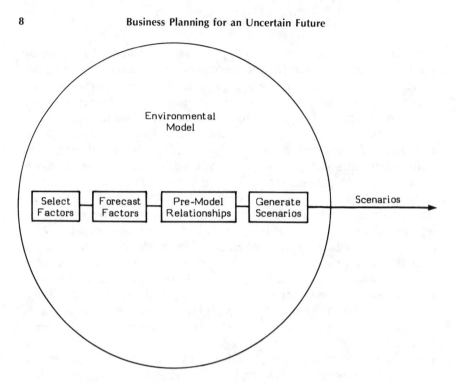

Fig. 1.5. Environmental Model

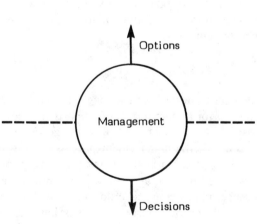

Fig. 1.6. Representation of the Management Function

all plant and equipment needed to carry out R&D, product/service design and development, and product/service production and marketing. Human resources are the pool of human talent and skills required to carry out corporate functions.

Management's major decisions are circumscribed by these three classes of resources; and such decisions are, of course, strongly interacting and overlapping. For example, management can raise capital through equity offerings, borrowings, or retained earnings by controlling debt/equity ratio and by determining what proportion of earnings to distribute as dividends to shareholders. It can choose the size and direction of its research and development effort, where to build a new plant, how large it should be, and what manufacturing processes should be used. It can determine the level and kind of marketing effort to be allocated on a product/service-by-product/service basis. It can decide who to hire, when to hire, who should manage what, and under what incentive structures; and *each combination* of specific decisions with respect to each major resource category — including acquiring or selling particular segments of a business — is precisely what we mean by resource allocation.

Normally, management explores and examines a very small part of the "option space" defined by the dimensions outlined above before decisions are made. Traditionally, the primary focus has been on *financial* and *physical* resource management — with far more emphasis on the former than the latter. The most elaborate corporate models are financial, followed by less elaborate models for planning and managing production resources. Corporate market forecasting and marketing models, and R&D planning models are somewhat less commonly used; it is fairly recently that initial attempts have been made to link the human resources area to corporatewide planning.

How, indeed, are corporate options normally generated by management? No simple answer can, of course, be given. In a majority of cases, the answer is by force of historical precedent or by *incrementalism* based on the experience of the last "learning period" and conditioned largely on a fairly simple-minded projection or extrapolation of that experience. In fact, operational incrementalism has long been recognized as a repeatable and effective approach to option or candidate strategy generation. The term "muddling through" (Lindblom 1959) was first introduced to describe the essentially "cut-and-try" small steps that are typically used by management in some form to feel one's way into a new direction. More recently, a more elaborate extension of this approach has been described (Quinn 1980) based on a study of strategic change in 10 major corporations. According to Quinn, "logical incrementalism" is a shorthand for an "artful blend of formal analysis, behavioral techniques and power politics to bring about cohesive step-by-step movement toward ends which initially are broadly conceived, but which are then constantly refined and reshaped as new information appears."

The likely runner-up position for generating options or candidate strategies is what some have referred to as the "key business value" (Peters 1980) and others have designated as the "driving force" (Tregoe and Zimmerman 1980, p. 39) approach. Some would claim that the process can hardly be termed "planning" at all. And they may be correct. In any event, through some undefined and intuitive or conceptual process — usually but not always linked to historical precedent — a dominant figure (usually the CEO) selects a "theme" on which corporate goals and objectives will focus. This may be "service" or "quality" or "productivity." In many instances, it is closely matched to what are perceived to be unique strengths for survival and growth of the organization or pivotal product/service characteristics on which consumers will make choices. In other instances, it may represent no more than an "intuitive leap" that proposes to set new directions.

Both "methods" for generating and evaluating options or candidate strategies share two common characteristics: heavy reliance is placed on "trial and error" in the real world to evaluate the "goodness" of a particular choice, and generation of options or candidate strategies and decision making become so closely intermingled that they become almost indistinguishable. In other words, it is through use of the lower (decision or tactical) feedback loop (Fig. 1.7) that the relative merits of options are determined.

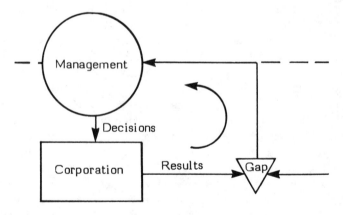

Fig. 1.7. Tactical Feedback Loop

Needless to say, when the external environment is changing rapidly or when major shifts in resource allocation approaches are required, both methods leave much to be desired. Not that incrementalism or "grand themes" should not be developed or used; they are simply not good enough when prior experience is less relevant in making judgments about options or candidate strategies or when time does not permit waiting for "results" to be available for monitoring.

What management needs to supplement its decision or "tactical" feedback loop is an option or "strategic" feedback loop. Management needs new and improved ways for evaluating options or candidate strategies such as those resulting from "logical incrementalism," an intuitive leap to a "grand theme," or generated by any other means. In short, management increasingly needs access to some means of simulating the future performance of a corporation that will permit it *both* to evaluate its options or candidate strategies and to stimulate generation of new ones. The outlines of such simulation means, using models of the corporation, will be described in the next section; here, we will dwell a bit on the general function of a corporate model vis-à-vis its option evaluation and generating capabilities.

A useful corporate model needs to be able to accommodate scenario inputs generated from an analysis of the external environment (as described earlier in this chapter). It also needs to reflect the dimensions of resource allocation choices outlined at the beginning of this section: financial, physical, and human. Each option may be characterized by "positions" of a series of knob settings (see chapter 3) representing each dimension of resource allocation. And, finally, it needs to be able to translate the interplay of scenarios and options or candidate strategies into specific consequences or measures of corporate performance.

With such a model of the corporation — even a very primitive one — we can easily visualize how it might be used for option or strategy evaluation and generation. The simplest and most direct method — and perhaps the most commonly used — for option or strategy generation is the use of *judgment,* individual or group. Generally, such methods rely heavily on formal aggregation of judgment. More importantly, such judgment may be applied to processes that do not reflect primarily strictly operational experiences.

The second method is to carry the process one step further: a plot is made of a composite output measure (see chapter 7) versus the positions of each knob setting defining each option being evaluated. The shape of this output surface may be used to suggest new options or candidate strategies that strike a better balance among the pattern of "knob settings" to achieve a desired output. In principle, such an approach attempts to *interpolate* from known to new options or candidate strategies.

The third continues the process one more step — that is, to construct a *metamodel* that describes the surface generated (composite outputs versus option or candidate strategy inputs for a particular scenario). This "supra" model can, in principle, be used directly to identify "better" options or candidate strategies in the space over which its outputs are considered valid.

In summary form, then, we have outlined the elements of an upper strategic loop for strategy generation in figure 1.8, and a strategic feedback loop in figure 1.9.

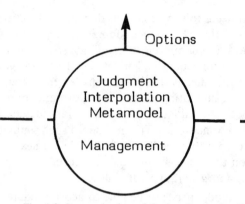

Fig. 1.8. Representation of Option Generation Process

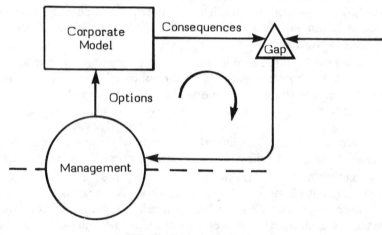

Fig. 1.9. Strategic Feedback Loop

CONSEQUENCES

The kernel of our planning framework is the interplay between scenarios and options. The problem is to evaluate the expected corporate performance of each option (that is, particular candidate allocations of financial, physical, and human resources) vis-à-vis each possible scenario. Assuming, for purposes of illustration, that we are working with three scenarios and three options, the representation may be similar to that found in figure 1.10.

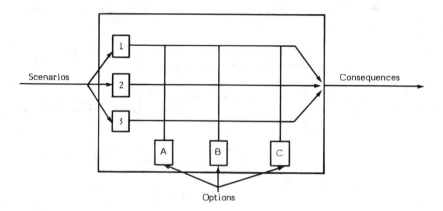

Fig. 1.10. Representation of Scenarios vs. Options

As previously noted, evaluations are in terms of impacts on specific (usually financial) measures of performance.

The most commonly used corporate models are financial models in which all inputs and outputs are basically expressed in financial terms. In such instances, scenarios of the external environment generally focus almost exclusively on economic factors (or factors that can be easily translated into financial terms), and options tend to focus on financial resources — control of capital budgets, borrowings, expenditures, and the like; and, of course, the output measures are also strictly financial — e.g., profits, sales growth, ROI. In recent years, financial models have become very sophisticated, the options available to the user have become considerably richer, and, in many instances, capabilities are being provided to deal with physical and even human resource choices.

In parallel with the development of financial models has been the evolution of judgmental models. As "mental models" that guide decision making of most corporate executives, they have, of course, been used from time immemorial. As explicit vehicles for aggregating group judgments, they are of more recent origin, particularly when such models focus on the impact of many of the noneconomic, softer variables in the external environment. And, of course, most often combinations of financial models and judgmental models are used to try to overcome the limitations of each.

At the third level of corporate model evolution, true corporate strategic models are developed that can deal explicitly and quantitatively with environmental variables and physical process (research and development, production, and marketing) variables, a range of options, and can formulate the interaction between such variables and options into impacts on both financial and nonfinancial measures of performance. Today, only a few corporations have approached this level of development.

In summary form, then, the principal ways for structuring corporate models are shown in figure 1.11.

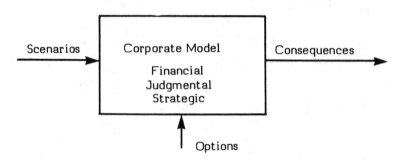

Fig. 1.11. Types of Corporate Models

ABOUT OUR APPROACH

We will now summarize — in terms of the corporate planning framework shown in figure 1.3 — the focus and approach of our book.

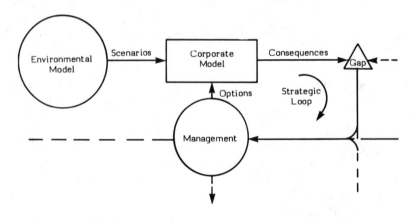

Fig. 1.12. Portion of Planning Framework on which this Book Focuses

The focus is on that portion of the total framework shown in figure 1.12. The kernel of the book is the "strategic" loop. A significant portion of the planning framework, which we are deliberately omitting from our primary purview, is the value model. This model deals with the translation of stakeholder interests into explicit representations — priorities as well as risk and time preferences — of corporate objectives. We will assume that such representations of objectives have been generated in a form suitable for making comparisons with the outputs (consequences) of the corporate model. An examination of some aspects of the "stakeholder-value model" representation will be given in chapter 9.

Our approach is different in three important ways:

First, we formulate a *comprehensive framework* for strategic planning that spans the simplest to the most complex processes and that integrates the viewpoints of the major practitioners into a single common process.

Second, we focus on *strategic management* for pivotal decisions rather than on the mechanics of budgeting, paper flows, or formal planning roles.

Third, we *simplify* by reducing planning to its essential elements without distorting the more complex processes that underlie these elements.

Comprehensive Framework

For too long, no comprehensive framework for planning has existed. The usual practice has been to allow each practitioner or each substantive discipline to define planning in its own terms. This piecemeal approach has made it difficult to visualize any coherent underlying or background process that knits the pieces together. It has encouraged "gimmickry" by suppressing the development of a unified picture of planning. And, worst of all, it has prevented useful communication of ideas across disciplinary boundaries.

Operationally, our proposed planning framework meets several basic requirements. First, the framework is heuristically attractive; that is, it seems "natural" or derivable from first principles. Second, the framework readily accommodates the enormous range of planning modes that may be used — from the simplest to the most complex. It portrays the major evolutionary levels of planning at the same time that it serves as a guide for the possible development of planning activities in an organization over time. Third, the framework is intended to stimulate further progress in developing more effective planning processes by encouraging rather than impeding communication among the principal practitioners — particularly communication that deals with critical judgments on the quality of the process. And, fourth, the framework is expandable and modifiable to include possible future changes in our perceptions of planning.

Methodologically, the proposed framework attempts to draw from four or five distinct activities that have on the whole grown up and existed in relative isolation from each other. The first is the considerable body of forecasting techniques that has been developed in the last 20 or 30 years. Of particular relevance are those tools that rely heavily on subjective judgments (as opposed to analysis of past trends) (Wheelwright and Makridakis 1980). The second is that part of probability theory and statistics that focuses on processes for extracting, quantifying, and aggregating individual and group judgment about uncertain quantities (Spetzler and Stael von Holstein 1975). The third major methodological component is option or strategy generation. Few areas related to planning and decision making have been as under-researched and unexplored. Most methodological guides are either silent on the subject or treat it every superficially. The most useful methods are basically heuristic search processes using constructs such as graphs, trees, and matrices, or using basically "cut-and-try" iterations (Royce 1979). The fourth major area — modeling (Naylor 1979) — serves as the coalescing element tying together the interplay of scenarios with options or candidate strategies for evaluation of consequences. And, finally, a fifth activity — the structuring of value models and the selection of objectives (or, more properly, value function specification and evaluation) — although not at the focus of our book, comprises still another critical element of our complete framework.

Strategic Management

Within our defined framework for planning, the focus of the book is directed to the most complex and richest part of that framework, namely, the interplay of scenarios and options or candidate strategies and scenarios. This is where the potential gains of strategic planning are greatest and the least exploited. These are also the levels at which strategic *planning* can become synonymous with strategic *management*.

Strategic management requires nothing short of total and sustained commitment to the process. It cannot be a tentative, part-time activity. It cannot deal primarily with the trappings of planning: budgeting, paper flows, mindless revisions of last year's forecasts. It cannot be a casual "on-off" effort dependent on the relative press of other activities. It is not a process for month-to-month or even year-to-year choices that are basically continuations of present strategies or that require only the most rudimentary attention. It can be undertaken only when it is viewed as *the* top priority of management involving major allocation of resources affecting corporate survival and setting long-term corporate directions.

To date, strategic management as defined has been practiced by only a few organizations. And yet, changing a corporate culture, developing new ventures, diversifying into new businesses, and developing new products cannot be the result of quick or easy choices. They inherently require the intensive involvement of the key individuals of an organization over a very long period of time. The making of such choices must also involve the "best" thinking tools and processes at our disposal. Such tools must include the capability, inter alia, to evaluate a rich menu of options or candidate strategies in the light of the most comprehensive picture of the changing external environment. Thus, by strategic management we mean the delicate orchestrating between "thinking" and "acting" using the tools that best match the unique requirements of each situation.

Simplification

All planning, except at the simplest levels, is fraught with an inherent flaw severely limiting its utility. The process can quickly become so complex and time consuming that only the most dedicated can be expected to have the stamina to stick with it. Furthermore, any benefits that flow from the process unfortunately often do not make themselves felt quickly. To overcome this problem, simplification is needed at all levels. Otherwise, the chances of the process "taking" or being accepted as credible and understandable are severely diminished. But, how can we simplify without emasculation or distortion?

The primary requirement is to select and focus on the truly important dimensions of the planning process as early as possible, especially in selecting external developments. To do this effectively, a strong linkage must be developed between the "so what" consequences (or output measures) and the "what if" external developments (or exogenous factors). The selection of the "what if" factors must be carefully screened for relevance, probability of occurrence, and importance vis-à-vis the output measures and the options being considered. Only those developments or factors that are clearly dominant should be included.

This selectivity, when applied intelligently and skillfully, will permeate the entire planning process. Fortunately, the analytical and processing tools for exercising selectivity are becoming more accessible and understood. These include qualitative methods relying heavily on subjective judgments elicited via structured interviews; quantitative methods using variants of pair-wise comparisons or multidimensional scaling; and interactive information systems that permit individualized trial-and-error sensitivity testing in the privacy of one's own office.

None of these techniques are, however, substitutes for the mental and analytical discipline needed to get quickly and directly to the most essential elements. Failure to do this will result in our drowning in a sea of detail and paper flows, clearly heading us in a direction worse than when we started. Unfortunately, the history of many planning efforts has followed precisely this course. Accordingly, one of our highest priorities here will be "simplification without distortion."

REFERENCES

Amara, R. C. 1979. Strategic planning in a changing corporate environment. *Long-Range Planning* 12: 2-16.

————. 1981. The futures field: Searching for definitions and boundaries. *The Futurist* XV, No. 1: 25-29.

Ansoff, H. I. 1977. The state of practice in planning systems. *Sloan Management Review* Winter: 1-24.

Braybooke, D., and Lindblom, C. E. 1963. *A strategy of decision.* New York: Free Press.

Henry, H. W. 1981. Then and now: A look at strategic planning systems. *Journal of Business Strategy* Winter: 64-69.

Hussey, D.E. 1974. *Corporate planning theory and practice.* Oxford: Pergamon Press.

Kerin, R. A., and Peterson, R.A. 1980. *Perspectives on strategic marketing management.* Boston: Allyn and Bacon.

Lindblom, C. E. 1959. The science of "muddling through." *Public Administration Review* Spring: 79-88.

Mintzberg, H. 1973. *The nature of managerial work.* New York: Harper and Row.

Naylor, T. H., ed. 1979. *Simulation models in corporate planning.* New York: Praeger.

O'Connor, R. 1976. *Corporate guides to long-range planning.* New York: The Conference Board.

Peters, T. J. 1980. Putting excellence into management. *Business Week* July 21: 196-205.

Quinn, J. B. 1980. Managing strategic change. *Sloan Management Review* Summer: 3-17.

Royce, W. S. 1979. *SRI Business Intelligence Program Research Report No. 620.* Menlo Park, CA: SRI International.

Spetzler, C. S., and Stael von Holstein, C. S. 1975. Probability encoding in decision analysis. *Management Science* 22, No. 3: 340-58.

Steiner, G. A. 1979. *Strategic planning: What every manager must know.* New York: Free Press.

Tregoe, B. B., and Zimmerman, J. W. 1980. *Top management strategy: What it is and how to make it work.* New York: Simon and Schuster.

Wheelwright, S. C., and Makridakis, S. 1980. *Forecasting methods for management.* New York: John Wiley.

CHAPTER 2
STRATEGIC PLANNING: DEFINITIONS AND EXAMPLES

DEFINITIONS

Planning is, simply, thought before action.

Understandably, planning has as many definitions as it has practitioners; a review of some of those definitions will provide a context for examining business strategic planning.

One of the best overall definitions of planning we know is the following from Donald Conover of Western Electric (Committee on Science and Technology 1976, p. 126): "The real planners are the managers who make the final decisions, and what we call planning is the support service intended to help make decisions better." The key message is the essential unity of thought *and* action, or planning *and* decision making. Even though thought precedes action, the interweaving should be so close that they become almost indistinguishable.

On a somewhat more philosophical level, it has often been noted that "the future and the past fight an endless battle of the present." Should thought before action be influenced primarily by the past or primarily by future expectations and possibilities that may be different from the past? Of course, the answer is "it depends." It depends to some extent on perceived rates of change; it depends to some extent on our willingness to take risk; and it depends to some extent on our "discount rate of the future" — that is, the

19

extent to which we are willing to trade future benefits/losses for present benefits/losses.

The role of intentionality in planning or "what we want to happen" is captured best by a definition from R. L. Ackoff (1970, p. 1): "Planning is the design of a desired future and of effective ways of bringing it about." Here the emphasis is clearly on the interventions that may be considered that are intended to increase the likelihood of achieving "a desired future."

Through the lens of intentionality let's try to examine in finer detail the "thought" component. Heuristically and as already noted in chapter 1, the three key questions any thinking must address are:

- What do we *want?*

- What can we *do?*

- What do we *know?*

The process of disaggregating the "thought" component may be usefully carried one more stage, expanding on the *iterative* sequence of questions presented above.

- What are our objectives?

- What principal factors and future changes may influence achieving these objectives?

- What choices do we have?

- How do we value these choices in light of the perceived consequences vis-à-vis our objectives?

Similarly, to round out the "action" component by an analogous set of questions:

- How do we best allocate our resources to achieve our goals?

- What do we monitor to improve the foregoing process by iteration?

These six questions will form the basis of a detailed heuristic look at the evolution of business planning in chapter 3.

Next, we would like to define two critical dimensions of planning that determine the dominant orientation of this text. Planning may be described along any number of distinguishing characteristics or dimensions: short-term versus long-term, quantitative versus qualitative, explicit versus implicit, centralized versus decentralized, and so forth (Steiner 1979, p. 12). Of these we consider two such dimensions as key.

The first dimension is the *number of individuals* involved in the process. In the simplest characterization we may picture this dimension extending from the *single* solitary decision maker at one end, to *multiple* (up to, say, 10 to 20) decision makers in the middle, and to purely *participatory* planning/decision-making modes at the other extreme. A variety of ways is normally used to describe positions along this scale: top down versus bottom up, centralized versus decentralized, hierarchical versus participatory.

The second dimension is the degree of *explicit rationality* employed in the process. At one end of this scale are purely quantitative, systematic, logical approaches; somewhere in the middle, processes akin to "logical incrementalism" (Quinn 1978) or "muddling-through" (Lindblom 1959); and, at the other extreme, purely qualitative, implicit, intuitive approaches to planning and decision making. Approximate descriptors that may be used to characterize different ends of this spectrum are "left" versus "right" brain, "hard" versus "soft," and even yin versus yang.

It is useful to portray these dimensions along orthogonal axes, both to illustrate a few "sample" points in the domain and to define the focus of this text. Figure 2.1 is a "map" of our planning domain, where the "top-down" versus "bottom-up" dimension is shown along the vertical axis and the "left" versus "right" brain dimension along the horizontal axis.

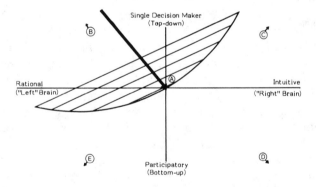

Fig. 2.1. Planning "Map"

The intersection of the axes, point A, represents multiple decision makers utilizing "logical incremental" or some happy combination of rational/intuitive planning processes. Similarly, point B represents the pure rational planner/decision maker; point C represents the pure intuitive planner/decision maker; point D represents intuitive group planning/decision making; and point E represents rational group planning/decision making. Other approaches may be placed at various other points in this two-dimensional space. The dominant view and approach of this text will be from the northwest quadrant, extending to the right of the vertical axis into domains of "enlarged rationality" and below the horizontal axis into domains of increasingly participatory planning processes.

Next, we would like to define and distinguish a subset of planning: *strategic planning*. In the past, the usual definitions have made such distinctions on the basis of the so-called tripartite model: strategic planning involves only top management levels of an organization, is long-term, and focuses primarily on external factors. Our definition is somewhat different and, we feel, more functionally related to the essential characteristics of strategic planning. Specifically, *strategic* planning (or thinking) is defined by the following characteristics:

- The contemplated actions involve the *integrated allocations of a significant portion of organizational resources;*

- The contemplated actions involve *large uncertainties* about possible outcomes;

- The contemplated actions *cannot be reversed,* except at great and increasing cost with time.

Even casual inspection of those defining characteristics reveals that strategies may also include decisions made at lower organizational levels, involving short-term outcomes, and focus on internal factors.

It is appealing to attempt to represent the "strategic" subset of planning along a third orthogonal dimension in the planning map of figure 2.1. This can be done only approximately in accordance with the level of resources that one can justify allocating to the "thought" (or planning) before "action." Clearly, such "thought" resources should bear some relationship to the "action" resources being allocated and should bear some relationship to the expected "benefits" (value-added or uncertainty reduced) that can be derived. A common-sense rule of thumb setting a lower bound is 1 percent of the resources to be allocated. A theoretical upper bound is set by the value of perfect information — that is, the worth of perfect information (no uncertainty) about the exogenous variables on which an outcome is dependent. Within this range, the planning or "thought" resource is clearly not a few persondays, but usually on the order of many person-months or even person-years. Decisions justifying only modest allocation of "thought" resources are thus excluded from our definition of "strategic planning."

EXAMPLES OF CORPORATE STRATEGIC CHOICES

Many examples of corporate strategic choices can be cited. We have selected 10 that illustrate different stages in the evolution or development of actual businesses or corporations in the early 1980s — from the most ambitious strategies involving drastic alterations of the internal culture of an organization (AT&T) at one extreme, to continuing the present commitment to a product (Polaroid, *Washington Post*) in the center, to possible liquidation of a business (Kaiser Steel) at the other extreme. In each example, the corporations involved are committing enormous resources, are faced with great uncertainties, and are making somewhat irreversible "one-shot" choices. Also, as will be described in detail in chapter 3, each candidate strategy actually represents a *set* of orchestrated choices, each choice dealing with a specific allocation of human, product, production, marketing, or financial resources.

Defining the Corporate Culture

Corporate culture is a shorthand for the sets of values instilled in employees and corporate practices that govern their internal and external behavior. Elusive as it may be to define precisely at times, it is the keystone in determining whether particular strategic choices will ultimately succeed or fail. Over and over, the lesson is being learned that corporate strategies must be compatible with corporate cultures.

A few examples will illustrate how pervasive and unique corporate cultures are: marketing and a service philosophy for IBM; financial discipline at ITT; entrepreneurship at ARCO; long-term loyalty at J.C. Penney; top-of-the-line engineering quality at Hewlett-Packard; and so forth. Purposefully altering corporate culture may be one of the most difficult and basic strategic choices a corporation makes in its lifetime. A case in point is the long-term effort by AT&T to change a dominant service orientation to one that places as much emphasis on marketing. Such changes are not easily made. At AT&T − and at other organizations involved with culture changes − changes are being made in organizational structure, in reward and punishment systems (or performance measures), and in the mindset that dictates response to a problem or an opportunity. For example, traditionally because costs for AT&T's services have been passed to customers easily through rate increases, establishment of lowest-priced services was never an overriding priority. However, in the increasingly competitive environment of the 1980s in which AT&T operates, far greater emphasis must be placed on marketing, competitive advantage, and costs. Thus, corporate managers must often decide the extent to which corporate cultures must be changed to be compatible with long-term growth or survival strategies.

Developing New Ventures

Among the most difficult strategic choices facing any corporation are those involving massive redeployment of its assets. For example, a number of major oil companies are today operating enormously profitable oil and gas businesses that have limited lifetimes − perhaps 15 to 20 years. This means that cash generated by such ventures must be fairly quickly and systematically applied to acquisition or development of new ventures that will be profitable in the future.

A major corporation that has been thrust in the 1980s into the role of finding new corporate investments for its "mountains of cash" is Standard Oil of Ohio (SOHIO). Unfortunately, few, if any, opportunities exist for further oil investments in the United States. Diversification must take place in other than conventional energy sources: synthetic fuels, coal, chemicals, nonfuel minerals, and even genetic engineering, semiconductors, and information processing equipment. The strategic options for SOHIO (and other oil companies) are complex, given the need to acquire and develop new management capability, to modify corporate culture to match its new ventures, and to steer skillfully through a maze of possible government reactions (for example, to synfuels production) because of majority ownership of SOHIO by British Petroleum.

Diversifying into New Businesses

Diversification choices can also occur less dramatically for reasons other than those requiring massive asset redeployment. They often result from more evolutionary changes stemming from the gradual decline of old businesses and the need to invest in the development of new businesses. Such shifts can be quite risky, particularly when the transaction proceeds from the firm ground on which a corporation enjoyed a commanding market share to new ground where no such advantage is necessarily guaranteed.

Du Pont is now involved in such a major calculated transition out of its familiar world of textiles and plastics into the less familiar world of biosciences. Its stated objective is to realize half its profits from its life sciences-related businesses by 1990, many times their present contribution. Massive infusions of capital investment and R&D spending are required to develop new capabilities and products in genetic engineering, drugs, and agricultural chemicals. This strategy represents a fairly sharp break with the recent past when Du Pont was struggling to save its ailing fibers businesses, with the resulting postponement of necessary investments to build new businesses.

Expanding into New Geographical Areas

Increasingly, businesses are preparing themselves to operate in world markets; and for many companies, such operation means more than exports, it means substantial capital investments for manufacture abroad. The most recent entries into multinational sales based on local production are Japanese companies.

In the past, overseas manufacture in host countries has been dominated by U.S. and European companies. In the next decade, the growth of overseas assets by Japanese companies is likely to make itself felt in many ways: manufacture of cars and trucks in the United States; joint ventures for producing jet engines in the United Kingdom; building of petrochemical companies in Saudi Arabia; joint ventures for the manufacture of refrigerator compressors in China; and so forth. In the decade of the 1980s, the United States is likely to become the biggest Japanese investment location in the world.

These developments represent a major strategic shift from export-led to investment-led growth. The implications are profound for the Japanese economy where investment will focus on knowledge-based industries and automation as well as for the world economy where heavier production will gravitate to the labor pools of the Third World.

Developing New Products

The development of new products (or services) that may represent either minor or major departures from current products is an ever-present set of strategic choices for virtually every corporation. And, naturally, the more radical the departure, the greater is the risk taken.

In the past decade, Intel Corporation has made two such major choices and is now on the verge of a third. The computer semiconductor memory chip was the first; and the microprocessor, or the computer on a chip, followed. Now, in the early 1980s, Intel has outlined plans for putting the equivalent of a mainframe computer on these chips at a fraction of the cost of a minicomputer. Equally important, Intel is planning to develop and market the software that will permit customers to use this computing power more cheaply and effectively in a wide variety of new applications. The implications of this kind of strategic option are staggering when it is recognized that Intel will be in toe-to-toe competition with the industry giants: IBM, Hewlett-Packard, Digital Equipment, and Texas Instruments.

Increasing Market Share

Market share has become the sine qua non of industry leadership. Increases in market share have almost always meant decreased units costs, while involuntary loss of market share has been equated to failure to meet competition.

Strategies for increasing market share are often built around marketing options, such as pricing, terms of sale, advertising, and so forth. An example illustrating the development of a new marketing strategy is provided by Bausch and Lomb on its soft contact lenses. Since the early 1970s, the market for such lenses was almost the exclusive domain of Bausch and Lomb until more aggressive competitors reduced that share from 100 percent to about 50 percent in the late 1970s. A turnaround strategy focusing on marketing initiatives was put in place in 1979. Aimed at reversing the downward trend in market share, its main features were: drastically cutting wholesale list prices on soft contact lenses, selling lenses on consignment, standardizing curvature of the lens, and embarking on a national TV advertising campaign. As a result, Bausch and Lomb's market share bounced back to 60 or 70 percent — at least temporarily.

Maintaining a One-Product Strategy

The decision to *not* diversify is as much a strategic choice as is one to do so. A number of companies have fared extremely well on a deliberate and calculated strategy to eschew other business opportunities to pursue a single-minded, one-product path.

An outstanding example of a very successful single-product company is Polaroid. For about 30 years, from the early 1950s to the present, Polaroid has dominated the instant camera market through sheer technical leadership. It not only chose to not diversify outside photography, but even avoided other business opportunities in its own industry.

Another example — equally successful in the past — is the decision (until the late 1970s) of *The Washington Post* to not enter new ventures of almost any kind. It decided in the early 1970s to *not* get into cable TV and even avoided creating a small chain of newspapers.

Increasingly, in both cases cited, the strategies have been put in place by strong-willed, dominant individuals (Edwin H. Land, Katherine Graham), and in both instances these one-product strategies have seemed to run their courses.

Turning a Company Around

Periodically, most organizations experience a gradual or abrupt decline in their operating effectiveness that requires making choices directly affecting their survival. These may stem from a changing external environment, from particular technological changes, or from complacent management.

By the early 1970s, the International Paper Company was netting only 2 percent in sales, barely enough to cover dividend payments. To stem this decline, the management put into place in the late 1970s a new, two-pronged strategy aimed at restoring its leadership in pulp and paper for the long run. The first prong was to make the necessary capital investments to become the lowest-cost producer; the second was to seek an increased yield from its timberlands by extending tree harvest cycles by 20-25 to 30-35 years. The implementation of this strategy has also involved massive organizational restructuring as well as a transformation of corporate culture. The real payoff for the new directions being set are expected to show up as impressive ROI in the next decade and beyond.

Phasing Out of a Declining Business

The term "cash cow" has become commonplace for describing the phaseout of a business to support the buildup of others. Portfolio management has raised this process to a fine art and science.

One of the most dramatic examples of such a phasing out is being implemented by B. F. Goodrich Company in the early 1980s as it attempts to switch its main business from tires to chemicals. The change is spurred by the long-time decline and lackluster quality of the tire business, coupled with the opportunity to exploit a product line — PVC — in which it has undisputed leadership. In almost all cases, such transformations are accompanied by great risk. In this instance, Goodrich is incurring very high debt and interest expenses on the input side to make the necessary capital investments in plastics. On the output side, the company is gambling on the stability of PVC prices for the long pull.

Liquidating a Business

Liquidating any business is always a painful process. No one wants to be identified with a failure, particularly when liquidation comes as the last choice in a long sequence of alternatives. Management of an organization facing the possibility of liquidation becomes a superhuman task.

In the late 1970s, Kaiser Steel Corporation attempted a turnaround strategy in the face of increasing foreign competition that resulted in several successive years of losses. Plagued by high labor and material costs, obsolescent equipment, and a poor location, the only other major option for staying alive is for Kaiser to limit its steel operations to those areas in which it does best — pipe and plate. Even so, the prospects of going out of business remain real, given the almost irreversible toll taken in the quality of management.

REFERENCES

Ackoff, R. L. 1970. *A concept of corporate planning.* New York: John Wiley.

Committee on Science and Technology, U.S. House of Representatives, 94th Congr., 2nd session. 1976. *Long-range planning.* Washington: U.S. Government Printing Office.

Egerton, H. C., and Brown, J. K. 1972. *Planning and the chief executive.* New York: The Conference Board.

Janis, I. L., and Mann, L. 1977. *Decision making.* New York: Free Press.

Lindblom, C. E. 1959. The science of "muddling through." *Public Administration Review* Spring: 79-88.

Linstone, H. A. 1981. *The multiple perspective concept.* Portland, Oregon: Futures Research Institute.

Paul, R. N., Donavan, N. B., and Taylor, J. W. 1978. The reality gap in strategic planning. *Harvard Business Review* May-June: 124-30.

Quinn, J. B. 1978. Strategic change: "Logical incrementalism." *Sloan Management Review* Fall: 7-21.

Sage, A. P. 1977. *Methodology for large-scale systems.* New York: McGraw-Hill.

Steiner, G. A. 1979. *Strategic planning: What every manager must know.* New York: Free Press.

CHAPTER 3
DEVELOPMENT OF
OUR STRATEGIC PLANNING
FRAMEWORK

In chapter 2, the "thought" and "action" phases of planning were broken out into a set of six component questions. We would like now to use these questions (see table 3.1) as a point of departure for developing in stages our strategic planning framework.

Table 3.1. Key Questions and Descriptors

	Question	Descriptors
	What are our objectives?	Objectives
"Thought"	What principal factors and changes may influence achieving these objectives?	Scenarios
	What choices do we have?	Options
	How do we value these choices in light of perceived consequences vis-à-vis our objectives?	Consequences
"Action"	How do we best allocate our resources?	Decisions
	What do we monitor to improve the process by iteration?	Results

Next, the activities described by the foregoing questions can be represented diagrammatically — exactly as they were shown in figure 1.3 of chapter 1.

Here, we will abstract and simplify that representation further as shown in figure 3.1, focusing primarily on the parts of the diagram in the solid lines.

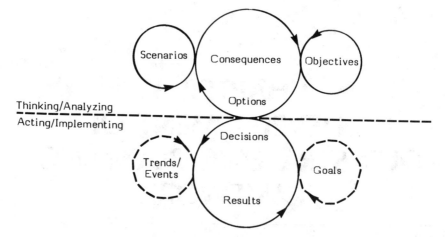

Fig. 3.1. Representation of Corporate Planning Framework

Several important features of the representation are emphasized. First, it represents a gross *simplification* of a very complex process. Second, the "thought" and "action" phases of the planning process are continuously *interweaved*. Third, the process is incremental and *iterative*.

It is also important to understand the different perspectives of the variety of actors who play dominant roles within the planning framework (see Fig. 3.2). For example, the chairman of the board normally views the *objective*-setting stage as key; the chief executive officer focuses first on the "what is the *decision*" (resource allocation) question; the chief operating officer is normally preoccupied with the monitoring of *results* of decisions that have been made; the natural starting point for strategic planners is the generation of candidate *options*; for decision or system analysts, it is the structure of a model for examining *consequences*; and for the futurist, it is the generation of *scenarios* (Amara 1981).

Each participant tends to view the basic process much as the early Bostonians' distorted view of the United States — the terrain is dominated largely by that portion with which each participant is most familiar. It is easy to see how such one-sided views can often contribute to enormous misunderstandings and communication problems among those involved in the process.

How can this fairly abstract cycle of six basic questions/activities be related to the pragmatic world of corporate decision making? A useful way to do this is to construct the complete process from the "ground up" in progressive stages.

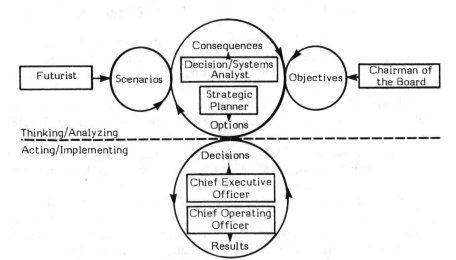

Fig. 3.2. Six Perspectives on Corporate Planning Framework

STAGE 0: LITTLE OR NO FORMAL STRATEGIC PLANNING

Not all action is preceded by thought — conscious or otherwise — nor should it be. In the most general sense, this category includes actions that have been preprogrammed from repetition or rote, or actions that stem from considerable prior experience that is still deemed to be a direct and useful guide to action. Diagrammatically, for our more limited purposes, this stage may be represented as shown in figure 3.3.

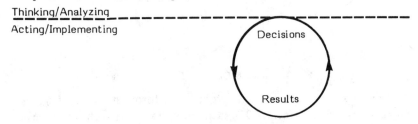

Fig. 3.3. Stage 0: Little or No Formal Strategic Planning

   The activity is entirely in the "action" domain. This is the most primitive "allocate-monitor" loop in which a very direct "hands-on" steering is done to achieve short-term tactical goals. It represents the ultimate in "seat-of-the-pants" management that can work reasonably well in a fairly stable or slowly changing environment. Decisions based on historical precedent or "muddling through" are perhaps the most common representatives of this mode of operation.

STAGE 1: OBJECTIVE-DRIVEN PLANNING

The conceptually simplest planning activity relies heavily on the linkage between powerful imagery and fairly direct (and often persistent) action. It is the most informal planning of all, and some would claim it is also the most effective.

Thomas Peters, a principal of McKinsey Company, has put it very succinctly: "The most effective executives give rather short shrift to (elaborate) planning. Instead, they spend much of their time on two other activities — first, playing with lofty ideas, searching for an enduring theme or metaphor to guide their businesses. And second, as they home in on the theme, they concentrate on mundane actions that will instill and reinforce their chosen metaphor in the furthest nooks and crannies of their organization." For Edward Carlson of United Airlines, the theme was close customer contact; for IBM, it was Thomas Watson's service theme; and for Thomas Clausen at the Bank of America, the focus was clearly on profits. In each instance, considerable evidence exists of the effective coupling of each image or metaphor to the "action" domain of each organization. (Peters and Waterman 1982.)

In terms of our developing framework, this level of planning is represented in figure 3.4.

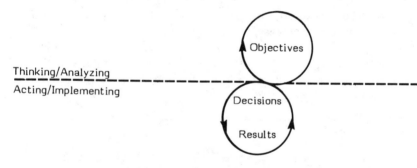

Fig. 3.4. Stage 1: Objective-Driven Planning

Corporate objectives can be stated in many forms at varying degrees of complexity (Hussey 1976, p. 103). Generally, however, such objectives can be divided into two broad classes: financial and nonfinancial. A generic representation of objectives and subobjectives is shown in figure 3.5. Those shown can, of course, be extended and disaggregated in considerably greater detail.

Considerable debate exists on whether or not corporations select objectives systematically (see chapter 9), whether the objectives selected are rational or nonrational, and whether corporations seek to satisfice (achieve satisfactory levels for) rather than optimize (achieve maximum levels for) their objectives. Whatever the case, it is interesting to note that objective-

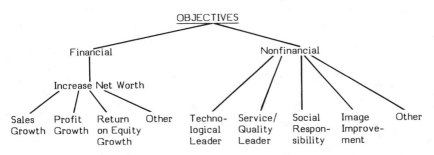

Fig. **3.5.** Generic Representation of Corporate Objectives

driven planning is as often concerned with achieving nonfinancial objectives as with financial goals, and that one of its distinctive features is the creation of a dominant and distinguishing corporate culture (Ouchi 1981, p. 225).

STAGE 2: FINANCIALLY-DRIVEN PLANNING

For most corporations, planning of any kind is synonymous with financial planning. This usually begins with a budgeting process tied to the statement of a set of predominantly financial objectives in terms of profitability or return on assets, equity, or invested capital. It represents the conceptually simplest planning mode that includes a formal feedback *evaluation* loop, as illustrated in figure 3.6.

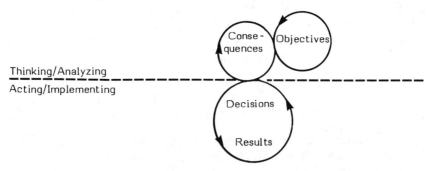

Fig. **3.6.** Stage 2: Financially-Driven Planning

Here, for the first time, appear the notions of trade-offs among particular objectives and an indication of how multiple financial targets might be balanced. At the top management level in a diversified corporation, the process may appear as some form of portfolio analysis (Allen 1978): matrices of company capability versus industry attractiveness dealing with "cash cows," "cash hogs," and so forth. Ordinarily, individual or group judgment informed by a simple financial model is used. Strategic options considered are very narrowly defined (ordinarily only financial), derivable directly from objectives, and are based on rather deterministic if not static views of the external environment.

STAGE 3: STRATEGY- (OR OPTION) DRIVEN PLANNING

The distinctive feature of option-driven planning is the richer range of strategic options provided to the decision maker. At this level, more elaborate corporate models are often used that may include corporate production and marketing functions as well as financial operations (Naylor 1979). On occasion, these may extend to R&D activities and even to human service or organizational characteristics of the corporation.

Options that may be orchestrated into candidate strategies by a corporation fall into three major categories: human, physical, and financial. A generic representation of elemental options is shown in figure 3.7. Most option-driven planning deals with physical and financial elements — product design, marketing choices, manufacturing or service delivery options, and methods of financing. In principle, each distinguishable corporate option may be visualized as specific choices along each of the 14 (or more) "control knobs" shown in figure 3.7. Any specific strategy — a sequence of options over time — may be directed at achieving an overall objective, such as "Redefining the Corporate Culture," "Developing New Ventures," "Diversifying into New Businesses," and so forth, as described in chapter 2.

In terms of our evolving planning framework, stage 3 planning may be simply illustrated as in figure 3.8.

In this instance, the iteration in the "thought" or "planning" domain may be far more extensive, deliberate, and formal before entry into the "action" domain for actual resource allocation.

STAGE 4: SCENARIO- (OR ENVIRONMENTALLY) DRIVEN PLANNING

At the most complex level of planning, the full array of external environmental factors are included: macrovariables such as GNP growth, inflation rate, and world oil price; basic demographic and labor force characteristics, particularly as affecting consumer behavior and human resource needs; descriptors of the regulatory climate; competitive variables such as competitors' strategies, and competitive pricing behavior; and indices of new technological developments and rates of technological diffusion. Since such factors or variables can never be forecast precisely, the treatment of uncertainty now becomes an explicit and pervasive feature of the planning process. A particular approach that has proved extremely useful is the use of multiple scenarios (Linneman and Kennell 1977).

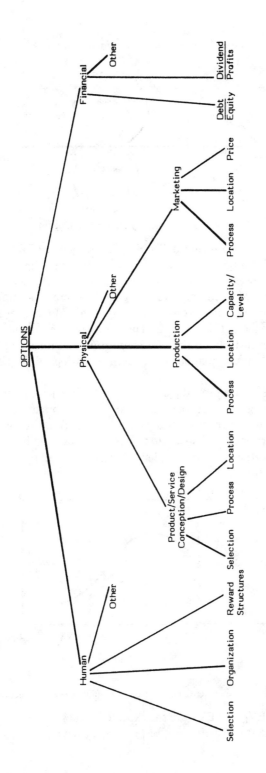

Fig. 3.7. General Representation of Corporate Options

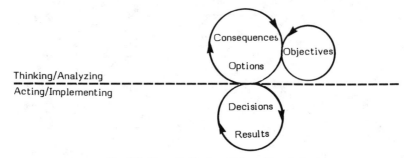

Fig. 3.8. Stage 3: Strategy-Driven Planning

In its simplest terms, a scenario is a plausible sequence of relevant events and trends to which a probability of occurrence may be assigned. Although for even the simplest environments the number of possible scenarios is very large, scenarios to be used for evaluating options must be pragmatically limited to less than five, and ordinarily no more than three or even two. As was noted in chapter 1, this places an enormous burden on the planner to focus attention exclusively on the *most important* variables and to employ methods of representation that portray as accurately as possible the perceived uncertainties.

Probabilistic trees have proved particularly useful in representing scenarios. The elements (or branches) of such trees may be either binary (occur or not) events, or trends with particular probability distributions at some point in time. Although probability distributions can be represented by such trees to any level of detail, the need for simplicity has encouraged the use of a two-valued representation as shown in figure 3.9.

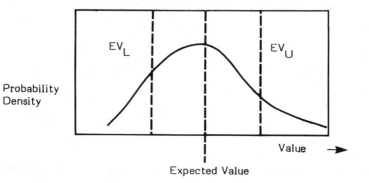

Fig. 3.9. Two-Valued Representation of Probability Density Function

The quantitites EV_L and EV_U are the expected values of the lower and upper portions of the full distribution, respectively, each with a probability of occurrence of 0.5.

Thus, for a tree structure of three variables, the first two of which are trends and the third the state of a binary event (S_0, S_1), we could represent a sequence as in figure 3.10.

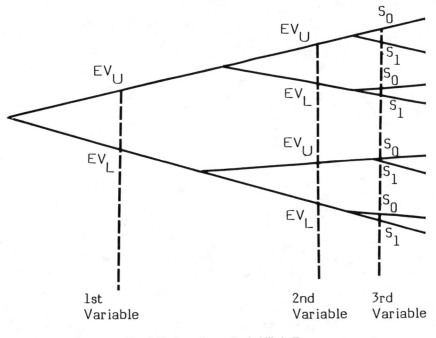

Fig. 3.10. Scenarios as Probabilistic Trees

Each branch is assigned a particular probability (0.5 for each trend variable), and in this instance the eight scenarios with their respective probabilities might be aggregated into a lesser number in accordance with, for example, the specific outcome of the trend variable. It is easy to see why pragmatically such trees seldom extend beyond four or five levels; the effort required to elicit credible values (conditional probabilities) grows geometrically with each level added. Again, the necessity to identify the *key* environmental variables or factors cannot be overemphasized.

Stage 4 planning adds the final element to our developing framework, so that it now appears in its most complete form in figure 3.11.

STAGE 5: STRATEGIC MANAGEMENT

The most advanced planning occurs when the full range of tools and approaches from all preceding stages is available to management. In such circumstances, a delicate balance can be achieved between the "thinking" and

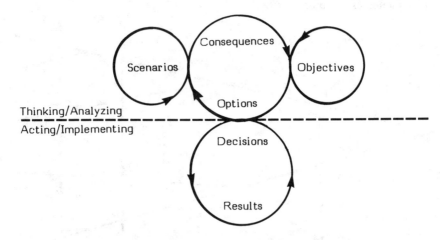

Fig. 3.11. Stage 4: Scenario-Driven Planning

"acting" components that matches the requirements of the situation. We refer to this stage as strategic management.

For the first time, the full range of environmental scenarios can now be played against a set of candidate strategies or options to compare consequences. Conventional financial models cannot be used for this purpose. Required are "extended financial models" or corporate strategic models that can handle the wide variety of environmental and decision variables that have been identified in stages 3 and 4. In some corporations, such models are being constructed by interconnecting models previously developed separately; in some instances, general-purpose modeling systems can be used.

Not all corporate decisions need the application and full power of the approach or tools of stage 5, but some clearly do; and it is this sensitive balancing and orchestrating among the appropriate stages that best describe the art and science of management. Several practitioners and students of management have described the essence of strategic management in different ways. Perhaps one of the best is the combining of rational and behavioral approaches to decision making (Quinn 1978). Some (Gluck et al. 1981) define strategic management in terms of a planning framework, a planning process, and a corporate values system. A key concept is the tight linking of "strategic thinking to operational decision making at all levels and across all functional lines of authority." Others have similarly stressed the basically iterative nature of both tactical decision making and strategic planning, including the need to monitor the external environment rather than trying to forecast it.

RECAPITULATION

We are now in a position to integrate the stages of planning defined in this chapter into our corporate planning framework, as shown figure 3.12.

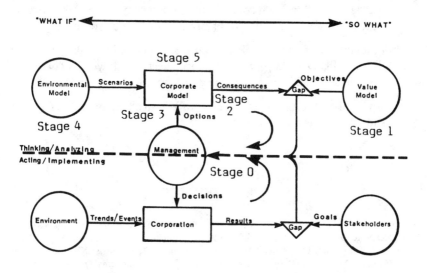

Fig. 3.12. Stages in Corporate Strategic Planning

A number of specific features of this framework should be noted:

1. The upper (analyzing) half of figure 3.12 includes the five principal stages of planning, stages 1 to 5; the lower (implementing) half includes the basically operational loop, stage 0.

2. From left to right, the upper framework reflects the three principal components of any planning framework: the probable (environment), the possible (options), and the preferable (values); or, alternatively, what do we know, what can we do, what do we prefer?

3. The management function is the centerpiece of the framework, straddling the line between the upper "strategic" and lower "tactical" half of the framework. This positioning graphically illustrates the essential unity and inseparability of tactical decision making and strategic planning.

4. The iterative nature of the basic planning processes is illustrated by lower tactical and upper strategic feedback loops, joined within the management function.

5. The principal flow between the upper and lower halves of this figure is information: options that inform decisions or resource allocations from top to bottom, results that monitor the outcomes of decisions previously made from bottom to top.

6. Symbolically, the upper strategic loop may be viewed as representing the "left brain" rational component of management while the lower tactical loop represents the "right brain" intuitive component.

7. Financially, the upper half of figure 3.12 generally deals with choices that are likely to impact the balance sheet, the lower half with decisions more likely to impact the profit-and-loss statement.

8. Any real decision-making situation will be an amalgam of the five stages shown and described earlier.

REFERENCES

Allen, M. G. 1978. Corporate strategy and the new environment. *Strategic leadership: The challenge to chairman*. London: McKinsey and Company.

Amara, R. 1981. The futures field: Which direction now? *The Futurist* XV, No. 3: 42-46.

Ansoff, H. I., Declerck, R. P., and Hayes, R. L., eds. 1976. *From strategic planning to strategic management*. London: John Wiley.

Banks, R., and Wheelwright, S. C. 1979. Operations vs. strategy: Trading tomorrow for today. *Harvard Business Review* May-June: 112-20.

Gluck, F. W., Kaufman, S. P., and Walleck, A. S. 1980. Strategic management for competitive advantage. *Harvard Business Review* July-August: 154-61.

Hussey, D. E. 1976. *Corporate planning theory and practice*. Oxford: Pergamon Press.

Linneman, R. E., and Kennell, J. D. 1977. Shirt-sleeve approach to long-range plans. *Harvard Business Review* March-April: 141-50.

Lorange, P., and Vancil, R. F. 1977. *Strategic planning systems*. Englewood Cliffs, NJ: Prentice-Hall.

Miser, H. 1980. Operations research and systems analysis. *Science* 209: 139-46.

Naylor, T. H., ed. 1979. *Simulation models in corporate planning*. New York: Praeger.

Ouchi, W. 1981. *Theory Z: How American business can meet the Japanese challenge*. Reading, MA: Addison-Wesley.

Peters, T.J., and Waterman, R.H. Jr. 1982. *In search of excellence*. New York: Harper and Row.

Quinn, J. B. 1978. Strategic change: "Logical incrementalism." *Sloan Management Review* Fall: 7-21.

Radford, K. J. 1980. *Strategic planning: An analytical approach*. Reston, VA: Reston Publishing Company.

CHAPTER 4
SCENARIOS – SHORTHAND
DESCRIPTIONS OF THE FUTURE

Scenarios can have many purposes. They can entertain, frighten, provoke reflection, or lead to action. Depending on the purpose that the scenario creator has in mind, scenarios are constructed using different techniques. We propose to concentrate on one kind only – *informative* scenarios; such scenarios try to organize available information about the future in an operationally useful manner.

We know that there is only one future. The trouble is, we do not know which. Out of the myriad of possible paths that the future could take, only *one* will be taken. If you happen to be a believer, then perhaps only the Supreme Being knows which particular scenario will occur. In decision analysis (Howard 1965), there is room for a parallel and useful, though less exalted, all-knowing personality – that of a clairvoyant who is assumed to possess perfect information. A clairvoyant knows what the future will be. But mortals like us see the future only through a darkened glass, a misty crystal ball. The real future is unknowable. Therefore, you may as well inquire, how can anything meaningful or operationally useful be said about the future? In response, let us suggest a conceptual parallel between an unknown future and an unexplored territory.

To recognize uncertainty, we will assert that the future is not one future, but rather a continuum of individual, rather improbable, future scenarios in which such future scenarios or "futures" reside side by side. The characteristics of the entire "territory" covered by the scenarios are more important than any individual, improbable scenario. It is as though someone

41

in the nineteenth century were trying to convey what Africa is like. He would tell you that, in Africa, there are mountains, deserts, and deep clefts, such as the Rift valley. Similarly, looking at the future of a country or a future corporate environment, we might encounter mountains and valleys where the individual scenarios differ in some important characteristics so that, instead of real mountains, the future may feature mountains of prosperity and valleys of depression. Seen from the viewpoint of a corporation, valleys of depression might represent instances in which a competitor has gained a commanding market share. This idea of the future as a territory is illustrated by the map in figure 4.1, where the present is a single point of known attributes; its height may indicate some convenient measure (i.e., current sales or profits). Because of increasing uncertainty, the paths diverge as we go into the future. Some paths will climb to high ground, others will continue on level ground, still others will descend into valleys that indicate economic depression. On such a map, if a large proportion of the paths were to climb, there would be a high probability of prosperous futures. If most were to descend, the corporation would be in for trouble.

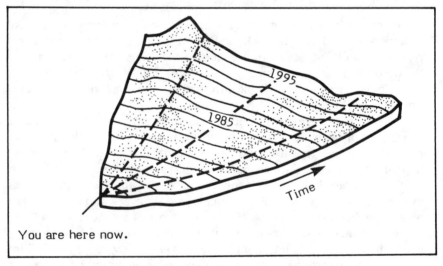

You are here now.

Fig. 4.1. A Map of the Future

The map in figure 4.1 will have hills and valleys, or just tilt to one side, if each individual scenario of small probability has been sorted according to some criterion. Otherwise, the map might look like a moonscape of sharp ridges and crevasses. For example, the scenarios can be sorted by the future price of oil. If a corporation sells recreational goods, high oil prices may result in lower disposable per capita income. Low disposable per capita income might then be the "low ground" in the territory. The individual scenarios can be reshuffled in any fashion, as long as the sum of their probabilities equates to one. That is, the horizontal dimension is always probability —

the probability domain of an entire lottery. Among them, whether sorted or not, the scenarios contain all the information about the future. The information content is unaffected by the reshuffling of the scenarios. It merely becomes easier to examine if the scenarios are ordered, either by a particular variable, or by a function of a variable, or by the joint utility — a measure of goodness — of several variables. The preferred measure will depend upon the character of the business and should be selected on the basis of what is "good" or "bad" for that business.

A real territory can be explored on foot, by camel, or by driving a jeep. But what are the means of exploring the future? Sometimes, but not very often, the exploration can be done by the use of a model. In most cases, it is done mentally. Models are used when two conditions are met: a small number of variables can capture the essence of reality well enough that we can safely ignore other variables *and* the relationships governing the interaction of the variables are well understood. Two examples illustrate how the use of models can produce useful results.

The operational problem of the artilleryman is to hit a distant target. The small world of importance to the artilleryman comprises gravity, wind velocity, atmospheric pressure, the size of the powder charge, the state of wear of the barrel, and the future position of the target. Most of these are known well enough so that the flight of the projectile can be modeled and computed. Even so, there will remain some residual uncertainty. If we think of the repeated shots that he might direct at the target as forecasting attempts, then some forecasts will miss the target (Fig. 4.2). The planning analog is to misestimate market size because some variables either cannot be computed or are very uncertain.

Fig. 4.2. The World of the Artilleryman

The other example is drawn from the world of celestial mechanics. Because of our excellent understanding of the motions of the planets and the action of gravity at a distance, and because only a few celestial bodies need be taken into account to describe the future position of the planets, the *Farmers Almanac* can tell us — with high accuracy — the time of sunrise over San Francisco on June 1, 1990. Whenever well-developed knowledge exists, when the underlying mechanisms are not too complex, and when there is little uncertainty about the interrelation between variables, models can provide useful results about the future. Unfortunately, such conditions are rare.

Usually we are interested in the workings of the economic system, the behavior of a competitor, the possible price of a key commodity — where our understanding of the basic phenomena is very poor. That is, we do not know which variables are key and which are not, and we often have only the haziest idea of the interrelations among variables. Often, we do not even know which model best represents the situation.

But the difference between forecasting the future of the physical environment and forecasting the future of the social environment is not simply due to the higher level of understanding of basic phenomena in the physical sciences vis-à-vis the social sciences. Man is not (yet) responsible for the vagaries of weather, but we cannot say much that is useful about the weather beyond a few days into the future. In modeling the social environment, the differences become insurmountable because of the human element. However, this is precisely what we face in trying to model the corporate environment: the future political climate, the behavior of regulatory agencies, and the actions of competitors are influenced by many individuals, each making his or her own essentially unpredictable choices.

In trying to forecast the future behavior of such "choice-rich" systems, the only useful alternative is to acknowledge the inherent uncertainty of the system by considering a number of possible scenarios. Preferably, these scenarios should span most of the relevant territory (or domain) of uncertainty, and there should be enough such scenarios to convey some idea of the profile or characteristics of the entire domain.

To restate our objective: The purpose of constructing informative scenarios is to capture the essence of the uncertainty about the future, i.e., the profile of the territory of the future, and to present that information in terms that will be operationally useful. Simply put, operationally useful information is information that we know how to use. We would like to use such informative scenarios to evaluate the consequences of the interaction between scenarios and a candidate strategy. So far, so good. The question we would like to examine now is how best to construct operationally useful scenarios. We will begin with the choice of structural components of a scenario and then examine the process of selecting the right elements.

STRUCTURAL COMPONENTS OF SCENARIOS

Scenarios may be composed of events and trends. An *event* consists of discrete states, rarely more than two. An example of a typical binary event would be a ruling by the Supreme Court for a corporation to divest part of its assets — the two states being a finding for or against a corporation. If the Court were likely to postpone a ruling, this alternative might be modeled by having a third state of the event — a delay. Then, next time around, there may again be a choice of a "yes" or "no" ruling, but this time with perhaps a negligibly small probability of a further postponement. Figure 4.3 shows how the one event and two time periods described above create four different scenarios.

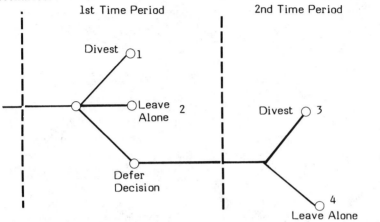

Fig. 4.3. One Event, Two Time Periods

A *trend*, on the other hand, is continuous rather than discrete. At any instant of time, not only two or three, but all intermediate states are theoretically possible. The annual rate of inflation or the annual growth of GNP for the next 10 years are examples of trends. Notice that no clear-cut division exists between the states of an event and the values of a trend. One can see that, as the number of states in the event increases, a multistate event gradually changes into a continuous variable.

The similarity between events and trends extends to their behavior over time. A sudden change in the state of an event can be described as a sudden discontinuity in an "event" trend: using the example already noted, a corporation is suddenly ordered to divest itself of its subsidiary (fig. 4.4). Because of this similarity, we should expect that events and trends will often be coupled (Mitchell, Tydeman, and Georgiades 1979, pp. 409-28). Thus, the Mount St. Helens explosion (a change of state of an event) corresponds to a sudden increase in pollution.

An event is fully described by a catalog of its possible states and the probability that it may assume any of these states at any given time. And, of course, the probability assignment may vary as time goes on. The instantaneous probability is the probability of a particular state occurring for the first time in any short time interval. Typically, it is very low for very short intervals. Each one of us can die today, but the odds against it are rather long. But the cumulative probability over time rises until it reaches some

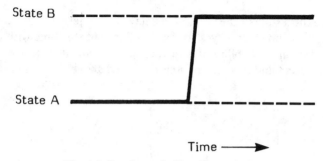

Fig. 4.4. Trend as a Sudden Change in State

specific value. Of course, in the case of death and taxes, it reaches unity: we will certainly die and the IRS will collect. There is often some confusion between cumulative probability over time and cumulative probability as a synonym for mass function (probability that a given value will be exceeded). As both are used in constructing scenarios, two examples may clarify the distinction.

Let us assume that cumulative probability over time describes the subjective judgment that a young woman will run a four-minute mile, ever. When she is a girl of ten, she might have already exhibited great potential, but odds makers may conclude that the odds are long against her ever becoming that fast. But, as she matures and keeps training hard and as her talent and achievements become obvious, the odds would shorten, and the cumulative probability would climb. It could be at a high value at an important time, like the time of the Olympic Games. If she does not make it then, the instantaneous probability will probably diminish. Thus, the instantaneous probability reaches a peak at the time of her first participation in the Olympic Games and then achieves a lower peak at her second participation. On the other hand, the cumulative probability over time, one that says that she could make it ever, in any event she participated in, rises even after the first Olympics and then settles down to some terminal value, less than unity (Fig. 4.5).

Cumulative probability or a mass function spans the range from zero to one. Its coordinates are probability and the value of a variable. There is no time dimension involved, although time may be the uncertain variable; for example, a mass function can describe the probability assignment that a new product will be late or very late. It is the probability of the value of an uncertain quantity being exceeded (the "right-tailed" mass function) or of the probability of the value being less than a particular value, in which case the function is called "left tailed" (Fig. 4.6). It describes the aggregation of probability over a range of possible values, hence the term cumulative. When differentiated, the left-tailed mass function becomes the probability density function. Most people are familiar with one particular probability density function, namely, the bell-shaped normal distribution (Fig. 4.7).

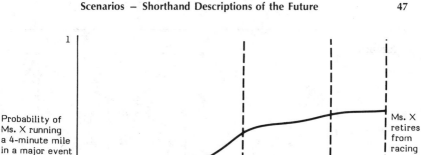

Fig. 4.5. Instantaneous and Cumulative Probability Over Time

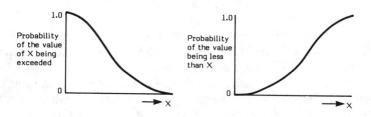

Fig. 4.6. Right- and Left-Tailed Mass Functions

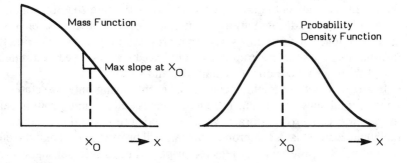

Fig. 4.7. Mass and Density Functions

To describe an uncertain trend, i.e., the behavior of an uncertain variable over time, we would need to employ several successive probability density functions spaced at time intervals, each one describing the probability distribution at a particular point of time (Fig. 4.8).

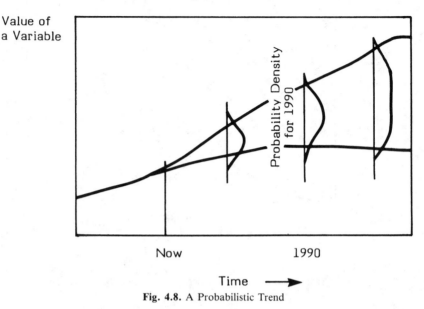

Fig. 4.8. A Probabilistic Trend

From the preceding, one can see that events are simpler to describe than continuous variables (because events have fewer states), and, consequently, that the probability that a state of an event would occur is a simpler concept than a sequence of probability densities. But the problem with using events as structural components of scenarios is that events, typically, are not very informative. This is because a brief description of the few states of an event leaves much unsaid. Referring again to the example of the explosion of Mount St. Helens, this particular event could have been given only two states: Mount St. Helens is quiescent (state A) or it has erupted (state B). But, unless we were to provide additional information in the form of other possible states, state B supplies no idea how severe that eruption may be. To provide that information, a less severe eruption should have been described as a state B_1, a slightly more severe one as a state B_2, and so on.

If we are lucky, we might encounter an event having only two states. An important bill may be pending in Congress that is quite unambiguous in defining a new excess profit tax rate. We also happen to know that there is (virtually) no chance that a compromise tax rate will be worked out, and therefore the bill will be either entirely rejected or passed in its original shape. Since we know the current rate of taxation and the rate of taxation that the bill proposes, the passage of the bill (a change in the state of an event) could be described as a sudden change in the value of the tax rate.

On further consideration of events that may be important to a corporation, we almost always encounter trends that are impacted by the new state of an event. The event itself, of course, creates the trend change, but it is the value of the trend that matters. Yet, in spite of the difficulties of interpreting the state of an event in operationally useful terms, early scenario builders were fond of event scenarios. The main reason was that, as we have seen in the example of figure 4.3, event-composed scenarios are easy to construct. But today, event scenarios are considered to serve the more useful purpose of exploring and challenging corporate flexibility and the speed of response to sudden developments. What if King Saud were assassinated tomorrow and what if the Soviet Union achieved control of the Strait of Hormuz in 1985?

Notice that the recipient of such a "what if" scenario would immediately try to translate the state of an event into a value of a trend or trends. He or she might translate the event scenario in the first example into the following equivalent trend: What if, as a *result* of King Saud's assassination, the price of crude oil rose to $50 a barrel and the U.S. inflation rate rose to 25 percent? In other words, he or she would have to enter the new state of the event into a model (which may be only a mental model) that would translate the event into a trend or trends. Then why not generate trend scenarios directly? This is not done because, as we have indicated already, probabilistic trend scenarios are more difficult to generate than probabilistic event scenarios. By probabilistic, we mean that the scenarios have a probability assigned to them. Using the image of the future as a territory, such scenarios would encompass a specified segment of that territory. Our next problem is to decide which events or trends should be selected to describe it.

SUBSTANTIVE COMPONENTS OF SCENARIOS

We will now devote considerable attention to the substantive content of scenarios. What factors should be included? In our experience, the options facing a particular business unit are usually affected by relatively few external variables. Yet, typically, corporations start environmental scanning by collecting mountains of information that managers never use because they do not know what to do with it. The focusing techniques we will describe are intended to help the manager identify key external developments and to evaluate their relative importance. We will describe two focusing approaches. The first approach is rather soft. It is intended to generate a ranked list of candidate components and, in addition, provide a soft measure of their relative importance. In the second approach, we use the resulting list of candidates and determine their relative importance quantitatively.

Ranking of Importance

To obtain the data from which the important scenario components will be drawn, we recommend that knowledgeable managers in a particular strategic unit (it could be a corporation as a whole or one of its strategic business units) be interviewed. To create a sufficient numerical base for analysis, about 20 interviews are needed. The purpose of the interviews is to establish the relative importance of key external factors needed for evaluating the consequences of options or candidate strategies. The method employed infers importance by measuring the frequency with which a particular development has been mentioned. That is, if a given development x is mentioned A times in all interviews and another development y is mentioned only B times, then development x ranks higher in importance. A somewhat weaker inference determines the relative importance of x and y by assuming that if x is mentioned n times more frequently than y, then x is n times more important than y.

The purpose of the interview design is to allow respondents an opportunity to identify any development they choose, in the belief that, if the development is important enough to them, it will arise in one context or another. To make the data from different interviews comparable, a common interview plan must be followed. Each interview consists of:

- The interrogation of the "clairvoyant,"

- A report on an unfavorable future environment,

- A report on a favorable future environment,

- The identification of pivotal decisions to be made,

- The identification of current management assumptions about the future environment.

The interviewer selects the time horizon for which questions will be posed. In each of the interview stages, the respondent plays a different role. First, the respondent questions an imaginary clairvoyant, then "reports" his or her perceptions of an unfavorable and favorable future environment, follows by identifying a few pivotal decisions on the horizon, and finally identifies some possible corporate "blind spots."

Interrogation of the clairvoyant. By definition, the clairvoyant "knows" the external environment of the corporation in the time frame of interest. Given the opportunity to question briefly such a clairvoyant, what information would the respondent seek? Of all the approaches used during the interview, the questioning of the clairvoyant is the most direct. What is important to the corporation?

Report on an unfavorable future. Asked to report on a future that has developed so badly for the corporation that there is only one chance in ten that it could have been even worse, the respondent first describes a gloomy future and later "reads" the What's News? captions from *The Wall Street Journal* written at the time (e.g., 1990) about the specifics of that future. We recommend that one caption include a fictitious character, say, a Mrs. Brown living in the town where the unit is located. The reason for including Mrs. Brown is to allow the respondent to describe, if he or she chooses to do so, important details of everyday life or life-styles possibly far removed from the typical concerns of the executive suite.

Report on a favorable future. This report is a mirror image of the unfavorable future. The future has developed so favorably for the corporation that in the respondent's mind there is only one chance in ten of its being even better. As before, the reading of *The Wall Street Journal* follows.

Identification of pivotal decisions. Each respondent is asked to identify one or two pivotal choices that the corporation as a whole or a particular SBU will have to make or should take the initiative in making in the next several years. For each such decision, the respondent must also identify how knowledge of future specific changes in the external environment would influence the choices to be made.

Challenging current management assumptions. Asked where a forecast of the future environment made by knowledgeable outsiders might differ from a similar forecast of the management team, the respondents seek to identify areas of corporate blindness, lack of sensitivity, or perhaps bias preventing an assimilation of important information.

Analysis. The interview notes are transcribed and sorted into initial categories, such as economy, technology, and competition. In each category, a preliminary list of more detailed developments is made (i.e., world economic growth is listed as a detailed development in the category of world economy). Then all "mentions" are assigned to the categories listed. The remaining "mentions" unassigned to any detailed development are used to develop a few new detailed developments that were not thought of at the beginning.

A simple count of the number of mentions results in a histogram. An example of such a histogram is shown in figure 4.9. Here, six variables form the first group in order of importance, followed by the continuously decreasing importance of the variables in the second group.

For most purposes, the identification of scenario components ought to stop right at the end of the first group. In the example we show, our recommendation would be to limit the scenarios to six components, ending with world energy prices.

To obtain a more quantitative measure of the relative importance of the scenario components (and thereby reduce the number of components even further), a pair-wise comparison method can be used.

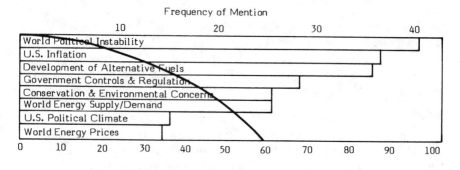

Fig. 4.9. The Histogram of Importance

Pair-Wise Comparison of Importance

The components identified as important (by the method just described or any other) are entered in a symmetrical matrix, similar to a cross-impact matrix (Fig. 4.10). In each cell, a judgment is entered about how much more important one development is than another (designating each column). A scale of 1 to 9 is used, 1 being equally important and 9 predominantly more important. Lesser importance is entered as a reciprocal: In the example shown, the entry 1/5 in the first rows denotes the dominance of variable *C* over variable *A*.

The variable below compares in importance to:	A	B	C	D
A = World political instability	1	3	1/5	5
B = U.S. inflation	1/3	1	5	4
C = Development of alternative fuels	5	1/5	1	3
D = Government controls	1/5	1/4	1/3	1

Fig. 4.10. Saaty's Pair-Wise Comparison Matrix

Computation includes the normalization of the entries and the calculation of the normalized eigenvectors that determine the absolute importance of each candidate as shown in table 4.1. The example, in which the judges rated the relative sizes of the GNP of different countries, permits comparison of the judgmental ratings with actual values as shown (Saaty 1977).

The method also allows for checking the consistency of the pair-wise entries. To reduce the number of candidates and the resulting tediousness of elicitation, Saaty recommends a hierarchical approach in which the relative importance of broad categories of candidate developments (e.g., economy over technology) is determined first.

Whichever procedure is used, interviews or pair-wise comparisons, the end result should be a small list of developments of real importance to the business for which the scenarios are being developed.

Table 4.1. Normalized Wealth Eigenvector

	Normalized eigenvector	Actual GNP* (1972)	Fraction of GNP Total
U. S.	0.429	1167	0.413
USSR	0.231	635	0.225
China	0.021	120	0.043
France	0.053	196	0.069
U. K.	0.053	154	0.055
Japan	0.119	294	0.104
W. Germany	0.095	257	0.091
Total		2823	

*Billions of dollars.

BUILDING SCENARIOS

We are well aware that an overwhelming majority of corporations that generate alternative scenarios employ informal methods for the purpose, using such terms as "most likely," "expected," and "worst case" to describe the approximate location of such scenarios within the entire probability domain; but such scenarios are usually generated without an adequate analysis of the full probability domain. However, with the aid of even the simplest approaches that will now be described, the assignment of probability estimates to informal scenarios can be vastly improved.

Simple, Probabilistic, Static Scenarios

The example we choose is the 1985 average crude oil price in 1980 dollars per barrel (the term average applies to both the time average during 1985 and an average of long- and short-term contract prices). Let's assume that because of the low credibility of models that would tell us what the 1985 oil price will be, we have decided on a short-cut approach and would rather ask experts what the alternative prices *might* be. Three examples of elicitation follow, from the simplest to the most thorough.

Assuming normal distribution. The simplest approach starts with the notion of a range of prices rather than a single price. We might obtain an assignment (it could be our own) of 80 percent probability that the 1985 oil price will lie between two values — for example, $30/B and $50/B.

Making a simplifying assumption that the distribution of oil price is normal (a reasonably good assumption if we do not have any other information of what that distribution might be), the range and the shape specify the entire distribution (Fig. 4.11). The center (median oil price) lies halfway in the range, $40/B. Assume that we would like to have three equally likely forecasts about the 1985 oil price, each of the forecasts being a single value of price. We already have one of these, namely, $40/B. To obtain the other two, we divide the area under the probability density function into three equal area (or probability) segments. With a little training, these may be determined by eye, the error being quite acceptable for our purposes. The two boundaries are approximately $36.5/B and $43.5/B.

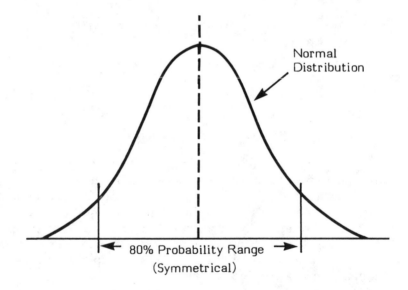

Fig. 4.11. Range and Shape Define the Distribution

The next step is to determine the expected value of the two outside segments. The expected value is the one value that we would be prepared to accept in lieu of the actual distribution of oil price within each segment — a single number that, unlike the median or the mode, tells us about the entire distribution. We can obtain the expected value of each segment by a fairly simple computation. Using $f(x)$ as the height of the distribution and $f(x)dx$ as the probability of a small width dx, the small increment of probability is multiplied by the value of x, the mean price of each segment dx. The expected value is the summation of these "first moments" in which probability $f(x)$dx becomes a weight at a distance x (Fig. 4.12). The mean of these moments is obtained by dividing by the denominator, the total probability of the segment — in this case, 1/3. If we were to cut that probability segment out of cardboard, the point of balance would be the expected value (Fig. 4.13). Knowing how to do it, we might approximate the expected value by guessing where that balancing point might be. The correct value is $32.2/B and $47.8/B but, as we have indicated already, a judgment of $33/B and $47/B, or even $34/B and $46/B would be quite acceptable.

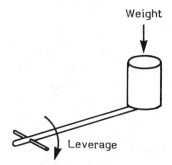

Fig. 4.12. The First Moment Concept

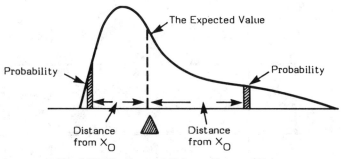

Fig. 4.13. The Expected Value as Center of Balance

If we have reason to suspect that the distribution is either not symmetrical or does not resemble a normal distribution, we will have to obtain more information about it by consulting experts on oil pricing. In the next section, we will assume that the experts are perfect assessors. That is, they know a lot about oil prices and can assign probabilities *perfectly* in accordance with their best judgment (Stael von Holstein 1972).

Full distribution, perfect assessors. The expert's opinion about oil prices is encoded as a mass function. In the example described, there are nine such answers corresponding to 9 points on the mass function. The questioning proceeds as follows:

1. Think of a 1985 oil price that is so high that, in your judgment, there is only one chance in a hundred that the actual oil price would be even higher. What is the price? (This is point 1 on figure 4.14.)

2. Now imagine a 1985 oil price that is so low that there is only one chance in a hundred that the actual oil price would be even lower. What is that price? (This is point 2 on figure 4.14.)

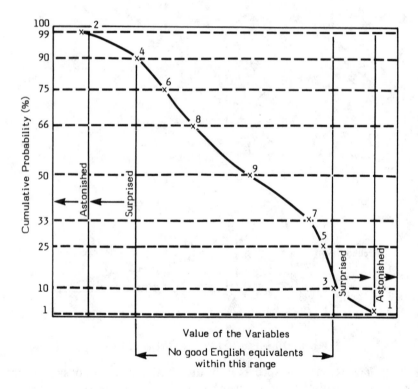

Fig. 4.14. Extraction of Nine-Point Mass Function from Respondents

The interrogation continues in this manner, alternating between the high and the low side of the oil price and gradually approaching the median price, one in which the expert assigns equal probability to the 1985 price being either higher or lower.

There are two caveats for the procedure: (1) we do not ask what the price will be, and (2) we do not show the expert the mass function or the probability density function resulting from his or her individual answers. The reason is that some experts would try to make the distribution look like a normal distribution.

In the third stage, the most complicated, we measure the characteristics of the expert and modify his or her judgment to try to compensate for imperfections in probability assignments (Morris 1977).

Full distribution, imperfect assessors. The "perfect" respondent possesses three kinds of knowledge: substantive knowledge in a particular field, assessing ability when faced with an uncertain extension of his or her substantive knowledge, and imagination. The first two forms of knowledge can be characterized numerically, but it is imagination that allows the expert to consider new interrelations among variables.

Substantive knowledge: Self-evaluation by "experts." Each expert can be asked to evaluate himself or herself using the set of criteria shown in table 4.2. Notice that the emphasis is on understanding of the subject and not on the ability to "guess right."

The joint distribution of several calibrated (in substantive knowledge) experts can be made from their individual judgments by probabilistic weighted addition (Winkler 1968). To help determine the weight accorded to individual judgments, we recommend the weights shown in table 4.3 because our measurements indicate that most corporate decision makers tend to assign weights in approximately that fashion.

In each interval of probability (for example, 100 intervals to cover the range of the random variable), the individual probability contributions, weighted by expertise, are then added (Fig. 4.15). The resulting joint distribution of all experts on that variable is then normalized so that the sum of probabilities equals unity.

Assessing ability: Evaluation by the interviewer. The "assessing ability" describes the expert's ability to assess the uncertainty about what he or she really knows, when his or her opinion is sought concerning a possible, but highly uncertain, extension of substantive knowledge into the future. The assessing ability test is an attempt to measure (or characterize) the way the expert communicates his or her beliefs.

In the assessing ability test to be described next, one attempts to "measure" how experts allocate probability to uncertain values of a variable (Morris 1971; Winkler 1969). On the basis of the test, it is possible to "translate" expert judgments to a common basis of perfect assessment and subsequently to merge them by the method just described.

Table 4.2. Self-Evaluation Criteria: Guidance to Self-Ranking of Expertise

Category

1.   You are *unfamiliar* with the subject matter if the mention of it encounters a veritable blank in your memory or if you have heard of the subject, yet are unable to say anything meaningful about it.

2.   You are *casually acquainted* with the subject matter if you at least know what the issue is about, have read something on the subject, and/or have heard a debate about it on a major television or radio network or on an educational channel.

3.   You are *familiar* with the subject matter if you know most of the arguments advanced for and against some of the controversial issues surrounding this subject, have read a substantial amount about it, and have formed some opinion about it. However, if someone tried to pin you down and have you explain the subject in more depth, you would soon have to admit that your knowledge is inadequate to do so.

4.   You are *quite familiar* with the subject matter if you were an expert some time ago but feel somewhat rusty now because other assignments have intervened (even though, because of the previous interest, you have kept reasonably abreast of current developments in the field); if you are in the process of becoming an expert but still have some way to go to achieve mastery of the subject; or if your concern is with integrating detailed developments in the area, thus trading breadth of understanding for depth of specialization.

5.   You should consider yourself an *expert* if you belong to that small community of people who currently study, work on, and dedicate themselves to the subject matter. Typically, you know who else works in this area; you know the literature of your country and probably the foreign literature; you attend conferences and seminars on the subject, sometimes reading a paper and sometimes chairing the sessions; you most likely have written up and/or published the results of your work. If the National Science Foundation, National Academy of Sciences, or a similar organization were to convene a seminar on this subject, you would expect to be invited or, in your opinion, you should be invited. Other experts in this field may disagree with your views but invariably respect your judgment; comments such as "this is an excellent person on this subject" would be typical when inquiring about you.

Table 4.3. Weighting of Experts' Opinions

Experts' Substantive Expertise Ranking	Relative Weight
1	1
2	2
3	4
4	8
5	16

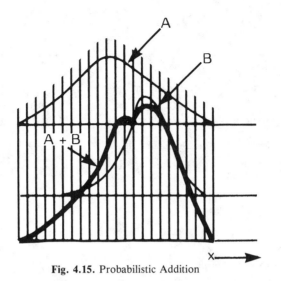

Fig. 4.15. Probabilistic Addition

The test we suggest consists of two parts. The first part (Morris 1971) requires the respondent to reply to 10 questions drawn from the *Guinness Book of World Records*, phrasing responses probabilistically. The respondent provides a high and a low limit so that there is, in his or her mind, an 80 percent probability that the real answer contained in the Guinness book will lie between the two limits. The questions are likely to be outside the expert's immediate field of knowledge, but his or her overall knowledge should enable the expert to allocate the limits more or less correctly, for example, in (approximately) 8 out of 10 questions or, even better, in approximately 16 out of 20 questions (for the 80 percent probability condition). It would be very easy to obtain a score of 10 out of 10 simply by quoting absurd limits, but getting 8 out of 10 is much more difficult. Table 4.4 is an example of the questions.

In the second part of the test, the respondent is asked to reply to another set of questions (preferably 20), this time from the *Statistical Abstract for the United States.* He or she is asked to give two sets of limits corresponding to 50 percent and 80 percent probability of capturing the correct result.

A perfect or perfectly calibrated assessor (we occasionally find that such people do exist) would capture approximately 80 percent of the correct results when quoting limits at the 80 percent probability level and 50 percent at the 50 percent level. At the first attempt, experts most frequently capture only 2 or 3 out of 10 correct results at the 80 percent probability level but quickly learn to increase the range of their responses so that on retesting their performance improves. With practice, scores can be improved and maintained;

Table 4.4. Self-Calibration Sheet

	Lower Estimate	Higher Estimate
1. Longest fasting record (days)		
2. Fastest measured speed of a spider (feet/second)		
3. Modern pole-sitting record (days)		
4. World's longest sermon on record (hours)		
5. Typical length of world's largest species of ant (inches)		
6. World's longest straight length of railroad track (miles)		
7. Weight of world's largest recorded gorilla (pounds)		
8. Longest recorded jump of flea (inches)		
9. Longest labor strike (months)		
10. Diameter of world's largest rope (inches)		

but, on each occasion, it is necessary to match well one's responses to his or her state of knowledge. The measurements of assessing ability are used later to process the judgment in the expert's substantive field of knowledge. Typically, the responses lead us to assign higher probabilities to both the lower and higher ends of the probability density function obtained from the direct elicitation.

Let us now assume that, given the information provided by the expert, we would like to project three equally likely scenarios of the 1985 oil price. We first translate (differentiate) the elicited mass function into a probability density function (Fig. 4.16). (The value of the slope of the mass function is the height of the probability density function.)

An example of such a probability density function representing, in this case, the joint judgment of several experts on oil price, each of whom has been interrogated and measured in the manner just described, is shown in figure 4.17.

The area under the probability density function is unity. To obtain three equally likely scenarios, we divide as before the entire area into three equal area segments and then compute the expected value of each segment. For the actual distribution shown in figure 4.17, the expected values are as follows:

(1978 dollars)

$19.2/B   (expected value of the entire distribution)

$10.8/B $17.4/B $35.7/B   (expected values of the three terciles)

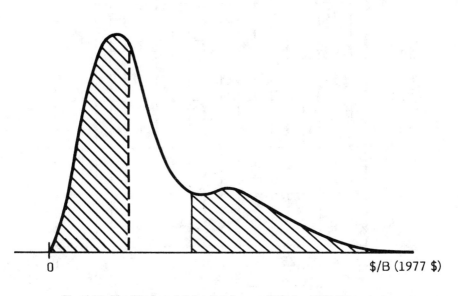

0 $/B (1977 $)

Fig. 4.16. The Terciles of Joint Opinion on Oil Price (1978 Elicitation)

The lower three values are the three equally likely scenarios we needed. If we can only deal with one value and suppress all the uncertainty implied by figure 4.17, the three values can be replaced by one number: $19.2/B.

Now let us extend the procedure to cover three time periods: 1985, 1990, and 1995. The scenarios will still be the most frugal in content, consisting of one variable only, the oil price.

Simple, Probabilistic, Dynamic Scenarios

One way (incidentally, the proper one) to extend the time frame to cover the 1990 and 1995 time periods would be to ask the experts for *conditional* forecasts. That is, their forecast of the 1990 oil price would be conditional on the oil price in 1985. But there are three such equally likely oil prices for 1985, so that for each one of these prices the expert would have to accept the 1985 situation and then reflect upon his or her uncertainty about oil prices in 1990. Figure 4.18 shows the sequence of such conditional projections. If the conditional mass functions of the 1990 oil price were again split into terciles (by the method already illustrated in figure 4.18) and if the procedure were again repeated for 1995, we would then end up with 3 scenarios for 1985, 9 scenarios for 1990, and 27 scenarios for 1995. The corresponding number of elicitations would be 1, 3, and 9. It is obvious that the condi-

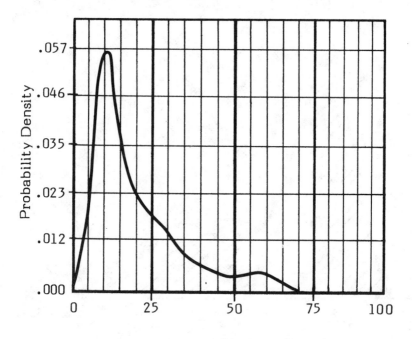

Crude Oil Price $/B (1978 Dollars)

Fig. 4.17. Joint Opinion on 1985 Oil Price

tional elicitation process results in a cascading number of scenarios and (unfortunately) geometrically increased expense of the cost of elicitation (table 4.5). However, there is a shortcut which, while sacrificing some resolution, could provide useful information at considerably less expense.

Table 4.5. Scenarios Assuming 3-Way Split

Number of Scenario Elements	1985	1990	1995
1	3	9	27
2	9	81	729
3	27	729	19,683
4	81	6,561	531,441
5	243	59,049	14,348,907

In this shortcut approach, instead of asking questions about oil price at a particular time, we would simply ask the expert to draw three trends of oil prices. The upper trend would be one in which the oil price at any given

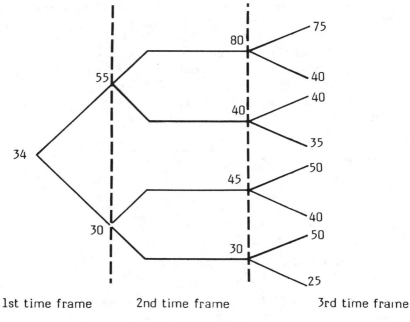

1st time frame   2nd time frame   3rd time frame

Fig. 4.18. Probabilistic Tree

time is so high that there is only one chance in ten that it could be even higher; the bottom trend would be one in which the oil price is so low that there is only one chance in ten that it could be even lower; and the middle trend would be one in which the oil price could be equally likely either lower or higher. Figure 4.19 illustrates the results of such an elicitation.

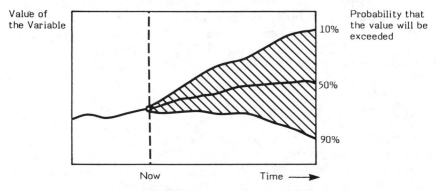

Fig. 4.19. Simplified Elicitation of a Probabilistic Trend

What have we sacrificed in order to save effort? We have lost the information about the dynamic behavior of the individual scenarios. Notice that some scenarios in figure 4.18 have a sequence of oil prices starting with a high price in 1985, then a lower price in 1990, and again a higher price in 1995.

In figure 4.19, however, these individual sequences are hidden in an envelope of high and low prices shown in the shaded area of figure 4.20. We don't even know if 80 percent of the same individual scenarios (as contrasted to 80 percent of oil prices) lie within the envelope. Some individual scenarios may have "escaped" from the envelope, and some others that were outside the range earlier may have "joined" the 80 percent range later on. And that is the information loss we have incurred in exchange for the simplicity of elicitation.

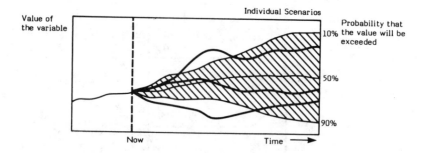

Fig. 4.20. The 80 Percent Probability Envelope and the Individual Scenarios

Is there yet another approach that would preserve the individual scenarios and yet be simpler and less expensive to conduct than the full, conditional tree treatment? Yes, but only if we are able to make two strong simplifying assumptions: (1) that the distributions are all of a particular type (e.g., normal), and (2) that the values of the variable in different time periods are stochastically independent, that is, the distribution of probability of the variable in time period number two is independent of the value of the variable in time period number one. For one or two variables that may be true. But more often it is not. For example, if variable No. 1 were oil price and variable No. 2 inflation, could we then say that a low value of inflation is just as likely even if the oil price were high or low? Probably not.

Complex, Deterministic, Dynamic, Mutually Consistent Scenarios

In the current state of planning, most corporations use one central set of variables — e.g., GNP growth, inflation rate, unemployment level, and energy prices — that are mutually consistent because they are generated by an econometric model provided, for example, by Data Resources, Chase, or Wharton. Other important variables, such as the future regulatory climate or competitors' prices, are then added judgmentally.

To check the sensitivity of a company's current strategy to an environment different from the central scenario, most corporate planners can only change the value of one variable at a time and then only an economic one, because corporate financial models can generally only accommodate economic variables. What we now propose is a method of generating alternative *sets* of internally consistent scenarios that include noneconomic variables. Furthermore, it would be nice if the "outside," borderline sets of scenarios could be gauged to capture a sizable chunk of future possibilities or, as we prefer to describe it, the "territory of the future."

A relatively simple and inexpensive tool for the task, which also allows the planner to span a desired segment of probability, is a DYCIM (*dynamic cross-impact model*) — a distant relative of Kane's Simulation (KSIM), which belongs to the family of cross-impact models (Kane 1972; Lipinski and Tydeman 1979).

To the planner, DYCIM may be thought of as a means of systematically recording judgments about the interrelation of future developments and producing a set of scenarios that are consistent with these judgments. Used well, it can produce useful insights into the future.

Using DYCIM. Utilizing DYCIM to generate alternative scenarios requires the modeler to follow seven steps:

1. Identify the important events or variables (this step has already been described).

2. Make preliminary forecasts for each variable or event (a trend or a cumulative probability over time for an event).

3. Select sources best qualified to describe their interrelations.

4. Elicit information about the interrelations.

5. Process this information.

6. Generate alternative forecast(s) for one or two of the important exogenous variables (e.g., GNP growth).

7. Rerun the model with these forecasts taken as a given to produce the remainder of the forecasts, which will automatically fall in line with the driving variables.;

The result of the first five steps is one consistent set of forecasts, or one corporate scenario. We recommend that this be the central set, comparable to the current scenario. The remaining two steps generate alternative scenarios. A fuller description of steps 2-7 follows:

2. Make preliminary forecasts. Once the important scenario components are selected, a preliminary, single-valued, dynamic forecast is needed for each. For the input variables, the forecasts should be the best available because they will influence the judgment of the participants regarding the cross-impacts and will later be used in computations. For the output variables, only the initial values and initial slopes will be used in DYCIM processing. The remaining values will be used only to elicit the cross-impact judgments.

3. Select best-qualified sources. The chief role of each expert participant is not to generate relationships between variables but, rather, to contribute to a discussion so that *all* participants will be better informed prior to registering their cross-impact entries. Thus, a well-informed participant who does not communicate his or her information to others will be of limited value, because the general level of the group's expertise will not be improved. Participants should cover a wide range of the competencies required for modeling the key interactions. As an example, in applying DYCIM to a manufacturing technology (composite materials) forecast, the assembled participants covered the following areas of expertise:

- Business environment (sales, profitability)

- Development and processing technologies of composites and plastics

- Manufacture of composite-making equipment and composites for aircraft industry

- Polymer structure, composites' performance and characterization

- Use of composites, bonding sealants, and elastomers

- Design/cost of lightweight structures for aircraft/aerospace and land transportation

- Use of composites in land and air transportation

- Metals manufacture and utilization

- Automotive design and materials selection.

4. Elicit information about the interrelations. The workshop moderator plays the crucial role in eliciting panelists' opinions on the interrelationships among the variables. He or she has already "pre-run" the exercise to determine which interrelationships are the most important and should be addressed first. The moderator focuses attention on the first interrelation by specifying that an impacting variable *A* has undergone a hypothetical sudden change (step function change) in its value, and the team ought to consider what effect this step change, by itself, will have on an impacted variable *B*.

Figure 4.21 shows a typical elicitation form. Note that the upper graph, that of the impacting variable, contains a step. The respondent's task is to judge the effect of such a step on the preliminary forecast of the impacted variable *B*.

To record his or her judgment, this respondent merely redraws the lower forecast and records his or her expertise on that particular interaction.

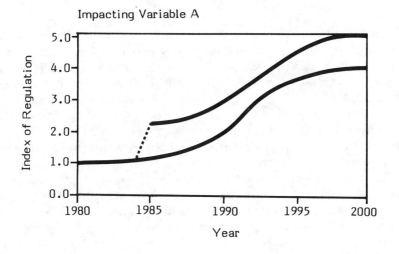

Impacting Variable A

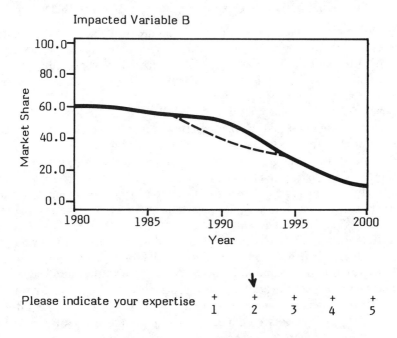

Impacted Variable B

Fig. 4.21. Typical Elicitation Form

So much for the technicalities of how judgments are recorded. But how are these judgments made? Think of a court proceeding. For each interrelation, a discussion that lasts an average of five minutes takes place. Each participant plays a dual role as both the participating lawyer and a member of the jury. The arguments presented deal with the effect of the step in the impacting variable on the impacted variable. Is there any effect? If so, in what direction? With what time delay? When all the arguments have been heard, participants switch to their jury roles and record their verdicts. Each verdict is anonymous. The moderator then invites the participants to look at the next interrelation. The process continues until all important interrelations have been discussed. Typically, the process requires a full working day.

The ideal moderator should have a sufficiently good understanding of the individual variables that he or she can detect when a discussion strays. This does not necessarily mean that all digressions should be stopped, for at times they may provide valuable insights (for example, identifying a "missing" variable that ought to be added to make the forecast more realistic). The moderator should also fully understand how DYCIM works, for, typically, participants will ask for clarifications of how their judgments (entries) should best be recorded and how they will later be processed. The two qualifications can be met by having both a "substantive" moderator and a DYCIM expert.

5. *Process the results.* The completed forms are then placed on the graphic panel of a computer; then, under computer direction, each participant's modified forecast of the impacted variable is traced. This procedure results in the automatic encoding of all responses for each cross-impact, which are then stored in a series of disk files.

When all the forms have been encoded, the processing begins. First, an expertise-weighted consensus of each cross-impact is established using the weights derived from the self-rankings of the participants. Second, the modified forecast of the impacted variable is compared to the original forecast, and the difference between the two is determined. This "departure" forecast is actually fitted to a five-parameter function to provide smoothing, to reduce storage requirements for the multiple-year array, and to allow extrapolation of the matrix elements. The values of the derivative or the slope, which could be different for each time period, will be used in computing a new value of the variable. This procedure is repeated for all cross-impact combinations.

Finally, the actual computation begins. Starting with the initial value and the initial slope of each variable, the appropriate cross-impact matrix coefficients are calculated, and the new values for the next time period are established. The process continues until one complete set of consistent forecasts (or a scenario) is established.

6. *Generate alternative forecasts.* This step is easy if one is willing to short-circuit a formal approach, but quite tricky if one is not. First, the easy way. Ask the best available source (typically, the corporate economist) what he

or she considers to be a good (say, only 1 chance in 10 of being even better) forecast for the economy and a bad (1 chance in 10 of being worse) forecast. The responses might look like those shown in figure 4.22.

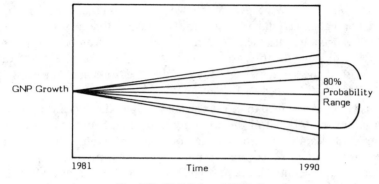

Fig. 4.22. Well Behaved GNP Growth

The formal approach is tougher because of the difficulty in allocating probability to time-varying trends. We have already described this procedure — but here we want to avoid it. Let's take the GNP example again. If one is lucky, the projections of GNP behave nicely, monotonically increasing or decreasing. If GNP is well behaved, it is easy to calculate, say, the boundaries of the 80 percent probability range. Unfortunately, most corporate economists subscribe to the theory of business cycles, and their alternative projections of GNP growth often look as shown in figure 4.23.

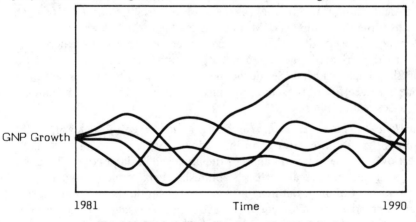

Fig. 4.23. Typical Alternative Views of GNP Growth

But one can rephrase the question and ask the economist to project a GNP forecast for the desired time frame that would be so good (note: good rather than numerically high, thus bringing in the notion of utility) that there is only 1 chance in 10 that it could have been even better. A mirror image approach in which the economist is asked to identify a "bad" GNP forecast would yield the low utility GNP scenario.

7. *Rerun the model.* Whichever of the two methods is used, once the range of desired probability is established and the "boundary" forecasts for the most important exogenous variables are identified, the model can be used again, but this time to make the forecasts of the other variables consistent with the new forecast of the leading exogenous variable. Let's assume that we start with the pessimistic forecast of the economy.

Because GNP is assumed to be the driving variable, the DYCIM program will not allow the forecast of the economy to be modified by the effect of the other variables. But the cross-impacts obtained from the participants are retained; as a result, all other forecasts must reposition themselves to preserve consistency with the initial cross-impacts. The computed output is a new set of internally consistent values of variables (or a scenario) corresponding to the poor state of the economy.

Limits of DYCIM. Earlier, we indicated that the use of DYCIM is one of the options in creating alternative, consistent scenarios. It is relatively inexpensive and not too time consuming. However, the user should also be aware of the limits of DYCIM modeling, and indeed modeling by other so-called family of "trend-impact" models (Cearlock 1977; Lendaris 1980).

"Short conditional" assumption. In common with all pair-wise comparison models, DYCIM disregards higher order dependencies, even though they may be critically important. If it takes two or more variables *jointly* to have an effect on the third, the DYCIM model is unable to include the effect. For example, if drastic advances in both computers and rocketry are needed to advance the arrival of space-weapon platforms, the participants in a DYCIM workshop might truthfully decide that neither the effect of computer advances alone nor the effect of rocket improvement alone would advance the number of space-weapon platforms.

Invariance of interrelationships over the entire range of values. DYCIM assumes that a unit change in an impacting variable would have the same effect over a large range of values of the impacted variables (large because, near both ends of the scale, effect is diminished by assuming a logistic function for each variable). But imagine a real-life situation: Is a 10-cent increase in gasoline price per gallon equally effective in decreasing travel at gasoline prices of 50 cents, 150 cents, or 300 cents? The participants at the workshop may have been asked only about the effect on travel at a price level of, say, 150 cents per gallon. Yet, later on, DYCIM quite happily uses the same cross-impact whatever the price happens to be. There are other, more complex models, such as Quick Simulation for Interactive Modeling or QSIM

(Wakeland 1976), in which a price elasticity might be entered as a function of price level. But imagine the complexity and tediousness of eliciting such judgments. In a typical DYCIM exercise, one might have to address 100 interrelations. In QSIM, each of these elicitations would have to be redone at several levels of the impacting variable.

Reversibility of DYCIM cross-impact. Using the previous illustration, DYCIM assumes that a 10-cent increase in price would have exactly the reverse effect of a 10-cent drop in price. For very small changes, this may well be true. For large changes it may not.

Linearity of DYCIM. DYCIM assumes that a 20-cent increase in price per gallon will have twice the effect of a 10-cent increase in price. Again, probably true for very small changes only.

Nevertheless, DYCIM and models similar to DYCIM are useful tools for developing alternative corporate forecasts. Their use lies about half way between using simple judgment and very complex modeling of alternative forecasts. If an alternative forecast from DYCIM proves to have a great effect on corporate performance, then one might wish to explore that forecast using a greater degree of modeling formality, but, of course, at a higher cost of elicitation and processing.

To recapitulate: We have demonstrated a method of generating trend scenarios by (1) building a succession of probabilistic trees, or (2) using a deterministic model that is then made to include alternative forecasts of the most important variable and readjust the other variables into internally consistent sets. Either method requires a nontrivial investment in acquiring the information (by the elicitation of expert judgment) and in computer resources. These expenses would preclude, we think, the generation of scenarios merely for the sake of "having" scenarios, and limit the use of the process to cases where operationally useful assumptions are needed in order to examine alternative strategies. In the next step, we address the problem of complexity by simplifying the information provided by the scenarios by sampling, pruning, and supplementary computations.

SIMPLIFYING SCENARIOS: METASCENARIOS

The processes described so far have one property in common — they generate a large number of scenarios, each of small probability of occurrence. But, to facilitate management's understanding of alternative environments and facilitate subsequent calculations of the consequences of candidate strategies vis-à-vis particular scenarios, the number of scenarios must be kept small — typically, two or three. We will now describe processes for generating such scenarios — to be called "metascenarios" to distinguish them from the low-probability scenarios we have been discussing thus far.

Metascenarios – Sampling the Probability Domain

Operationally useful metascenarios are a planned set of explorations that sample the territory of the future. Once again using Africa to visualize the process, instead of one explorer we would send three voyagers southward – one through the center (starting from Libya), one from Algeria, and one from Egypt (Fig. 4.24). The information to be collected is increased by a factor of three. But, if the three voyagers never stray from a straight north-south path, we might still gather a very inaccurate picture of what Africa may be like. Further improvement in information would result if each expedition were to set up camp at intervals and, making systematic detours east and west from its planned path, summarize its impressions before proceeding farther south. The methodological equivalent is the averaging of the information obtained from many neighboring scenarios. These averages or aggregations are metascenarios.

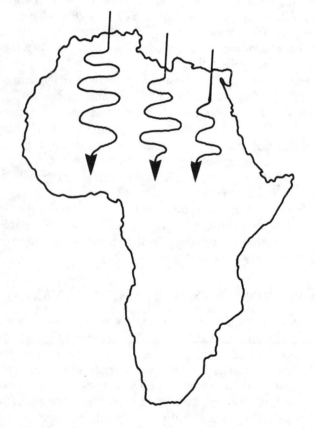

Fig. 4.24. Three Journeys through Africa

Metascenarios can differ in the number of scenarios they aggregate and, hence, in their respective cumulative probability. Such arbitrariness — or freedom — of communicating the "profile" of uncertainty is illustrated by the two examples shown in figure 4.25. Note that the basic information about the future is exactly the same in each of the examples, but is merely presented or aggregated differently.

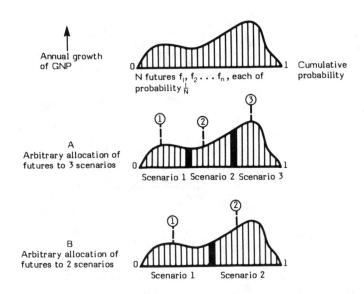

Fig. 4.25. Equally Valid Means of Presenting an Uncertain Future

The probabilities of the metascenarios are determined by arbitrarily chosen methods of bundling them (Fig. 4.26). There is no a priori reason why the center metascenario should have higher aggregate probability than the side metascenarios. A metascenario will acquire a higher probability only by aggregating more, lower probability scenarios. But aggregating more and more scenarios into one metascenario incurs a penalty: the high-probability metascenario becomes a more uncertain indicator of the future in the sense that it encompasses a wider assortment of individual scenarios. Thus, the probability increases that the values in any actual future will be further away from the value indicated by the metascenario.

In figure 4.26, at one extreme, the more probable metascenarios are more "uncertain" metascenarios — they have a greater potential variation of GNP growth values. At the other extreme, the very specific, unaveraged, "point estimate" scenario has a negligibly small probability of occurring, but will be "dead-on" if such a future does occur.

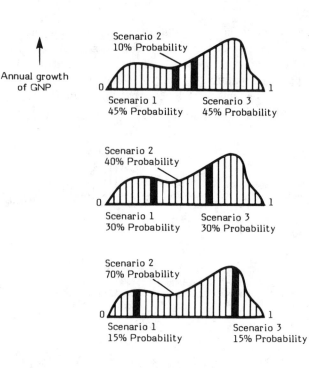

Fig. 4.26. Uncertainty and Probability

We would like to make a clear distinction between single scenarios of low probability, such as one of our many constituent scenarios, and metascenarios that average many such single scenarios. We do not consider the first type of scenarios particularly useful. A single, "what if" scenario of *negligible* probability ought to have *negligible* operational significance for business managers unless the consequences are truly disastrous and unless something can be done about the scenario. Thus, a hydrogen war of a small probability should still be disregarded if management can't invent a strategy to accommodate to it or cope with it.

But when a single metascenario is offered *in exchange* for a segment of the entire probability domain, then it behooves us to treat it more seriously. Metascenarios convey operationally useful information about the future because they are few in number and yet they capture the uncertainty surrounding the future.

But there is a limit to simplification. When a single metascenario is offered in exchange for the *entire* map, it becomes very uncertain because it tries to aggregate all possible futures (Menke 1979). The seeming precision of such a single metascenario — quoting, as it may, a single inflation rate of 6.2 or 9.7 percent — does not mean what it implies. The metascenario constructor knows that the inflation rates in the bundle of scenarios of which the metascenario is composed vary from 4 to 18 percent, and the 6.2 or 9.7 percent figure is simply an average of the entire, very wide distribution of different rates of inflation.

Knowing that most senior managers seem to prefer certainty — even though they know better — it is better *not* to arrange the center metascenario to be the most likely metascenario. We are afraid that if the center metascenario is designated the most likely, managers will tend to disregard the side ones. Herein may be the underlying reason why a number of corporations prefer only two. A compromise is to portray the future as three *equally likely* metascenarios. Equally likely literally means that they are completely interchangeable from the standpoint of probability of occurrence (Fig. 4.27). One can visualize metascenarios as paths through the segments of the map of figure 4.1, which are shown as dotted lines.

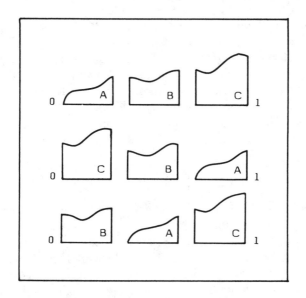

When groups of scenarios are equally likely, they can be juxtaposed any which way. The concept of a center scenario is divorced from the most likely scenario.

Fig. 4.27. Equally Likely Group of Scenarios

Before averaging, low-probability scenarios should be sorted so that one end of the probability domain is "worst" and the other is "best." The histogram of figure 4.9 provides a powerful clue on how to determine the best combination of developments. Using that example, the best individual scenario as seen by the managers of that corporation consists of a high degree of international stability, low U.S. inflation, rapid development of alternative fuels, low level of government controls, moderate degree of environmental concerns, reasonable world demand for energy, benign U.S. political climate and slowly rising world energy prices.

A simple way of deriving a joint utility (a measure of goodness) is to use the value of importance derived from the histogram of figure 4.9, or, if pairwise measurement of importance has also been made, the value of the normalized eigenvector (see table 4.1). For example, the histogram of figure 4.9 yields the following values of importance (judged by frequency of mentions):

World Political Stability	41
U.S. Inflation	37
Development of Alternative Fuels	36
Government Controls and Regulation	28
Conservation and Environmental Concerns	26
Balanced World Energy Supply and Demand	26

Then, if the value of each of the variables were to be at its *maximum* normalized value (e.g., 1 for complete world political stability), if the direction of "good" and "bad" were as indicated (in parentheses below), and the importance readings were as above, the total utility U_T of maximum settings would be:

U_T = 41 (good) + 37 (bad) + 36 (good) + 28 (bad) + 26 (bad) + 26 (good)

or

U_T = 41 (1) + 37 (0) + 36 (1) + 28 (0) + 26 (0) + 26 (1) = 103.

The best scenario in which all of the values are best or scale readings are at 1 will have the total utility of 194.

Derivation of the total utility (subjective, of course, in that it simulates the value model of the corporation) is fraught with difficulty (see chapter 9). But, for the purposes of sorting the small probability individual scenarios, the simple method just outlined seems adequate enough. The inevitable occasional inconsistencies in the computed utility of individual scenarios will diminish in the process of averaging them.

Let us assume that we would like to have three metascenarios with the following properties: a center metascenario averaging the middle region of the utility domain, and the two outside ones spanning 80 percent of the entire utility domain. The averaging of the sorted scenarios would then proceed as shown in figure 4.28 in which the territory is divided into segments of 20 percent, 60 percent, and 20 percent, and the average of each segment produces the desired metascenario. Note that, once the information about the entire domain is available, the range of choices of metascenarios is very wide, and they can be chosen depending on the intended purpose.

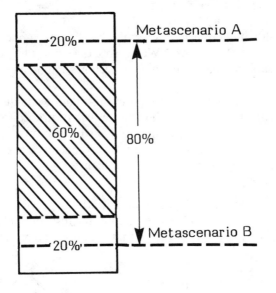

Fig. 4.28. Two Corporate Assumptions 80 Percent Probability Apart

We are now at a point where probabilistic scenarios arrived at by using probabilistic trees yielded, after relatively simple processing, operationally useful metascenarios. The drawbacks of the procedure are (1) the tediousness of the elicitation of conditional probabilities, and (2) the need for computer-processing capability (see table 4.5).

We continue with more examples of how to simplify scenarios. Now that we know how to make metascenarios, we can use that method as one means of pruning.

Pruning Probabilistic Trees

Probabilistic trees have a habit of growing an enormous number of branches (e.g., scenarios) rather quickly. An example uses just the six variables derived from the analysis of an actual interview process already described (the histogram of figure 4.9). Let's assume that each full distribution is used to generate only three expected values of each variable. Even so, the end number of scenarios N_I in the first time period is

$N_I = 3^6 = 729$.

If we were to continue the tree into the second time period and build more scenarios in a similar manner to that used in the first period, then for *each* end branch of the first period there would be 729 more scenarios depicting the situation at the end of the second time period. Thus, the number of scenarios N_2 in the second time period is

$N_2 = N_1 \times 729 = 531,441.$

Now, half a million scenarios seem to be about the upper limit of current computer file size "tolerance." Well before this limit, the problem of elicitation of such a number of judgments becomes impossible.

Pruning by metascenarios. Using the shorthand technique implicit in the generation of a metascenario, the first tree can be pruned to a small number of end branches. If we are willing to live with just three metascenarios to describe the first time period (and use these to obtain conditional assessments for the second time period), then N_2 becomes

$N_2 = 3 \times 729 = 2,187,$

which, by comparison, isn't bad at all. The arbitrary division of each distribution into three terciles makes sense only if the distribution does not exhibit a bipolar character (Fig. 4.29). For that situation two branches will suffice.

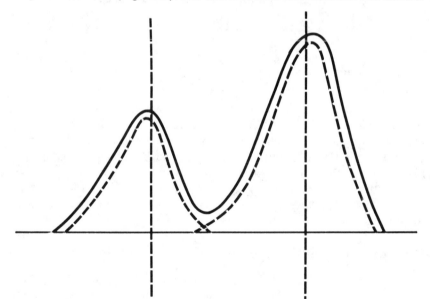

Fig. 4.29. Example of Bipolar Distribution

Pruning by simple, "within-the-tree" computations. The number of elicitations required to build a "fully conditional" tree is only one order of magnitude less than the number of variables. Again, using the previous illustration in which each distribution was divided into terciles, the number of elicitations E_l required to describe the first time period is

$$E_l = 3^5 = 243,$$

which is still about 10 times too large (i.e., too expensive) to be practical.

Fortunately, quite often very simple relationships can replace conditional elicitations. The example here is the price of crude oil and the price of natural gas in the United States. We might be able to conclude that, whatever the price of natural gas happens to be, higher oil prices will always tend to drive the price of natural gas higher; therefore, there is no need to elicit distributions that would allow the probability *distribution* of the natural gas price being shifted downward under conditions of higher oil prices. Instead, a simple relation could describe one's belief — for example, that the price of natural gas (in dollars per thousand cubic feet) will, in the long run, be some specified fraction (e.g., one-tenth) of the price of crude oil (in dollars/barrel).

If the first variable in the tree sequence were to be the oil price, one elicitation of the probabilistic distribution of the natural gas price, given low oil price, would suffice. The other probabilistic distributions will simply shift that distribution up in value as the oil price increases, so that the tree would still have multiple scenarios of natural gas price *given* alternative oil prices (Fig. 4.30).

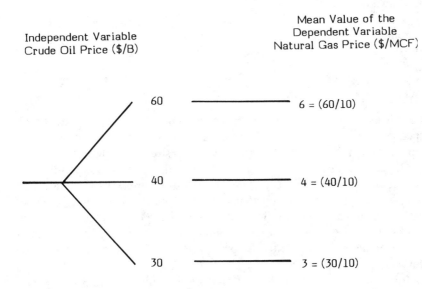

Fig. 4.30. Functional Dependence

Another way of simplifying scenarios is to avoid unnecessary elicitations altogether.

Avoiding Elicitations by Occasional Use of Convolutions

We have already indicated that elicitations of conditional probabilities need not be performed if the variables are stochastically independent. The definition of stochastic independence is that the probability *distribution* of a variable does not depend on the value of the other variable. In our interdependent world, such independence is seldom completely true, but it may be true enough for practical purposes. Using the previous example and arranging the variables in a symmetrical matrix (table 4.6), we can identify those that are (almost) independent of each other, as shown by X's.

Table 4.6. Searching for Stochastic Independence

	The Impacting Variable					
The Impacted Variable	WPS	USI	DAF	GCR	CEC	BWESD
World Political Stability (WPS)	—					
U.S. Inflation (USI)	X	—				X
U.S. Development of Alternative Fuels (DAF)	X	X	—	X		X
Government Controls and Regulations (GCR)	X			—		
Conservation and Environmental Concerns (CEC)	X				—	
Balanced World Energy Supply and Demand (BWESD)						—

One way to ask questions in order to judge the degree of stochastic dependence is as follows: If world political stability were to change by a small amount, such as occurred after the Soviet invasion of Afghanistan, would high U.S. inflation be any more likely (or less likely) than before the invasion occurred? One might conclude that the distribution of U.S. inflation is *predominantly* determined by an interaction of economic variables, whether domestic or international, and is relatively unrelated to changes in international stability. Of course, for truly dramatic changes in stability (for example, a war between the United States and the Soviet Union), it would be another matter.

After a little reflection and rejecting the temptation to find dependencies everywhere, no matter how feeble they seem to be, one might also be tempted to put zero dependence against the following:

- World political stability and U.S. development of alternative fuels
- World political stability and U.S. government controls
- World political stability and U.S. conservation movement
- U.S. inflation and the development of alternative fuels
- U.S. government controls and regulations and the development of alternative fuels
- World energy demand and U.S. inflation (this, however, is a close call)
- World energy demand and (within the time horizon of the tree) the U.S. development of alternative fuels.

The elimination of the above still leaves 22 cells exhibiting: (1) a probabilistic dependence on each other that can be addressed by a full elicitation of conditional probability, or (2) a conditional dependence in the form of a mathematical relation. Stochastically independent variables can be entered by convolution.

Convolution is a probabilistic multiplication. For each value of variable 1, all the values of variable 2, obtained from an unconditional elicitation, are possible. Figure 4.31 shows an example of convolution. In the example, two R&D departments independently develop components for a joint project. Each individual project could be on time (O), late (L), or very late (VL) with equal probability.

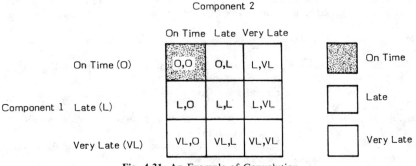

Fig. 4.31. An Example of Convolution

As a result of the independent outcomes of the probabilistically described efforts of the two departments, we would assign 1/9 probability of the project being on time, 1/3 being late, and 5/9 being very late.

We are again ready to summarize. By using metascenarios, simple computations replacing conditional elicitation or, alternatively, by assuming stochastic independence, we should be able to reduce the number of individual, small probability scenarios to a tractable number. Then, again by using metascenarios, we can present the information in the form of a few useful operational scenarios that can be used to explore the consequences of candidate strategies.

REFERENCES

Cearlock, D. B. 1977. Common properties and limitations of some structural modeling techniques. Ph.D. dissertation. Seattle: University of Washington.

Howard, R. A. 1965. Bayesian decision models for systems engineering. *IEEE Transactions on Systems Sciences and Cybernetics* SSC-1, No. 1: 36-40.

Kane, J. 1972. A primer for new cross-impact language — KSIM. *Technological Forecasting and Social Change* 4: 129-42.

Lendaris, G. G. 1980. Structural modeling — A tutorial guide. *IEEE Transactions on Systems, Man, and Cybernetics* SMC-10: 807-40.

Lipinski, H., and Tydeman, J. 1979. Cross-impact analysis — Extended KSIM. *Futures* 11, No. 2: 151-54.

Menke, M. M. 1979. The dangerous quest for certainty in market forecasting. *Long-Range Planning* 12, No. 2: 52-62.

Mitchell, R. B., Tydeman, J., and Georgiades, J. 1979. Structuring the future — Application of a scenario-generation procedure. *Technological Forecasting and Social Change* 14, No. 4: 409-28.

Morris, P. A. 1971. Bayesian expert resolution. Ph.D. dissertation. Palo Alto, CA: Stanford University.

———. 1977. Combining expert judgments: A Bayesian approach. *Management Science* 23, No. 7: 679-93.

Saaty, T. L. 1977. A scaling method for priorities in hierarchical structures. *Journal of Mathematical Psychology* 15: 139-49.

Stael von Holstein, C. S. 1972. A bibliography on encoding of subjective probability distributions. Menlo Park, CA: Stanford Research Institute.

Wakeland, W. 1976. QSIM2: A low-budget heuristic approach to modeling and forecasting. *Technological Forecasting and Social Change* 9: 213-29.

Winkler, R. L. 1968. The consensus of subjective probability distributions. *Management Science* 15, No. 2: 61-75.

———. 1969. Scoring rules and the evaluation of probability assessors. *Journal of the American Statistical Association* 64: 1073-78.

CHAPTER 5
CANDIDATE STRATEGIES

A candidate strategy has been defined as an orchestrated set of candidate decisions over time. Therefore, both the decisions and the timing of the decisions are important ingredients of a candidate strategy. In this chapter we will consider: (1) the process of arriving at candidate strategies; (2) the hierarchical structure of such strategies — that is, the process by which strategies are translated or better defined as they progress down the corporate ladder of responsibility; and (3) the integration of decisions affecting human as well as physical and financial resources. We will then address the robustness of strategies and how to document them.

In chapter 9, we will examine the task of generating corporate objectives. Here, we assume that the individual business unit or the corporation as a whole "knows" what it would like to achieve or, at the very least, knows how to distinguish relative goodness of outcomes or consequences. These consequences, we should remind ourselves, result from the interplay of scenarios and alternative strategies. The scenarios have been structured by methods described in chapter 4.

THE PROCESS OF GENERATING CANDIDATE STRATEGIES
Recognizing a Need

We must admit that thinking about options and candidate strategies is expensive — more expensive than thinking about and constructing scenarios — and that, as we have just seen, was complicated enough. Therefore, it is perfectly natural that corporations would devote very little of their intellectual resources to thinking about new options unless there were some compelling reason to do so. If the business seems to be doing well — sales increase each year, profitability is so-so but not all that bad in comparison to what the competitors seem to achieve — then a search for new strategies may be either perfunctory or nonexistent.

But occasionally there are such compelling reasons. The external reasons are normally bad news of some kind, e.g., the corporation's profits are down, while the competition seems to be doing fine; market share has dropped precipitously; a major contract was lost; *The Wall Street Journal* carried an article concluding that the management is inept and that the company doesn't seem to have any strategy at all; or the board is unhappy. Alternatively, a new CEO has come on board and believes it is high time to start thinking about alternative strategies.

Thus, the need for an alternative strategy can stem from external or internal sources. However, that need has to be recognized at a high corporate level. It is pointless to dream up strategies at a planning staff level when the climate for strategic thinking is not yet established by senior management. But that is precisely a good time to prepare, to learn how to think about choosing and defining strategies, because, when the trumpet to action finally sounds, there will be no time to prepare.

Unfortunately, what may appear to be the current "strategy" of an organization is sometimes a disjointed, instinctive set of responses to a changing environment. Not only are the business units going their own way, but the responses of the functions within a business unit lack correlation. If that is the case, then it can be called a "strategy" only if one stretches the meaning a bit. Nevertheless, one could argue, it is a strategy of sorts, a null strategy — "Do not think ahead, react when the pressures develop." The problem with such reactive responses is that their consequences cannot be analyzed until the decisions are taken, and then there is no time to do so.

Generating Candidate Strategies

Of at least two distinct methods of generating candidate strategies, *the incremental method*, by far the easier, starts from current strategy or, to use our analogy, a consideration of the current options in terms of the knob settings. The knob settings are then "improved" — by a more systematic choice of R&D options (Merrifield 1977), better choice of marketing options (Abell 1979; Kottler 1980), more effective manufacturing processes (Skinner 1978), and so forth.

In the other, *the conceptual method,* there may or may not be a recipe for generating candidate strategies. The origination of strategy may spring directly from perceived environmental changes, from analysis of the competition, from new or modified objectives, or from all three. For example, future growth in particular sectors of the economy, important shifts in the proportion of minorities in the United States, or deregulation of certain business sectors may spur ideas for new options or strategies. The options may be viewed as ways to move the equilibrium in the market place to favor the corporation. On the other hand, there may not be any obvious starting point. That is, the origination of a strategy comes about as a result of an intuitive leap — an idea, a hunch, or even a pet peeve. "Why do we always have to conform to what the competition does?" runs the complaint. "Let's do something different for a change!"

Because of their inherent originality, such proposals for change are traditionally resisted, principally because candidate strategies appear risky and the amount of risk is difficult to quantify because of the difficulty of relating it to current experience. It seems a folly to try the new strategy "for real," on a real business unit or a real corporation. But the situation changes completely if one can have a corporate model to simulate a risky strategy. With a model, experimenting may be expensive but not risky.

The individuals who are best at improving existing strategy or the "incremental strategy generators" are mostly drawn from operating management. They, more than senior management or staff, are likely to have a clear idea of possible improvements in the current settings of the decision knobs (and a better notion of the cost of those improvements). Therefore, proposals in which, for example, an improvement in sales, or market share, can be achieved only by a disproportionate increase in the cost of sales would be questioned early.

By the same token, operational managers are placed under great disadvantage in trying to come up with innovative strategies. To start with, these are by their definition unsound: "We have never done things like that." Secondly, the proposed strategies may entail significant changes in the corporate structure and the current division of responsibilities. It is inevitable (and perfectly natural) that operational managers would take into consideration their own future, or at least the future of their departmental projects. Thus, to suggest and explore broad conceptual strategies, we look to those who are not as tightly bound to more narrowly defined interests. That usually limits the field to senior executives (typically, members of the senior management "club," such as the executive committee) and sometimes a few members of the board, the corporate planning staff, and management consultants.

For a business unit, the generation of options and candidate strategies by incremental improvement can be initiated in meetings lasting several days or in a series of one-day sessions (Royce 1979). The suggested agenda is as follows:

- Identification and description of the option "knobs"

- Description of the position of each knob

- Maximum and minimum feasible setting of each knob

- The cost of incremental steps in the setting of each knob

- The benefit resulting from changing the position of each knob

- Organizational implications of changes in knob settings

- Identification of typical candidate strategies implied by knob resettings

- Individual knob settings corresponding to a couple of seemingly good strategies

- The rough cost of implementing these candidate strategies

- The approximate benefits of implementing these candidate strategies.

By contrast, the second method of strategy generation, that of developing new concepts, will be much less structured but should include a preliminary stage of analysis of the market, the corporate position in the market, and the strategy of its competitors (Biggadike 1976; Henderson 1973; and Porter 1980). The actual process of strategy generation might start with a day-long planning meeting or a more lengthy meeting incorporating: (1) a review of the analytical data, (2) generation of unorthodox candidate strategies, and (3) preliminary discussion of the steps that might be involved in the implementation of a few promising strategies.

Later, for the top few candidate strategies, the staff might make a translation into corresponding knob settings and the best guess about the associated estimated expenses and benefits (sales, profits, etc.) under some assumptions of competitive responses (Porter 1980). Then follows a second meeting, again attended by the senior executives and the senior staff, in which these conclusions would be presented, discussed, and the candidate strategies further improved. The result of the second meeting ought to be a list of new, improved strategies and their relative attractiveness.

Both approaches to strategy generation result in candidate strategies that need to be further defined before being tried in a corporate model. The conceptual approach needs more work, particularly in laying out the analytical base, but the framework presented below can also be used to examine the completeness of incremental strategies.

HIERARCHY OF CANDIDATE STRATEGIES – FROM CONCEPTS TO KNOB SETTINGS

In chapter 2, we introduced examples of very broad, conceptual strategies, such as "developing new products," "increasing market share," or "expanding into new geographical areas." Such notions are too broad to be translated directly into operationally useful terms. They are as imprecise and broad as scenarios describing an "unstable environment" — that is, they provide an initial image that must be developed further by adding more detail. Even as a concept, broad candidate strategies need additional clues before they can be "fleshed out."

For example, "developing new products" could be interpreted by an energy company as moving away from making basic chemicals (e.g., sulphuric acid) toward making intermediates (e.g., polypropylene), or, alternatively, as moving two full steps closer to the customer, from basic to intermediates, and then from the intermediates to the final product (e.g., articles made from polypropylene, such as computer terminal casings or ski boots). Similarly, "increasing market share" could mean more primary sales, adding the after-sales service (e.g., maintenance of equipment) or, moving even further, assisting customers in the solution of their problems by providing software packages. In the third example, an additional, clarifying hint could mean that the geographical expansion should take place only in Europe, or South America.

A "strategy tree" is shown in figure 5.1. Notice that in the second level from the top, the strategy has already become more specific. We move from the conceptual alternative ("expand into a new geographical area") toward a more concrete operational objective: expand into South America.

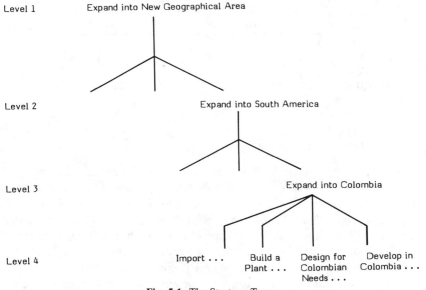

Fig. 5.1. The Strategy Tree

The next (third) tree level may specify a country, Colombia, for example. The fourth level might address the question: "How?" Here several alternatives might be considered, which can be taken singly or in combination:

- Import, and sell, our product(s) made in Germany

- Build a plant in Colombia and make a German-designed product in that plant

- Design a new product in Germany, especially suitable for Colombian needs

- Start a development activity in Colombia to develop or use locally available skills.

This is as far as a tree approach should take us. Beyond the fourth level of the tree, we need another conceptual tool — a strategy as a series of decisions over time. The tree ends in outlining: (1) departmental responsibility for decisions that need to be further fleshed out (e.g., to import, which is a marketing decision), and (2) the dimension of the decision (e.g., build one large plant in Bogotá rather than several smaller plants in different cities).

In contrast to the tree, table 5.1 shows the new interpretation of a candidate strategy: the functional responsibility (vertically) and the time for making the decisions (horizontally).

Table 5.1. Responsibility and Timing of a Strategy

Functional Responsibility	Time				
	1983	1984	1985	1986	1987
Marketing Strategy	X	X	X	X	X
Construction Strategy		X	X		
Product Strategy				X	X
Research, Strategy, etc.					X

At this stage of strategy definition, the Xs merely indicate the timing of the individual decisions needed to implement the candidate strategy. We will start marketing activity in 1983, start building a plant a year later in 1984, and start product activity in 1986. Research will begin in 1987. Notice that we are already a long way from "expanding into a new geographical area." But it is not enough. The marketing, construction, and product functional substrategies have to be more explicitly defined.

For example, in defining marketing (or any functional) strategy, we are assisted by several concepts: (1) decisions to allocate (or to reallocate) financial resources as changes in decision "knobs," (2) productivity of the applied resources, and (3) the inertia, or to use an engineering term, the "time constants," of the operation involved. Continuing with our marketing example, marketing embraces market planning, market development, and sales support. These, in turn, can be more finely divided. For example, market planning includes analysis of the competitor's strategy, competitive products, estimating sales volume and the cost of the sales effort, determining prices, and so forth. Similarly, market development will include advertising, preparation of promotional material, pilot trials, etc. These are then the final decision knobs that will have to be set at particular levels of annual expenditure.

The extent to which the knobs will have to be "turned up" (raising the expenditure level), will depend on the estimated productivity of a particular function. Thus, it will take so many salespeople, or agents, to sell a required volume of products (or services).

Finally, the concept of inertia will alert us to a possible delay between making the resources available and seeing the results of the resource allocation. Thus, it may take some time, possibly years, before the sales effort in a new territory results in the first sale. Therefore, a sustained effort over a considerable time, possibly more than one year, may be needed.

Analysis of delayed effects will be considered more fully in chapter 6. Here, however, we will note that a fully explicit candidate strategy must define resource allocations as a function of time. An example is shown in table 5.2.

Table 5.2. Timing of Resource Allocations

Marketing Strategy	\$ Expenditures		
	1983	1984	1985
Development of agents	50	30	20
Advertising	10	15	20
Preparation of promotional material	25	20	15
Direct sales effort	5	50	100

It is increasingly clear that we are developing information that looks very much like a business plan that, if approved, will be set in concrete by means of a budget (Steiner 1979, ch. 12). But there is a difference: our information resembles a budget (or, more to the point, successive budgets) if that particular marketing strategy were to be implemented. Whether or not it will be implemented will now depend on practical constraints on the candidate strategy — whether a particular level of proposed total expenditures in, say, 1983, is supportable by the cash flow, profitability, or manpower.

The point we would like to make now is that only after a marketing strategy (to continue the example) has been defined to the approximate degree of detail illustrated are we ready to check whether other functional substrategies — for example, construction, production, research — are consistent with marketing strategy. Quite often, the examination will show they are not. For example, because of local licensing problems, a plant cannot be constructed in the time originally assumed in the development of the sales strategy. And, if shipments cannot commence until year X, the advertising effort must be rescheduled to allow for the slippage in the shipping schedule.

But, after adjusting expenditures iteratively and after further analyses, a consistent strategy can emerge. It will be represented by a setting of an array of detailed decision knobs, one array of settings for each year. But there is more to generating a detailed candidate strategy than establishing expenditures; it is deciding what price to set.

Pricing Strategies

A pricing strategy is an essential element of all strategies (Dean 1980). Specifying a pricing strategy is also essential to the running of the strategic model because, without knowing about prices, the model cannot compute revenues. We cannot bypass the problem by simply extrapolating past revenues and determining net profits by using historical cost information. If such a simple procedure is credible, the business is so stable that there is no need to build either alternative scenarios or a model. But, in the more common situation of uncertainty, the required alternative — that is, postulating future prices — seems at first overwhelming. To make it less formidable, we will now consider methods by which future prices can be estimated. Let us review the candidates.

Long-term price trends. In many industries, there are reliable long-term price trends. Typically driven by technology, the prices (in real terms) drop each year in a very stable manner. Examples are the prices of semiconductor elements, such as random access memory chips. Other products using such components, e.g., calculators, also decrease in price. In other cases, the demand for constantly higher performance may offset the experience curve and act to keep prices increasing; for example, each new fighter plane costs more in real terms than its predecessor.

Cost plus a markup. Industry practices may set prices based on the costs of production plus a certain markup for profit. The more efficient producers can either reduce the prevailing price level or maintain a higher markup. Economies of scale and/or experience curve effects may suggest a strategy of setting a lower price, even below current cost, in the hope that the higher future volume will reduce future costs.

Cost related to alternative means of supplying the demand. Often, prices of products that may be substituted for each other are interdependent. For example, prices for crude oil, gas, and coal are loosely coupled now but could be more tightly coupled when natural gas is deregulated.

Price determined by regulation. Although forecasting regulated prices requires forecasting the regulatory environment, for a given regulatory environment the pattern of prices might be well defined.

Prices determined by the market leader. Here, analyzing the market, we forecast future prices (to recognize uncertainty, probabilistically) that might be charged by the price leader. Then, for each outcome (i.e., price charged by the market leader) we would set our own price in historical relation to that charged by the price leader — for example, 10 percent less.

Price determined by the intersection of supply and demand. According to traditional economics, given an idea of what the supply versus price and the demand versus price would be, the intersection establishes the price of the product or service that would clear the market. This works well with commodities.

Prices within a broad pricing strategy. Within the broad requirement for adequate profit, prices of individual products produced by a corporation may bear no discernible relation to costs, demand, or other variables. Products that can bear high prices are deliberately "overpriced." Other products become "loss leaders" (in a supermarket) or destroy competition by "predatory pricing" (partially regulated utilities).

Price based on the customer perception of value. If the customer believes that the product is of high value, the customer will be prepared to pay a price commensurate with this valuation. This strategy applies when there are no alternatives or when the characteristics of a product allow the purchaser to realize a high value added. Fertilizers, herbicides, and satellite solar cells are examples.

FULLY ORCHESTRATED STRATEGIES

Although strategies can be conveniently represented by knob settings that operate on dollars — turning the flow of money on and off — every manager knows that, in real life, it is people who influence whether or not a strategy succeeds. Therefore, we will examine briefly some "human" dimensions of strategy formulation.

Personality Profile Consonant with a Strategy

If a strategy calls for attacking, then, to lead it, choose a person with an aggressive frame of mind, a Patton instead of a Montgomery. Recognizing this need for synchronizing business strategy with personnel selection strategy, some corporations are beginning to include a careful appraisal of personnel profiles before determining who should be in charge of which strategy (Levinson 1980; Mills 1979).

Arranging Rewards for Thankless Strategies

Defensive strategies within one business unit (such as "milking cash cows" to provide funds for growth in other businesses) are not likely to offer enough psychological rewards or internal brownie points to the manager in charge of such an operation. It then becomes the task of the CEO to provide adequate incentives and to convince the manager that his or her personal prospects will not be adversely affected vis-à-vis his or her peers.

Laying the Groundwork for Candidate Strategies

Several internal and external groups may influence the implementation of a new strategy because they expect that the outcomes may harm them: employees, customers, shareholders, government, and public interest groups. Adequate preparation must be done by a number of staff and line groups to lay the groundwork, communicate and explain, or secure approval of (or at least ensure less hostility to) any new strategy.

THE ROBUSTNESS OF A STRATEGY

Changes in Pacing

We may expect that a candidate strategy may have to be changed if future circumstances change and make the decisions entailed in the original strategy no longer attractive or feasible in the ways originally conceived. The changed circumstances may simply be that the budget is tight and the investments required in order to implement the strategy have to be curtailed or stretched out. Yet, these "unforeseen" developments always seem to happen. They do not force a major strategy change but merely modify the original plan. The initial definition of a candidate strategy ought to recognize that such modifications may happen and allow some slack in the implementation.

Abandoning a Strategy

A more serious possibility is that the external circumstances will change drastically enough to make the original strategy completely untenable. The modeling problem is to recognize what such circumstances might be, to assign probabilities to them, and — this is most important — to identify a fall-back strategy. When this is done, the strategy "path" itself becomes probabilistic, with forks down the road. At each fork, the new direction will be determined by the circumstances derived from the external scenarios and, therefore, these scenarios must contain elements that would force the abandonment of a strategy and the putting in its place of a new strategy (Fig. 5.2). Similarly, actions of future management can be treated as external circumstances. For example, if one of the several possible candidates for the new chairman of the board is most likely to adopt a different strategy, the probability that he becomes chairman is one of the "external" scenario elements. Otherwise, the model will pursue blindly a preconceived strategy, disregarding the information about internal politics currently known (even if only probabilistically) by the executives.

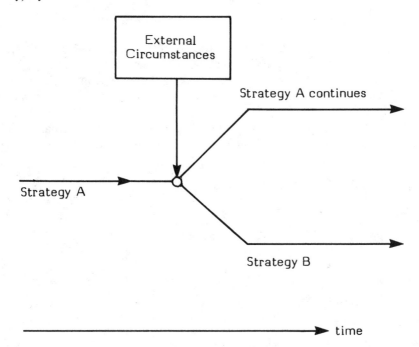

Fig. 5.2. Replacement of a Strategy

VERBAL ENCODING OF A STRATEGY

We have seen how, for the benefit of later quantitative analysis, a candidate strategy can be expressed as a series of numbers corresponding to the knob settings of the detailed decisions. But, unless there is a corresponding English language description of the candidate strategy created by these knob settings, the amalgam of numbers will be quite unintelligible to most people. A document — called a Business Direction Paper (BDP) in some corporations (Neubert 1980) — can be used to crystallize and present the strategy, and its truncated version can be used as a "comment" accompanying the numerical strategy file of the strategic model. Such a document would consist of:

- A general description of the business

- The market

- Competitive position in the market

- The results desired

- The strategic approach

- Means of detecting if the strategy works as planned.

For the purpose we have in mind, each of these headings should be compressed into a few sentences. This can be done because the compressed version is intended only as a master blueprint — the full document describing the implementation of a strategy as a series of annual plans is on hand elsewhere.

We are now ready to address the problem of translating the scenarios and candidate strategies into estimates of corporate performance by modeling the characteristics of the business.

REFERENCES

Abell, D. F.; and Hammond, J. S. 1979. *Strategic market planning: Problems and analytical approaches.* Englewood Cliffs, NJ: Prentice-Hall.

Andrews, K. 1971. *The concept of corporate strategy.* Irwin: Dow Jones.

Biggadike, E. R. 1976. *Corporate diversification: Entry strategy and performance.* Boston: Harvard University Press.

Dean, J. 1980. In Kerin, R. A., and Peterson, R. A. *Perspectives on strategic marketing management.* Boston: Allyn and Bacon.

Henderson, B. D. 1973. The experience curve reviewed: IV. The growth share matrix of the product portfolio. *Perspectives*, No. 155. Boston: The Boston Consulting Group.

Hussey, D. E. 1976. *Corporate planning: Theory and practice.* New York: Pergamon Press.

Kottler, P. 1980. *Marketing management analysis, planning and control.* Englewood Cliffs, NJ: Prentice-Hall.

Levinson, H. 1980. Criteria for choosing chief executives. *Harvard Business Review* July-August: 113-120.

Lorange, P., and Vancil, R. F. 1977. *Strategic planning systems.* Englewood Cliffs, NJ: Prentice-Hall.

Merrifield, D. B. 1977. *Strategic analysis, selection, and management of R&D projects.* New York: AMACOM.

Mills, D. Q. 1979. Human resources in the 80s. *Harvard Business Review* July-August: 154-162.

Neubert, R. L. 1980. Strategic management the Monsanto way. *Planning Review.* Journal of North American Society of Corporate Planners.

Porter, M. E. 1980. *Competitive strategy.* New York: The Free Press.

Rothschild, W. E. 1979. *Strategic alternatives.* New York: AMACOM.

Royce, W. S. 1979. *SRI Business Intelligence Program, Research Report No. 620.* Menlo Park, CA: SRI International.

Skinner, W. 1978. *Manufacturing in the corporate strategy.* New York: John Wiley.

Steiner, G. A. 1979. *Strategic planning: what every manager must know.* New York: The Free Press.

CHAPTER 6
THE CORPORATE (STRATEGIC) MODEL

Scenarios are like stories: informative, stimulating, and perhaps even thought provoking. Options and candidate strategies are also interesting because, in the course of generating them, one cannot help but reflect on the character of one's business and the elements of that business which come into play in defining different options. But what we need to make each far more useful are ways by which either options or candidate strategies can be tested against scenarios. This, of course, is the purpose of corporate (strategic) models.

DEFINITION OF A STRATEGIC MODEL

A strategic model should be able to accept a scenario and an option or a set of options (a candidate strategy) and, presumably, show the consequences of that conjunction. Let's build on that and slowly add to this very simple yet almost adequate description. We have said earlier that candidate strategies created for the purpose of trying them against alternative scenarios need not be real. They certainly should be plausible; otherwise, the effort would be a waste of time. But very rarely would we expect to hit upon an initial strategy that cannot be improved upon by trying it against different scenarios. Because even good candidate strategies are unlikely to finish as final strategies, we add to the definition of a strategic model: the model is an exploratory tool.

The strategic model cannot tell us what strategy *ought* to be. We have already seen how complex the description of a candidate strategy becomes as soon as we leave the level of broad generalizations. A large number of decision knobs had to be set, and we had to decide not only the magnitude of their settings but also the time sequence in which they are to be "engaged." When there are many decision variables (i.e. many knobs), it is very

96

difficult to determine how to optimize the magnitude and the timing of settings. That's why a strategic model cannot tell us what the best strategy is. It always leaves the improvement of strategy to intuitive judgments made by managers to whom the responsibility rightly belongs. No one will ever know what the *best* strategy is, but some candidate strategies will be shown to be better than others.

The next notion we would like to introduce is that of simulation. The actual external environment and the actual strategy will impact on a real corporation — an immensely complicated amalgam of human, physical, and financial resources. The (admittedly ambitious) aim of strategic modeling is to capture the essence of the corporate behavior, that is, its behavior as far as its response to options or candidate strategies is concerned.

In a strategic model, we are trying to capture the gross behavior of the corporation or a large corporate unit. We are not interested in the daily tactical responses that management at lower levels (and, surprisingly enough, even at higher levels) feels compelled to make in order to meet the sudden actions of a competitor, a letter from an important senator, or a ruling from a department of a regulatory agency. These are the minor nuisances of corporate life, and, statistically, they average themselves out. Otherwise, no long-range strategy would have been possible. Indeed, if all the long-range decisions are at the mercy of last month's operating results, no strategy is possible. Fortunately, that is very rarely the case, although, at times, it may seem like this to every manager.

A useful parallel to the strategic model of a corporation or a corporate unit — because most of the action takes place at the level of corporate units whether they are called business units, strategic business units, or whatever — is the Link trainer, a device in which a pilot can fly an imaginary airplane. One can think of the strategic model as such a trainer. We select a flight path (corresponding to a candidate strategy) and the weather through which we are going to fly (corresponding to a scenario) and then observe the consequences — have the wings dropped off, or has the engine stalled as a result of severe icing and wrong flight altitude?

Continuing with the simile, the corporation is analogous to a fleet of airplanes, some very fast but carrying only a few passengers, others slow cargo planes, while the rest might be modern, high-speed, wide-body jets with economical engines. The function of the simulator is to tell the flight commander how many and which planes of his fleet have made it safely to the intended destination.

Thus, every exercise of a strategic alternative can be compared to a flight test. Instead of a pilot in the cockpit of the Link trainer, the manager may sit in front of the computer terminal. It would be useful to preserve this analogy because one of the tasks of building a strategic model is to organize the cockpit instruments so that the model is "easy to fly." The control knobs that we have encountered in trying to define the strategy have their counterpart in the controls of the airplane — the throttle, gas mixture, flap setting, and so forth. Obviously, to make the airplane easy to fly, these controls should be as few as possible and yet, between them, able to accomplish all the essential operations: take off, bank, climb, land, and so on. In the real cockpit of a four-engine plane, the four throttle levers are connected so that the pilot can move them with one motion. Using this same principle, we will try to design corporate strategy control levers in the model so that a generalized instruction can be relayed to more than one business unit.

We said that the model is a simulation of the actual corporate unit. But how well does it perform the task of simulation? If it does it poorly, the whole exercise would be a waste of time. In the airplane industry, it is possible to validate the simulator. We recall reading a story about one of the latest fighter planes that had been designed by computer simulation. Later on, a mockup cockpit was made and equipped so that a test pilot could "fly" the plane, the gravity forces being simulated by inflating and deflating, as appropriate, the G-suit of the pilot. Still later, the real plane was made, and the test pilot flew it. Afterward, he made the engineers very happy by observing that "it flies just like the simulator." That was a nice compliment, testifying to the credibility of the simulation.

We can't afford the luxury of "flying" the real corporation in order to test the simulator, so the validation must rely on the judgment of experienced managers who, testing alternative strategies, will decide whether the results are believable. It is possible to think of some trial runs simulating the known past external environment and the past strategy to gauge whether the model replicates past behavior. We would not recommend that the model be released for "real" use unless it has been flight tested under such circumstances. But the ability to reproduce the past does not necessarily imply the ability to simulate the future with its different combinations of candidate strategies and external environments.

Let us now list the essential ingredients that ought to be included in a strategic model. The model must be able to:

- Accept a scenario and options or candidate strategies and show the consequences of that conjunction

- Capture the essence of performance of the entire corporation (or a corporate unit) in response to a candidate strategy

- Serve as an exploratory tool with the aid of which a manager can derive a better strategy than the current one

- Be used easily by managers

- Be credible to managers.

To recapitulate, we have addressed the following questions: (1) Why build strategic models?, (2) What are they?, and (3) What do they do? Only four more questions remain. They are:

- What are the main components of a strategic model?
- How do we best model a corporation?
- How do we build a strategic model?
- How do we use a strategic model?

The answers to the first three questions will be addressed in the remainder of this chapter. The fourth question will be taken up in chapter 7.

COMPONENTS OF A STRATEGIC MODEL

Again, using the Link trainer analogy, we picture ourselves in the cockpit. We want to select the weather (scenario), the flight path (candidate strategy), and look at the results (consequences of the conjunction of a candidate strategy and a scenario). So, at the gross design level, there are four main components or modules (as shown in figure 6.1):

- The scenario module
- The candidate strategies module
- The corporate unit module
- The display module.

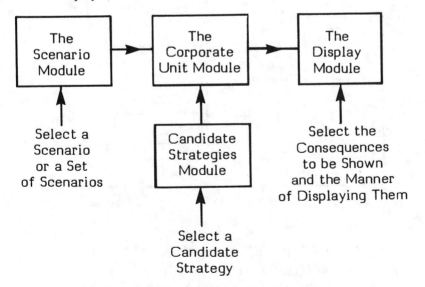

Fig. 6.1. Components of a Strategic Model

We have learned enough about scenarios and candidate strategies to make a good guess at the contents of their respective modules. For instance, we know that the scenario module will contain the metascenarios, that the strategies module will contain the candidate strategies, and we also know how a candidate strategy might be defined in detail. The display module accepts instructions about the results that the user needs and the ways of displaying them; it then finds the appropriate numbers in the files provided by the model of the corporate unit, arranges them into a desired format, and displays them (or stores them for later display). Thus, these three modules are rather straightforward in structure and do not warrant detailed descriptions. But the term "corporate unit module" is new. So let's concentrate on it.

The Corporate Unit Module

Many would call the corporate unit module "the strategic model," but it is not very useful without the other modules, two of which are driving it (the scenario and the candidate strategies modules), and one that receives the results of the simulation (the display module). But the corporate unit module is the core of the model or the model itself, depending on the definition. Typical organization of the corporate unit module is shown in figure 6.2.

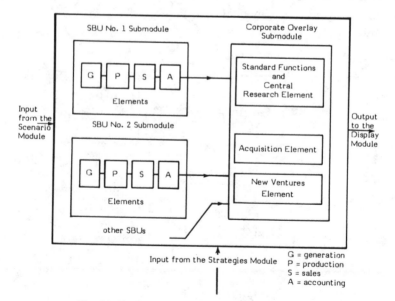

Fig. 6.2. Typical Organization of the Corporate Unit Module

Here, we encounter again the question of hierarchy. The smallest unit worth simulating is the smallest unit that can have an independent strategy. Typically we would call it, for that reason, the Strategic Business Unit (SBU). We don't mean to imply by the use of the word "independent" that the SBU runs amok in the corporate family. It is assumed its strategy is likely to be coordinated with the corporate strategy as a whole — at least it should be. But there are, in our experience, few corporate units that are truly SBUs. More typically, the corporation holds some strings over the unit. For example, it may allocate research and development funds from a central coffer. If the units need R&D, they must justify the need for such funds from corporate level. Also, typically, major capital investments are approved at corporate level, so that the SBU is not really capable of exercising a truly independent strategy; but, once the strategy is agreed upon, it is capable of implementing it — at least for a limited time.

For obvious reasons, it is very unusual for an SBU to be able to secure its own financing. In principle, the corporation can secure better terms from either the investment community or the banks. The reverse is sometimes also true. Thus, for example, Rolls-Royce Motors would have no trouble securing financing on its own, while Rolls-Royce as a whole couldn't raise adequate financing, went broke, and had to obtain government support. However, we will take it for granted in simulating that the only umbilical cord connecting the SBU to the corporation is common financing. Thus, any restrictions on capital expenditures will be accommodated as a component of a strategy by an expenditure limit (which may be, in principle, infinitely high).

We have compared the corporation to a fleet of airplanes. The individual airplanes are the SBUs. We will defer the problem of simulating the action of the fleet and concentrate on the strategic model of a single business unit. This is not necessarily easier because, from the modeling point of view, most business units are rather untidy. That is, SBU activities are often combined for any number of reasons: geographical location, common source of inputs, historical precedent, or the aggrandizing power of a particular executive. But let's start with a somewhat idealized concept of what an SBU is like and how it can be simulated.

MODELING A CORPORATION

We begin this section with a prescription: make the model as simple as possible. To bring the lesson home, we will paraphrase the saying of Lord Falkland, a member of the pre-Cromwellian British aristocracy. Lord Falkland has said, in the true conservative tradition of resistance to change, "When it is not necessary to change, it is necessary not to change." Applied to structuring a strategic model, we may paraphrase as follows, "When it is not necessary to include, it is necessary to omit."

There are several good reasons why the model ought to be simple.

First, typically, simple models require few inputs. A strategic model is intended for continuous use by many people. The input data has to be kept current and, if the model is small in size, it will be easier to keep it up to date.

Second, and equally important, simple models are easier to understand, and in order that the model be credible it must be understandable.

Third, after each SBU model has been individually debugged and approved, it will have to be run together with other models to simulate the behavior of the entire corporation. The simpler the individual models, the easier will be the task of mating them.

Fourth, occasionally each model might have a probabilistic element in it. For example, a competitor might lower the price, but we don't know if or when it might be done, although we might be willing to assign a probability to that possible action. To reproduce the effect of uncertainty, the model may have to be run several or even a hundred times in order to gauge the average effect of a strategy that is subject to uncertainty. Running a complicated model many times will take a long time and will be costly.

And, fifth, we believe that if the model is made interactive (and "friendly," of which more later on), there is a greater chance that it will be used more. And simple models tend to be "friendlier."

The first instant, almost gut reaction is that a simple model will not do. Why? Because our business is *so* complicated that its complexities cannot possibly be captured by a model that has to be simple. One of us has developed a standard ploy to overcome this common tendency. It is easy for an outsider — more difficult for an insider. "Assume," he would say, "that you are explaining your business to someone who knows little about it; how would you describe it?" Almost universally, the amazing response is, "Well, actually our business is rather simple." Then follows a description of the business in ordinary English, and it seems to make a lot of sense.

This anecdote has two important implications. The first is that only the senior managers of the business have accumulated enough experience to be able to cut out the frills and describe the real core of the business, and only top management has enough confidence to admit that the business is rather simple. The second is that modeling should start in English, with simple statements of its logic and not even a suggestion of computereze (at least not at this stage). Therefore, if willing, the manager is the best person to do the modeling. Preferably, he or she should do it by describing the business to someone who knows how to program. Let that someone worry about how to translate it into an appropriate system of equations using SIMPLAN, EMPIRE, or whatever. (As might be inferred, we do not accord a great degree of preference to any modeling support languages — the subject is really unimportant compared to our central purpose.) As the manager begins to describe his or her business, certain features of it occur repeatedly enough to be worth recording as standard elements. We begin with a model of a business unit.

Modeling a Strategic Business Unit

Most SBU models are likely to contain the following four elements: (1) product generation, (2) production, (3) marketing (including sales), and (4) accounting. For the purpose of simplifying the descriptions, we will address the task of modeling a business unit that makes products, but the modeling procedures will also be applicable to organizations that provide services.

Product generation. The basic concept is deceptively simple; but in strategic modeling that is precisely the assumption that can be made: Money injected into development of a product eventually produces designs that are ready for production some time later. Figure 6.3 illustrates the concept. The box of figure 6.3 specifies the efficiency of conversion: How much money at the input produces how much of a product design at the output? We can apply this concept to products of entirely different characteristics. For example, the rule of thumb in making battleships in World War II was that one person-year of input resulted in one ton of battleship. Similarly, $100,000 may result in one producing oil well. One geologist may discover so much in resources over the course of one year. It may take $1 million to invent a new drug and $1 billion to design one airplane, $5 billion for a 100,000 barrels-per-day oil shale plant, and so forth.

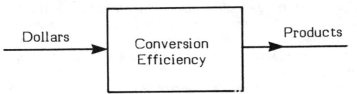

Fig. 6.3. The Simplest Model of Product Generation

In many businesses, managers know these rules of thumb, which they themselves use to establish reasonableness of new product generation proposals. We will now gradually elaborate on the simple concept. The first elaboration will be to introduce a time delay between cause (the injection of funds) and effect (product design ready for production). This immediately raises the question of selecting the appropriate values of time delays or intervals. The selection proceeds something like this: (1) Think of the longest individual product life time for any of the products that might be envisioned in any of the likely strategies; (2) add to it estimated total product development time, starting from early R&D; and (3) add the longest production run that such a product might experience.

We think you might be surprised to find how long the total time estimate will be. We know of companies that habitually think in terms of an initial product life of 20 years, followed by another 20-year life during which the product will be produced more cheaply by larger versions of the original plant. With such a time horizon, the model could probably step along in one-year time increments. On the other hand, if a company is in the business of producing highly perishable products (like hoola hoops), we might want to step the model in weekly intervals. The time delay between the injection of funds and the appearance of the product at the other end should be expressed in whatever time intervals are chosen.

Still more elaboration is needed. Some products may take more than one time interval to generate (several years to design a plane, for example). Therefore, unless a sustained effort is applied for the required number of time intervals, the results will not be proportional to the funds injected. Similarly, if the project is delayed beyond a reasonable time, it may be in danger of being cancelled altogether. That is one of the reasons why we suggest stopping the product generation cycle at the point where the product is ready for production. If the design is late, the product might never get into production, and the whole effort may be a washout.

Once we have these basic elements of product generation in place, it is time to think about constraints; unless some constraints are put in place, there will be nothing to prevent the model that is given enough money from generating a mountain of new products. Typically, there are constraints on how many designs can proceed concurrently. The amount of skilled effort may be limited, test equipment may be limited, and so on. If more is needed, additional delays may be encountered. These constraints have to be recognized and modeled. There may also be constraints in the opposite direction. Unless there is enough development work, engineers may leave and be difficult to rehire.

A question often arises: "But each of our products is unique; therefore, don't we have to specify all the products that happen to be on the drawing board now and enter the characteristics of each?" The answer is that, if this indeed is so, and there is no commonality between products, then the unit is truly dependent on the ability of designers to come up with the right idea at the right time. Also, since no one knows what the characteristics of future products will be, nothing sensible can be said about their sales either. In such circumstances, how can the decisions be made to expend or not to expend more development funds? If they are made on "hunch" then perhaps we should try to model the amount of those past management hunches. We must remember that the model is a simulator; it does not have to assume any logical or even explainable behavior from the managers of the enterprise.

An example: In modeling one business unit, we encountered what appeared to be a "leaky faucet." Money was put in every year, but (using the manager's own words) "no results were ever expected" — at least no tangible results. The amount of money was relatively small — only a couple of million — and the process was sanctified by tradition. Perhaps one important virtue of modeling is that it tends to shed a spotlight on such "leaky faucets."

Seriously, we doubt if any organization cannot find observable characteristics for its product generation. If new products are few and far between (aircraft, for example), the statistical base will be scanty, and the error of averaging might be large. The next plane might take twice the time to design as the last one. However, by using average trends characterizing product design, we will at least start at the best possible point to try to model products that have not yet been invented.

Before we leave the subject of product generation, we should remind ourselves of the need to clearly identify the decision knobs. Where are they in the model of product generation? Obviously, as we have already seen, we can adjust the development budget up and down. We can probably spread the same expenditures more thinly over time until the model will tell us that we have overreached ourselves and will come to the market too late.

We can assume that we can improve the productivity of new product generation — make our technical people come up with "more bang per buck." However, if we do that, we had better explain to the model how we have achieved it, without expending any additional money, that is.

Typically, in any one operational unit, there will be more than one kind of a product. The products will have different gestation times, and the productivity of the development people will vary. So we may have to repeat the basic relations or equations several times over, inserting appropriate parameters of development time, productivity, and whatever else that will have to be parametrized. As an example, illustrating the modeling of new product generation, we will use an actual case drawn from an SBU of a large diversified corporation (Lipinski 1964). Its charter is to produce telecommunication transmission equipment (equipment that processes signals for transmission and then transmits them). At the time of modeling, the three major product groups within the SBU comprised about 40 individual products. The major product groups were: (1) analog multiplex equipment, (2) microwave transmission equipment (both analog and digital), and (3) data transmission equipment.

At the time the study was made, the key developmental characteristics of these product groups were as shown in table 6.1. An examination of table 6.1 shows that the analog multiplex equipment returns the highest ratio of dollar sales per dollar of development expense — four times as much as microwave transmission equipment. One might be tempted, therefore, to pursue a strategy in which resources are shifted from microwave and data to multiplex. But that simple-minded approach would ignore a known fact — digital transmission was beginning to replace analog equipment. Because of the large amount of existing investment, the replacement process would take several decades (as a matter of fact, it will continue for two decades). Secondly, marketing knew that many customers were already in the process of transition

Table 6.1. Developmental Characteristics of Product Groups

	Development Time (years)	Product Life* (years)	Ratio of Dollar Sales/ Development Expense
Analog multiplex equipment	3.0	12	50
Microwave transmission equipment	2.0	7	12
Data transmission equipment	1.5	7	10

---

*From first year of sales (excluding demonstration sales) to year in which sales dropped to 10% of the maximum annual volume.

and, consequently, were buying all three groups of products. The inability to provide modern microwave and data equipment products might induce such customers to shift their purchases to competitors who offer a complete line of new products.

The purpose of modeling product generation for this organization was to examine the trade-off between short-term profitability and long-term growth. The task of the CEO was to determine the allocation of development funds among the three product lines. His task was complicated by pressures for short-term results from the corporate parent. A computer model was used to explore the consequences of alternative development allocations and to provide ammunition for dealing with headquarters. To establish future sales volume resulting from new product generation, we first needed to distinguish between the hypothesized sales of old and sales of new products. To model the sales volume of old products, we assumed that all development stopped, say 10 years ago, and plotted sales of all products older than 10 years. The procedure was then repeated on the assumption that all development stopped 9, 8, 7, etc., years ago. The surprising result was that the sales curve of old products looked very similar (Fig. 6.4).

As the company grew, total sales volume became larger, but the old sales volume maintained the same shape, composed of a rising linear component and an exponential decay. The approximation for old sales (OS) in year k was of the type:

$$OS(k) = S_{(k-l)} (1 + at) - F(t),$$

where $F(t)$ was the "decay" function shown shaded in figure 6.4. It is immediately apparent that, to preserve growth, the new products should fill the shaded area. New product sales were simulated as follows:

A. First year sales (FYS) of new products (in this case, analog multiplex) in year k, $FYS_{(k)}$ were given by:

$$FYS_{(k)} = \sum_{i=k-3}^{i=k} f(i)S(i)$$

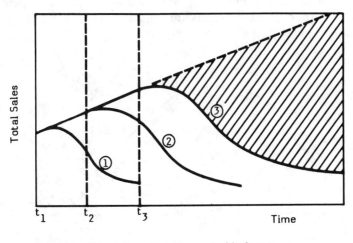

Graph 1 - Sales of products generated before t_1
Graph 2 - Sales of products generated before t_2
Graph 3 - Sales of products generated before t_3

Fig. 6.4. Decaying Curve of Old Sales

where *f(i)* is the fraction of sales revenues in the year *i* contributing to the product's first year sales in year *k* and *S(i)* are the sales revenues of the company in year *i*.

B. Given constant marketing effort, the first year's sales historically resulted in the succeeding year's sales (SYS) rising above the first year level to *M* times the volume of the first year sales and eventually falling to the point (*T* years after first sales) when the sales dropped to 10 percent of peak volume and were discontinued. The approximations used were:

$$
SYS_{(k)} = \begin{cases} M \cdot FYS_{(k-t+1)}(\sin(\frac{\pi}{L})t) & \text{for } 1 \le t < L \\[2ex] M \cdot FYS_{(k-t+1)}(\sin(\frac{\pi}{L})l)(e^{-a(t-1)}) & \text{for } 1 \le t < T \\[2ex] \text{and, } 0 & \text{for } t > T \end{cases}
$$

Figure 6.5 shows how the sales at times *l, L,* and *T* were determined. *M* is the ratio of peak product sales to the first year sales. Generation of other product groups used equations functionally similar but having different parameters *l, L,* and *T.*

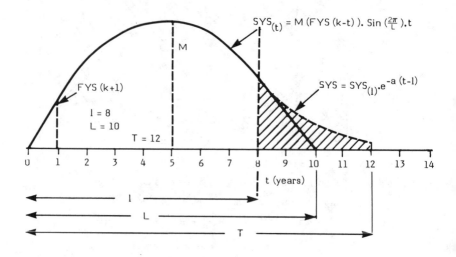

$$SYS_{(t)} = M\,(FYS\,(k\text{-}t)\,)\cdot Sin\,(\tfrac{2\pi}{L})\cdot t$$

$$SYS = SYS_{(l)}\cdot e^{-a\,(t\text{-}l)}$$

FYS (k+1)

l = 8
L = 10
T = 12

t (years)

Fig. 6.5. Characteristics of Product Life

When, in modeling new product generation, we have subdivided new products into different product lines as shown in the above example, we have invented another control knob — we can now change the proportion of funds allocated among product lines in development. When we finish, we might have the following decision knobs in place:

• Amount of money budgeted each year for product development

• Proportions in which the above is split among different product lines

• Willingness to hire or train more people or to expand facilities.

Now a word about dimensionalities, such as the dimensions of "product design." Certainly the input is dollars, but what is the output? Of course, the output of development, in real life, is a stack of drawings, perhaps a pilot model. What dimensions should we assign to it? We suggest the use of a "currency" that best approximates what actually takes place in an organization. It will probably be called something like "average product information package for the product type XY" — for example, a typical set of manufacturing drawings for an airliner. It probably has cost considerable money to develop. Now it will be the task of manufacturing to translate it into hardware and the task of marketing to translate the hardware into revenues at the market place.

Production. In some corporations, there currently is no product or process development going on. No one remembers the time when the current production process was developed. It seems that it has gone on forever and that it will go on forever. An example of such a stable, unchanging process is a sulphuric acid or a low-density polyethylene plant. In such plants, major changes in the process occur only over long intervals, perhaps only a few times in a century. In such instances, within the time horizon of the model, we might well be in between major changes in the nature of the production process, and part of the model that addresses "new process generation" would be missing.

A lack of changes in the process makes modeling a production plant much easier. Because it is much simpler we will address it first. Let's assume we are simulating a continuous flow process. A refinery is a good example. In come the feedstocks. Out go the finished products. We may insult the refinery production engineers if we compare their plants to sausage-making machines, but from the modeling point of view there is a great degree of similarity. It might seem to be a horrible caricature because, all the time, a great deal of very sophisticated adjustments go on in plants of this type. But they are all tactical! Responding to a new demand profile for heating oil, gasoline, etc., the refinery continuously adjusts its complicated operation. Similar readjustments follow changes in prices of feedstock, quality of crude that is being processed, and so on. But, from the strategic point of view, these technical adjustments do not matter. In the model, we take it for granted that the managers of the refinery will make such skillful adjustments. The only strategic variables are: whether or not to expand the refinery; whether or not to change the basic processes; and whether or not to get rid of the refinery altogether. Of course, implicit in each choice are also deciding how much each alternative would cost and deciding at what rate to implement the change. But, in this simplest case, no major process change is envisaged. Thus, we are left with a sausage machine. The simplicity of modeling is shown in figure 6.6.

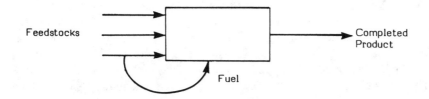

Feedstocks

Completed
Product

Fuel

Fig. 6.6. A Simple Model of Production

The example omits some of the details that are bound to creep in, if only to pacify the ego of the manager who describes the process. Note that some of the input is fed back to fuel the process. There are fixed costs and variable costs. The input is volume, and the output is also volume. The scenarios will tell us how much to pay for the input and what the output will fetch.

The critical strategic variables are whether to build a new plant and whether to dispose of a plant in any given year. Because plants come in different sizes, it may be necessary to assume, from the modeling point of view, a "standard plant package." The decision knob will then simply instruct the model that so many standard packages should be built or disposed of. In an option that would not even use such a knob, we might be able to reproduce the existing practice of incremental expansion. Knowing that 20 plants are in operation and that most of them (remember, only the higher-level manager will be able to make such broad judgments) are up to a high level of capacity utilization, we can safely assume in the model that another plant will be built. If the model is made to represent such standard management practices, it will run automatically, reacting to the level of demand and other significant variables in the scenarios by building or disposing of plants.

The building of a plant takes time, and a plant is useless unless completed. A plant-building program resembles a new product development program because the development has to be completed before a new design can be placed in production. Similar qualifications apply to the effects of a delay in construction — a delay would allow the competitor to complete his plant first and thereby command a larger market share from which it might be difficult to dislodge him. If a plant comes up to capacity slowly, the gradual increase of production can be simply simulated by the percentage of full capacity rising asymptotically to its final value.

Other than continuous-production plants must be simulated by reproducing their special characteristics. These will depend on the nature of the business. No general guidance can be given here except that there will be some statements about plant size, its construction time, its operating costs, and so forth. Managers of a manufacturing plant will have engineering department staff who can provide all the details needed.

We mentioned the occasional need to upgrade the manufacturing process in a continuous production plant. In other plants there may be a similar need to upgrade manufacturing technology by, say, an introduction of CAD-CAM (Computer Assisted Design-Computer Assisted Manufacture), or programmable automation by robotics, etc. The decision whether to upgrade or not can be implemented by providing a suitable decision knob, which will cause appropriate subroutines to be exercised. Also, even though there may be many dissimilar plants within control of one operational unit, these generally can be grouped into a few broad categories.

When the plant finishes producing a product batch, and the product is not perishable (e.g., electricity), it is typically stored in the warehouse. Here, we encounter one of those nice philosophical points of dispute so often occurring in simulation of real-life processes. When the plant is given an order to produce a quantity of goods, the size of the order is based on the best sales forecast available at a time. The best forecast may be dead wrong, and the unwanted goods will pile up in inventory. That's real life. But in modeling we can be too clever. If we take the demand forecast from the scenario file and pass it to the plant element, the plant element will produce exactly the right number of goods to meet the demand — no more, no less. The warehouse in the model will stay empty. Therefore, in order to be realistic, it is better to simulate imperfect forecasting, perhaps by using a random number generator to modify the scenario forecast before issuing orders to the plant. Now the inventory will be used. The stock in the warehouse can be valued at a nominal internal price, or in number of units. In the next part of the model — the simulation of marketing and sales — a price strategy will determine at what price the goods will be offered to the market. The number sold at the price will establish their dollar value.

Marketing and sales. One of the most valuable activities of marketing is the most difficult to simulate. This is market planning: helping to decide product characteristics; defining the potential customer; establishing price structure of the product line (for example, whether the price of some products or some product and service combinations ought to be bundled); determining the scope of the after-sales service, advertising, promotion, and so forth. The simplest way to represent these manifold activities is via their associated expenses because adequate records normally exist on how much they have cost in the past. The results of these efforts will be sales volume or so many units sold. If a product or a product line has had a stable history, it is often possible to determine the proportionality between the marketing/sales effort, the dollars spent, and the resulting sales volume. Thus, in the model, a dollar of marketing/sales will result in a certain unit volume of sales. But, such stable products are rare. Typically, it will be more realistic to agree that a great deal of uncertainty exists in the amount of unit sales that a given dollar effort might produce. The extent of the uncertainty can be captured by using a probabilistic routine, such as a probablistic tree, expressing the best judgment of what sales might be at a given price and marketing/sales effort. This judgment ought to come from the best informed people within the company (typically, the people in the field) and from any consultants that one might wish to employ. In chapter 4 we saw an example of how such judgment might be elicited.

To determine the sales volume, other variables besides the sales effort and price might have to be supplied: the state of the economy and the behavior of competitors, for example. These will come from the scenario file of the model. Similarly, prices and the extent of market coverage (which will determine the cost of the sales effort) will come from the candidate strategies module.

We know of companies who (rightly so) spend an inordinate amount of effort in forecasting their sales productivity. Others do hardly any forecasting of productivity at all. Those who do appreciate that marketing and sales are important ingredients in the total cost of sales and should be added to manufacturing costs and the costs of engineering associated with the product generation in order to determine the profitability of a particular product line. Modeling these separate cost contributions will identify potential improvement areas. Sometimes it is better to improve marketing productivity than to hope that all will be well if we could only generate more sales.

After developing the flow of logic for each product line (or service), we should consider any possible synergies between products (or services). Often, one product or service supports another. That, after all, is the advantage in having a comprehensive product line. While the salesman is visiting one customer, he might just as well visit the buyer in another department. But synergies are difficult to model. In contrast to the relative ease of obtaining good records relating to individual products, hard information about the interdependence of products in the market place is almost impossible to obtain. One is left with opinions. One must be careful here — a lot of "dogs" are justified on the basis of synergy. One check on such claims is to find out how often customers have been placing several products on one order, and whether orders for separate products come from the same department or the same buyer. If there appears to be a genuine interdependence of one product on another, modeling will have to reflect it by postulating a constraint: Unless a certain amount of product X is sold, the sales of product Y cannot exceed a given amount. Similar considerations apply to the interdependence of prices of different products, but that is best done in the strategies module.

A rough block diagram of the marketing/sales module is shown in figure 6.7. The circles along product paths show how the effort of any individual activity (e.g., advertising) affects volume. To develop such relations, it is best to start with the nominal or reference case, i.e., an average advertising effort, and then consider how an augmentation or diminution of that effort might affect sales volume. In econometric terms, we are dealing here with partial cross-elasticities of demand to advertising, promotion, and so forth. Information about partial cross-elasticities is notoriously difficult to assess because rarely do changes in one factor alone result in changes in demand — normally several factors combine so that the individual effect of any one is hard to disentangle. Typically, the effect of any single factor is overestimated. For example, if all partial effects were to be positive, if, say, each

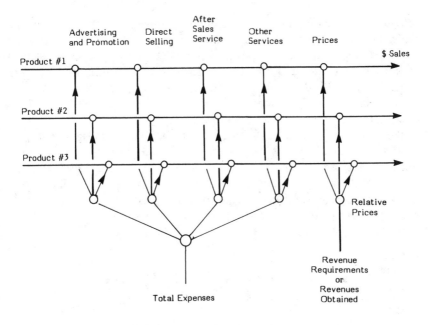

Fig. 6.7. The Marketing/Sales Module

of six functional departments were to increase its effort by 5 percent, the conclusion might be that the volume would increase by the sum of the individual contributions, that is, by 30 percent. Overestimation of partial effects is precisely what the individual departments of marketing rely on at budget time — if we were only given the extra funds, etc.

The larger circles in figure 6.7 are the decision inputs. The lowest layer allocates funds among the departments, implements product price strategy, and inputs other marketing strategies such as discounts, allowances, commissions, dealerships, licensing, etc. The next layer of heavy circles above allocates departmental funds among product lines, establishes relative prices of products, and deals with whatever funding is required for the other activities, such as licensing. We should be reminded that figure 6.7 is merely an illustration of what the block diagram of the marketing/sales element might look like. It will be different for different businesses, reflecting their special characteristics.

To summarize, the marketing/sales element draws goods out of the inventory and converts them into dollars of net sales, that is, sales revenues less discounts, commissions, and allowances, if any. We are now able to put together a profit and loss statement because we have arrived at both the expenses and the revenues of the operation. That determination will be the task of the accounting element, which is described next.

Accounting. The first task of the accounting element is to collect results that typically have to be passed on to "headquarters." In the model, the real headquarters is replaced by the corporate overlay. This is one reason this element is called an "accounting" rather than a "financial" element. In most corporations, individual business units rely on corporate headquarters to perform the financial functions. But each business unit is expected to provide financial (and other) results of its operations.

The block diagram of the accounting element is shown in figure 6.8. Principally, it produces the P&L statement, but it also provides information required to arrive at a corporate balance sheet and corporate cash flows. If the corporation is in the habit of computing Discounted Cash Flow (DCF) or similar projections for individual projects or products, the accounting element will also be expected to produce such computations.

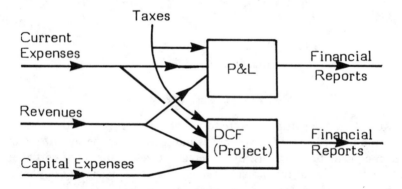

Fig. 6.8. The Accounting Element

We will now address the functions of the accounting element one at a time.

P&L. A typical profit and loss statement begins with gross sales and subtracts discounts, allowances, commissions, etc. (which, of course, may be different for different groups of customers) to arrive at net sales. The difference between the two is one measurement of the efficiency of marketing and sales.

The cost of sales (actual terms may vary between corporations) combines the cost of all activities that are directly traceable to the individual products or services.

Costs that cannot be allocated to individual products or services — such as research that is common to many products, marketing planning, general production engineering, plus the cost of general management and of the supporting services of personnel, payroll, etc. — are typically grouped as the administrative cost. Most often, they will bear some relation to the overall volume of the business in question, and these relations are generally quite stable over time.

Subtracting the cost of sales and administrative expenses from net sales yields before tax income. For some computations, like that of the discounted cash flow, taxes will have to be computed and added to other disbursements, even though taxes are actually being paid at a corporate level. It may be necessary, therefore, for the corporate model to "inform" the accounting element of the appropriate tax rate to use. However, the unit may have to pay its own taxes (e.g., state taxes or foreign taxes). Practices vary among corporations, and the accounting element should reflect these practices.

Cash flows. This element aggregates revenues and disbursements — that is, cash coming in and going out in any time period. Of particular importance are disbursements associated with investments, for example, investments in plant construction. Because we are describing a strategic model rather than a financial model, some of the finer points of cash management, such as moving deposits in and out to improve the return, can safely be omitted. If cash flows per product or per product line are needed by the DCF subelement, they must be so identified by the previously described elements.

DCF. Corporations differ in the method of analyzing relative profitability of projects. Some specify the required discount rate and compute the present worth of the net cash flow stream using that prescribed rate of discount. Others compute the internal rate of return (IROR) at which the present worth is equal to zero. Another index is the payout period, a point in time at which the total of nondiscounted revenues just balance the total nondiscounted expenses. The finance manager will specify the algorithm or algorithms that should be used in the computations. The time horizon of computation of DCF is very critical for projects where the revenues are well in the future and the investments are both heavy and early. Development of oil shale is a good example. Most of the oil shale revenues will occur in the next century, and yet billions will have to be spent in the next few years in gearing up for the operation. Unlike other elements that submit their report year by year, the DCF element has to wait until the model has reached the end of its time horizon.

Treatment of uncertainty. When circumstances demand a specific recognition of uncertainty — be they in external conditions or internal developments (i.e., R&D being ready in time) — the individual runs of the model will produce different answers, each accompanied by a probability assignment. The question then arises on how to treat and present such information. Typically, of course, uncertainty is being entirely suppressed in corporate financial projections and budgets. If the system — meaning the management culture, etc. — can only digest single numbers, then the accounting element should compute only the *expected values* (or averages) of sales, expenses, and so forth. However, care must be taken because expenses and sales may be probabilistically dependent. If that is the case, modeling suddenly becomes more complicated, requiring assignments of joint probabilities to combinations of revenues and expenses. In addition to examining the expected values, management may also wish to see the "best case" or the "worst case" projections, or even a "Lottery Profile" obtained by ranking the individual present worth streams by their respective probabilities (Fig. 6.9). The concept of the certain equivalent shown in figure 6.9 will be treated in chapter 9.

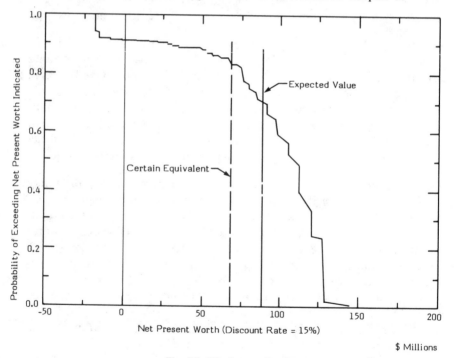

Fig. 6.9. The Lottery Profile

An interesting and, to some planners, a politically bothersome point arises when uncertainty has been explicitly recognized. That is, none of the runs of the model may correspond to budget projections. Therefore, for credibility reasons, if for no other, it may be necessary to redistribute the probability assignments in such a way that one outcome does track the "standard" projections, whatever these might be. But this is one of the finer points of the politics of modeling on which we shall comment later.

At this point, we have traced the development of the business unit model. Now we will describe the corporate overlay, the master model that accepts the results from the individual business units, "performs" corporate financial services for them, gives them strategic directions, and is often the modeling unit from which new businesses are spawned.

Modeling the Corporate Overlay

If it were not for the simulation of acquisitions and new ventures, corporate model building would be simpler than business unit modeling — merely accumulating financial results, arranging for the financial support of individual businesses, and taking care of the interests of shareholders and the government. We will first discuss such standard corporate activities and then comment on the modeling of acquisition and diversification activities. These are important in strategic modeling because opportunities exist here for developing new imaginative strategies.

Standard corporate functions. The corporate overlay element that deals with "current" business consists of two parts: (1) a "catch-all" to accumulate shared corporate expenses, and (2) a financial section. These would correspond roughly to the responsibilities of the Vice President of Staff Operations and the Vice President of Finance.

Staff operations may include central research and development. Modeling central research becomes more imperative than ever as corporations are finding that their research strategy seems to be disconnected from their corporate strategy and that the productivity of research seems to be falling. By the productivity of research, we mean research contributions to eventual corporate sales.

We should distinguish between modeling basic research and advanced research. Obtaining useful results from basic research is often a matter of faith and luck. One acquires very good scientists, supplies them with the facilities and the right working environment, makes sure they know about the corporation and its basic charter, arranges for occasional visits to the operating units, but more or less leaves the scientists alone to decide on appropriate research projects. From time to time, significant research findings may result from which the corporation, or the industry, or the nation, or even the entire world will benefit. But the process is largely unpredictable, and, unless the research center is very large, the statistical base is too small to describe its success in probabilistic terms based on experience.

Advanced research, on the other hand, can work toward achieving a particular corporate strategy by developing a profile of projects that can enhance the corporate business in years to come, typically a decade or more ahead. Here, one ought to be able to assign significant probabilities that one or more of these projects may generate future sales. The question is not to try to predict which product and how much sales but rather to decide how much should be invested in order not to deprive the corporation from access to future products or markets. These future products could be simply described in a model as product family "X" with an expectation of a certain sales volume, the expectation being based on the forecasted productivity of advanced research. Most vice presidents of research have a good notion of what this productivity has been and, alas, how it seems to be slipping. Figure 6.10 shows a simple model of advanced research productivity. An investment, typically lasting several years, results, after a fairly extended period, in new sales. The key parameter is the ratio of future sales to the current investment. Both are indicated by the area under the respective curves. Because future sales may have to support a somewhat larger corporate entity, the higher the desired rate of growth of sales, the larger the ratio must be. Also, if development time can be reduced, the ratio need not be so large. Finally, a longer product life helps to keep the ratio large. The very worst combination is expensive development, a long gestation period, and a short product life. We are sure that managers in some industries will recognize this as a familiar pattern.

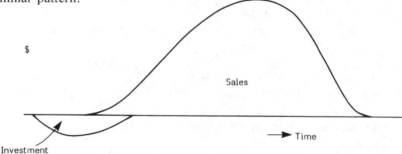

Fig. 6.10. A Simple Model of R&D Productivity

The objective of advanced central research is to feed promising prospects to the development laboratories within the business units. These might be products, processes, or even techniques. The latter two will reduce expenses and increase the productivity of operations. It is obvious that the modeling of such central resource activities will have to reflect the actual nature of the business and that no general rules are very useful.

Other staff operations, more mundane in nature than advanced research, may also be active participants in overall strategy. For example, personnel may have to expand its hiring operations if corporate strategy requires an increase in marketing. Similarly, the legal department will have to assume larger responsibilities if the corporate scenario envisages increased amounts of government regulation. For these reasons, it is dangerous to assume in the model that the historical ratio of staff expenses to overall sales volume will necessarily hold.

The financial subelement must compensate the shareholders for investing in the corporation, pay interest on outstanding loans, borrow funds by issuing more shares or contracting new debt, and compute corporate tax obligations. The requirement for funds will come from the requests of individual business units (their needs shown in the model by the negative cash flow projections) and from the corporate needs to finance acquisitions. The critical strategic variables are the payout ratio, which will determine the size of internal funding available, and the debt/equity ratio, which will determine the amount of new obligations, in terms of either new equity or new borrowing. Financial strategy will reflect corporate strategy regarding the direction of the business units and will take into account management preferences regarding payout practices and the amount of debt management is willing to incur. That is, as far as the conduct of the "standard" business is concerned, we see financial strategy as being subservient to business strategies by providing businesses with necessary sustenance and logistical support. In contrast, financial management plays a large part in acquisitions by developing a description of required financial characteristics for promising acquisition candidates. Such characteristics may include anticyclical behavior compared with current businesses, or cash-generating capabilities for financing current businesses.

Acquisitions and new ventures. It is almost impossible to model acquisitions for the very simple reason that not enough is known about them to model them prior to acquisition. Ideally, we would like to be able to borrow the model of the company we wish to consider as an acquisition candidate. In friendly takeovers, at some time in the future, such borrowing of models might be entirely feasible. But today, the best that can be hoped for is to create in a model a "black box" having a range of the desired characteristics of the acquisition candidate or candidates and assign a probability that such a candidate can be found in a given time period.

Let us be a bit more specific. The black box will produce financial reports similar to those produced by the business units but in considerably less detail. Probably they will include only the sales, total expenses, and the cash flow requirements (or, hopefully, cash flow contributions). The corporate unit module will then add the results of the black box or boxes to the results of the individual business units to show the effect of adding the newcomer to the entire corporate family. If the net result looks attractive, the search for a candidate more or less fitting the description will be intensified.

New ventures are, from a modeling point of view, much like basic research. That is, the results are far into the future, and only the early expenses can be seen with any clarity. The contributions of new ventures to future sales are probabilistic, each of them usually a long shot; however, if there are enough new ventures in gestation, the probability is much higher that one or another of them will produce useful sales. Nevertheless, the modeling of new ventures is at least as shaky as the modeling of acquisitions. A sophisticated corporate model user will know about the differences in the credibility of modeling a well understood business and modeling a poorly understood one.

BUILDING A STRATEGIC MODEL

In this section we address the technical and political aspects of building a strategic model.

The Technical Aspects of Modeling

The preceding section on the corporate overlay model completed our description of the model components of the corporate unit. Throughout our description of modeling we have almost managed to avoid equations or computer statements. That was deliberate because we feel that managers ought to model their businesses even though they may lack the specialized skills. Moreover, unless managers do modeling for themselves and are familiar with the model's logic and structure, they will not trust its findings and will not use it.

Managers can model perfectly well in plain English. However, computers can't understand English. Therefore, we need professional help to translate managers' statements in English into statements in the language of the computer.

The software language. In addition to standard higher level languages (such as FORTRAN) in which models may be written, several computer decision support systems, each using a convenient language, have been specially developed for financial or strategic modeling. A few of the more common languages are CUFFS, EMPIRE, EXPRESS, FCS/EPS, IFPS, REVEAL, SIMPLAN, and XSIM. Altogether, there are about 80 such decision support systems being offered.

These languages come as packaged software systems. They vary widely in price. Most corporations are already using one such package and have acquired experience in modeling in a particular language. In order not to complicate matters by introducing another (noncompatible) language into the company, it is suggested that, unless there are strong reasons to the contrary, the strategic model should be built using the software package with which some groups in the corporation are already familiar. But what could be these strong contrary reasons?

To answer that question in a roundabout way, we will now outline a set of desirable *system* characteristics for a strategic model. By system, we mean a computer plus a network of terminals, most likely geographically separated, that will be available to managers running models of their business units or a corporation consisting of several business units.

Corporate strategic model: desired system characteristics.

1. *Purpose.* The strategic model will be a planning tool enabling management to explore the financial consequences of alternative strategies under different forecasts of the external corporate environment.

2. *General description.* The model will consist of several Strategic Business Unit models and a corporate overlay model.

3. *Users.* The users of the models will typically be the planning managers in each group and in the corporate planning staff. It is estimated that the total number of users will not exceed N and that no more than n users will use the model simultaneously.

4. *Access to the model*:
   4.1. Access will be via hard-wired terminals, acoustic couplers, or modem-equipped terminals by dialing a telephone number(s) in the corporate headquarters area.
   4.2. The use of the model will be restricted to certain computer accounts. Each individual using the model will have a separate account and password.
   4.3. At any given time, only one version of the model will be the current operational edition and will be read-only. The custodian of the operational edition will be a designated member of the corporate planning staff. The operational edition will carry the date it became operational, and its validity expiration time will be specified and displayed to users.
   4.4. The custodian of the model will designate the users who can have access to the entire corporate model. Similarly, in each group or SBU, a custodian of that group's or SBU's model will be able to designate additional users who can have access to their model only.
   4.5. There will be a usage monitor that will generate and keep a log noting the name of each user, time of access, running time, the files used and read, the models employed, and the programs listed.

5. *Use of the model.* The model will be used for (1) generation of standard operational results and (2) experimentation.

Standard operational results will be the output that will take into account a set of the standard metascenarios and the currently approved and budgeted strategy. To compute standard operational results, the model will use the current operational edition of the model and its files describing the current set of metascenarios and the current strategy. These files will be read-only and dated.

Experimentation runs can use any combination of files (input and output) and programs, and both the programs and the files can be amended or generated by the user. Any user can declare such files and programs to be private (to be read or rewritten by him/her only) or semiprivate (to be read but not written by others).

Users can list files or programs that are accessible to them.

6. *Man-machine communications*:

   6.1. There will be an assist program that will respond to a call for help and respond to any difficulty a user may have at that point.

   6.2. Most entries that a user makes should be tolerated. If not typed in the approved manner, the program should inform the user how the last entry is interpreted and ask for an approval to proceed with this interpretation. The program will not abort unless the user requests it to terminate. Reasons for stopping will be given. (Example: file FILENAME needs 20 columns of data but only 19 were supplied.)

   6.3. If a run is expected to last for more than a minute or two, the expected time of completion should be printed. On no account must the user face prolonged silence. During a lengthy computation, "progress" reports should be printed from time to time.

Now the answer to "Why can't we use the currently used system software?" is clear. Before committing oneself to a particular software package, the company's professionals (operations research, computer center, etc.) ought to very seriously address system specifications. If the present software system cannot be made to fulfill the desired system specifications, it might be better to start afresh. The investment in modeling is likely to be considerable, involving time of fairly senior managers, and it would be unfortunate if a well modeled system were to be unused because of deficiencies in networking, file operations, etc., caused by an "unfriendly" computer environment.

Thus, the work of building a model proceeds along several parallel paths. While the managers are modeling, the senior professionals in operations research are likely to be working on the system design. Meantime, the corporate planners will be addressing the problem of developing scenario and candidate strategy files of general relevance to the corporation, while the planning managers at the SBU level will make corresponding preparations for scenario and candidate strategy files particular to their operations.

Size of individual models. We mentioned that the investment in modeling is likely to be considerable. Let's be more specific. How big are the individual models likely to be? How much should a corporate planner allocate for the entire effort? We will assume that a typical SBU makes three different product lines that will require differing modeling approaches. For example, the model of one product line may be much more probabilistic than the others, and therefore the model will be quite unlike the other two. We would be surprised if managers who model each product line cannot describe the model in fewer than 100 computer statements. Synergies between product lines, etc., may add 50 more statements. So we are not talking about huge models. Then, of course, there are the files, the strategies compilers (we have seen an example of one in chapter 5), and the display module. Still, the overall size of an SBU model is likely to be much less than that of a typical engineering or production model currently in use.

The model of the corporate overlay is likely to be similar in size to the model of an individual SBU. The corporate scenario file is likely to contain two or three sets of forecasts, each consisting of about 20 individual projections (e.g., strings of numbers for the GNP). Depending on the time horizon of the model, the strings will be from 15 to 50 numbers long. The corresponding scenario files at the SBU level are likely to be shorter, perhaps only 10 additional projections each.

The candidate strategies files, which contain algorithms translating a broad candidate strategy into individual knob settings, are likely to be comparable in size to the scenario files. Then we must remember that, for credibility reasons, both the scenario and the candidate strategies files will have to be extensively annotated. (We will address this problem in the next chapter.)

The display module extracts the desired results from the individual model runs and presents these in a manner most congenial and informative to the individual user. Depending on the degree of sophistication required (for example, if color CRT is needed, or color printers), the display module could be either of the same size as the scenario and candidate strategies modules or very much larger. Our recommendation is to start by making it simple and to add sophistication only after the success of the model is demonstrated — i.e., it is being used by managers.

The three modules (scenario, strategies, and display) are the equivalent of the cockpit controls we mentioned earlier. They bring together the appropriate programs and files, and they instruct the display module about the results desired and the manner of presentation.

Completing the system will be the administrative network overlay consisting of a monitor program, security provisions, and perhaps a section for billing individual users. In all, we should assume that for, say, six SBUs, the overall model size will be on the order of 5,000 computer statements. Budget estimates should be made for the modeling effort and the debugging of operations.

If, as a rough guide, writing and debugging 10 to 20 statements is assumed to take one professional person-day, then we are estimating one to two person-years of effort.

Modeling effort. The initial development of the model requires the modelers to:

1. Describe operations at each SBU and corporate level in a concise manner.

2. Translate these descriptions into a small number of statements and equations.

3. Write computer programs incorporating these statements into equations.

4. Develop files for handling the scenarios, candidate strategies, and the results of computations or consequences.

5. Design a communications interface between individual SBU models.

6. Write a user's command program that would bring into play the appropriate programs and files.

7. Design the file control program.

8. Write the usage monitoring program.

As important as the technical aspects are the political aspects of modeling.

The Politics of Modeling

Building a strategic model requires cooperation of several groups within the corporation: managers of operational units, corporate planning staff, and the professionals in the operations research or computer services group. Each of these groups has its special objectives and interests, and the individuals within each group have interests of their own. Each group looks for and reads key signals emanating from top management: Is the building of a strategic model or, even more fundamentally, is strategic planning to be taken seriously, and will engaging in the planning activity (to the detriment of other activities) contribute to the individual's brownie points or to the success of his or her organizational unit?

A strong supporting climate for strategic planning is the ideal condition. However, we should distinguish here between "real" strategic planning — elucidation and determination of a strategy, testing of alternative or candidate strategies against the changing environment — and paper work that in many corporations substitutes for the planning activity. The paper work may appear very impressive — for example, it may be titled "Five-Year Strategic Plan for the Corporation" — but it may contain only the marketing projections of the individual divisions, the corresponding revenues and expenses, and the computed financial results. Emphasis is placed on accuracy, i.e., whether the numbers add up correctly. These exercises consume an inordinate amount of management time, and if they serve any useful purpose it is to establish performance objectives. These would only be met if future conditions hold more or less to the assumptions made. So much time may be spent on the paper work of planning that none is left for thinking about strategy.

Ideally, the chief executive fosters strategic planning. To establish such a climate, he or she must ask managers to respond to strategic questions. When the chief executive directs strategy by requiring that each enterprise prepare and follow a Business Direction Paper (described in chapter 5), this short but effective document replaces the masses of paper used in more formal planning exercises. However, the preparation of a BDP requires much thinking and homework; its preparation can be improved by using formally derived scenarios (chapter 4) and the outputs derived from a strategic model.

Sometimes, however, the climate is mixed. Senior management is as yet uncertain whether strategic planning is really necessary, and it is worried that a diversion of the managerial effort to long-range planning can be only detrimental to the short-term corporate performance. Faced with a mixed corporate climate, the planning staff must decide how much effort can be justified.

Typically, operational departments have large enough budgets and considerable freedom in pursuing their planning. Therefore, it is often possible to charge the modeling activity in each unit to its own planning without the entire cost (which, as we have mentioned before, can be considerable) becoming too obvious. Sooner or later, however, the activity must surface because of networking charges and overall security arrangements.

The cooperation of operational groups is essential to the success of the modeling effort, but that's where snags can occur. Even when encouraging signals from above are fairly clear, one or more of the groups may not want to participate. Let's examine several possible reasons:

- The unit is under pressure and cannot afford the diversion of good people to the task.

- The local manager simply doesn't believe any good will come out of the exercise.

- Previous attempts at modeling have been disasters (too complex, needed too much data, etc.).

- There is a fear that the corporate planning will operate the divisional model in order to nitpick the unit's proposed strategy.

- The managers of the unit have set performance goals that will surely be challenged or "disproved" by the model.

It is not necessary for us to advise corporate executives on how best to diffuse or overcome these objections. They are problems with which most managers are only too familiar and have effectively addressed in the past. Assuming that they will do so again, we now turn our attention to the uses of the strategic model.

REFERENCES

Benson, F. S. 1978. The corporate model: Has management met the challenge? *Managerial Planning* 27, No. 3: 13-16.

Coates, J. F. 1976. The role of formal models in technology assessment. *Technological Forecasting and Social Change* 9.

Forman, L., and Lawrence, W. J. 1977. The case against corporate planning models: A rebuttal. *Business Economics* 12, No. 3: 54-57.

Lipinski, A. J. 1964. Planning for the company growth. *NAA Bulletin* XLVI, No. 3:37-41.

Lipinski, A.J., Ross, D.W., and Salmon, D. M. 1968. Development and application of a simple product development and marketing strategy model. *Digest of the Second Conference on Applications of Simulation*. New York: 57a-57b.

Naylor, T. H. 1976a. A survey of users of corporate planning models. *Management Science* 22, No. 9: 927-37.

———. 1976b. Corporate planning models: A survey. *Planning Review* 4, No. 3: 8-12.

———. 1976c. The state of the art of planning models. *Planning Review* 4, No. 6: 22-27.

———. 1977d. Why corporate planning models? *Interfaces* 8, No. 1, Part 1: 87-94.

———, ed. 1979. *Simulation models in corporate planning*. New York: Praeger.

CHAPTER 7
USING THE CORPORATE
STRATEGIC MODEL

The model has been built. A lot of grief, considerable funds, and a great deal of intellectual effort have been expended by operating managers, by computer and operations research professionals, and by planning staffs both at the operating units and at corporate headquarters. The simulator is ready and the controls are in place and seemingly working. The scenario file is full of scenarios, the candidate strategies file has at least the current strategy, and the display module is ready to print or show the results of the simulation. Like a new airplane glistening on the tarmac, the model is waiting for the test pilot to take it up in the air. But before flying the plane, we must prepare a flight test program. In its gradualness, it will be very similar to the test program of a new plane — first taxiing to check its brakes, then trying the nose wheel to see if the plane can change its direction on the runway. We will describe the test program, operate the controls, and go on some typical flights. Finally, we will comment on how the existence of a model will impact corporate communications.

THE TEST PROGRAM

We will assume that normal debugging has been accomplished, that is, the individual programs run and communicate with each other. The computer can be dialed up, the appropriate files can be transferred from the SBU model to the corporate model, and so forth.

The first model tests resemble the action of the test pilot who makes sure that the seat is comfortable and the seat belts fit. The modeling equivalent is to try the handshake commands, logging in and logging out, changing one's private identification code, and finding and reading the comments in the scenario and candidate strategies files. In other words, the user is in a "show-me" mood — "show me the standard strategy in the candidate strategies file; guide me into the successively finer level of detail within the file so that I can understand what the strategy really implies."

Next, the scenario file must be examined. Let's look at the corporate scenarios and the scenarios specific to the individual operating units. Hopefully, the comments will explain how the scenarios have been generated and when. Let's familiarize ourselves with the display module. We will order it to print the standard scenarios for the next 10, 20, or 30-year period. Then we will change the format from tables to histograms to graphs.

Now the model will be asked to "explain" the equations that determine its workings. We pick one assumption, say that of the GNP, and ask to be shown all the statements that use the GNP variable. We will probably have to use the text editor for the task, and that may be a good time to familiarize ourselves with the editor commands. All the above sounds easy but isn't. It will take several days to accomplish. Only then will we gain sufficient exposure to the "mechanics" of the model to be able to question its workings on the current strategy and a current scenario. The remainder of the test program is summarized in the following 10 steps:

1. Run the corporate model through current environmental scenarios and current strategies to detect possible logical errors.

2. Experiment with the effect of shifting individual SBU strategies in the designated year of the model run.

3. Experiment with the effect of delays in implementing some actions at the SBU level in otherwise current strategies.

4. Improve the software as a result of the experience gained in steps 1 through 3.

5. Develop the alternative scenarios data file.

6. Develop the alternative strategies data file.

7. Develop the alternative scenario selection program (one that would select or allow for modification of scenarios).

8. Develop the candidate strategies selection program (one that would select or allow for modification of the desired strategy).

9. Develop a consequences selection program (one that can portray the results of an interaction of scenarios and candidate strategies).

10. Improve the computer/communications infrastructure to reflect the incorporation of modules developed in steps 7 through 9.

When the model has been thoroughly tested, each of the operational group managers will be in a position to "sign off," in effect testifying that the model simulated his or her operation well enough to be used for strategic purposes (but, note, not for setting short-term goals or determining the budget).

Once the model has been officially approved, the approved copy is frozen and made into a "read-only" version. If any authorized individual wants to experiment with the model, a personal copy can be made. The official copy stays in operation until the next revision, typically six months to a year away. Thus, at any time, several personal copies of the model may be available, with individual managers trying to construct better versions or experimenting with alternative strategies.

It is easy to imagine how the model might be in constant use, provided, of course, that it is easy to use it. That's where the interaction with the user becomes all important. To illustrate the aspects of human interface, here is an imaginary account of one use of the model:

Watch Ms. Jones Use One

She dials a number and (one of the options) plugs the telephone handset into the terminal. The program she asks for comes up.

"This is the March 1982 version of the strategic model of the XYZ SBU of the company. May I have your name?"

The manager types her name and the model checks it against a preregistered list of authorized users.

"Please type your personal identification code."

Manager types something odd like AGYO (the terminal does not print or show the personal code).

"Thank you, Ms. Jones."

"By the way," types the model, "since the last time you ran this version, Joe Blow in the economics department (ext. 3374) has made some pretty important changes in the forecasts of the Aaa bond rate. There are also some minor changes in . . . . Would you like to see the changes in: (1) Aaa rate, (2) others, (3) both, or (4) none?" The model asks for the selection.

"Selection?"

Ms. Jones types "1" and decides that the changes in the Aaa rate projections may have been important to Joe Blow but probably to no one else in the division.

This introduction finished, the program brings up the model that Ms. Jones is authorized to run. The conversation continues:

"You have a choice of modifying:

1. scenarios
2. candidate strategies

　3. consequences you would like to explore

　4. method of presentation

Unless directed, the program will automatically follow current versions on all four choices. Please specify the category or categories you want to change (type zero if none)."

Ms. Jones types: "1 and 2." (Note that the programming is tolerant because it would have accepted 1 2 or 1, 2 equally well.)

"Current environmental scenarios consist of statements about:

1. the economy (you have just seen those)

2. demography

3. regulatory climate

4. raw material prices

5. competitive actions

Which one(s) would you like to change?"
1

"The economic statements consist of 1981-1990 forecasts of:

1. rate of growth of GNP

2. inflation (CPI)

3. discretionary income

Which one(s) would you like to change?"
1

"The current statements are as follows:

year:	1982	1983	1984	1985	1986	1987	1988	1989	1990
% growth:	1.0	3.5	2.0	2.5	4.0	4.0	3.0	2.5	2.0

Please retype the number(s) you want changed (year growth)."
1982 1.5
1983 3.0
1990 4.0
"Any other environmental changes? (Y/N)"
N
"Current candidate strategy consists of the following programs:

1. R&D

2. plant expansion

3. marketing

4. fuel acquisition

5. capital allocation

6. pricing

Which one(s) would you like to change?"
2
"The plant expansion program assumes the following authorizations:
1. 1983 — 120,000 lbs/yr
2. 1987 — 150,000 lbs/yr

Please type in changes."
Defer 1 to 1984
Cancel 2
"Any other strategic changes?"
Y
"Which category?"
5
"The capital authorization program assumes:

1. spending limit of $100M 1983-1988

2. zero after 1988
Which one(s) would you like to change?"

1
"Please type in change."
1982-85 change to 20
"Any other strategic changes?"
N
"Following consequences can be displayed (for any year or specified time period):

1. P&L

2. balance sheet

3. cash flow

4. employment

5. ROE

Please indicate categories and period you want displayed."
3, 5 82-90
"You have the choice of the following displays:

1. tables

2. histograms

3. graphs

Type C after choice for comparison with the current consequences."

3 C

"It will take me 6 minutes to display results. Do you prefer to see the results now or see stored data later on (N/L)?"

L

"The results will be stored in file JON341. Thank you and goodbye." Ms. Jones hangs up and later retrieves the results.

The internal monitor takes note that Ms. Jones has used the model on that day, that she has made some specific changes, and that she has opened a new file. Depending on the internal climate of the organization, these notes that the monitor has made to itself may be available for inspection by the security people, by someone else, or by no one.

USES OF THE MODEL

Now that we have seen how the model communicates with the user, we might imagine how it will actually be used. The simplest uses of the model will be to improve the current routine procedures. As the users become more sophisticated, the model will open new horizons, permitting exploration of general corporate strategies, improving the existing strategy, and even forcing a reexamination of corporate preferences.

Routine Uses

The most routine use of the model will be to prepare the manager for the annual ritual of budget setting. As our model is strategic, it can only paint the expected situation in the broadest of terms. But that is, in itself, an advantage because one can see the forest rather than the trees, and many broad options can be tried rather quickly. Many of the support languages in which the model might be built allow for optimization and therefore permit fine tuning. This is precisely the activity used in the budget preparation. Let's consider an example in which a business unit has three product lines. Their individual productivity measurements have been programmed into the model. Let's assume that management insists on cutting the expenses by a given amount. What is the best allocation of salespeople by product lines in order to optimize the revenues, or to optimize the profits, or to optimize the use of inventory?

We are not saying that the conclusions of the model will be directly translatable into the budgetary plans (although, with skill, they might be), but they will suggest a reasonably good plan, consistent with the circumstances, and, hopefully, reduce some of the tedious work that currently consumes so much of the manager's time.

The second routine use will be to answer, ahead of time, some of the anticipated "what if" questions that are sure to be raised during the budgetary review. A manager who has done his or her homework using the model will have an edge over those who have not. In the final analysis, however, any conclusions reached must appeal to common logic.

The third routine use of the model will be to answer or at least throw some light on the answers to the actual "what if" questions by the senior executives. The daily news will make certain of that. Let's suppose that a new oil price has been announced by the OPEC producers. As a result, the corporate economist revises his future price forecasts. What would be the effect of these new forecasts on the selected measures of corporate performance?

The fourth routine use will be to raise problems that might arise at a later stage beyond the typically short time horizon of budget setting. Again, the ability of the model to explore the delayed time effects comes to the manager's assistance. As a result, selected remedial measures might be started in time to do some good.

Exploration of Across-the-Board Strategies

When times are bad, corporations tend to trim development and investment expenses more or less uniformly across all operating units. Conversely, when business conditions are favorable, most units can expect easier approval of projects involving major expenditures. Having a strategic model allows planners to explore the effect of such general, across-the-board changes. One of the planners we know expresses modes of management behavior as follows:

- All lights are green; planners of each business unit should assume that all reasonable (that is, obviously well conceived) projects will be approved. Therefore, please incorporate all such projects in a candidate group of strategies.

- The corporate climate is that of "prudent investment." New projects will receive a thorough examination, and only those meeting strict criteria of, say, Internal Rates of Return of X percent, will be approved.

- Assume that there will be no new investments at all this year, the hatches to be battened down, waiting for the financial weather to clear.

Apart from generating information about the effect of a temporary hold on investment, these instructions to the unit planners will result in formulating three alternative candidate strategies for each unit.

Using a Strategic Model's Output to Arrive at an Incremental Improvement in a Candidate Strategy

It is inevitable that, as soon as a candidate strategy is formulated, one can use the experience gained thereby to improve upon it. The strategic model permits an evaluation of how much improvement is likely to result from the new insights. The sensitivity checks will soon reveal the identity of the main variables affecting the outcomes (or the expected value of the outcomes if the model has probabilistic components). The investigation is most likely to conclude that only a few decision variables will make most of the difference in the goodness of the outcomes. In such a case, one might map the values of the outcomes against these important variables, as shown in figure 7.1.

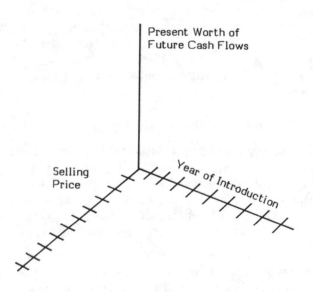

Fig. 7.1. Concentrating on Crucial Decision Variables

Enough runs should be made to sample the outcome space so that the shape of the territory, including a possible single peak or several peaks, would be revealed (Fig. 7.2). The preferred outcome will probably be a Present Equivalent capturing important indicators of success.

Using a Strategic Model to Determine the Robustness of the Value Model

When alternative strategies closely compete, it very likely may be that a small difference in the parameters of the value model (of which more will be said in chapter 8) do make the essential difference in the relative ranking of the candidate strategies. If found, this sensitivity is a signal to examine the value model. Does it correspond to management's perceptions of the relative importance of the components of an outcome, of their relative contributions over time, or of the risks involved?

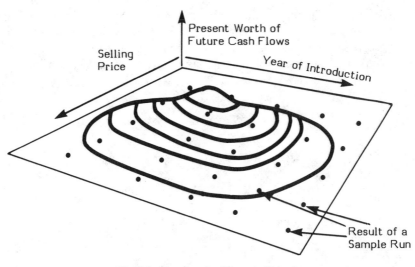

Fig. 7.2. Mapping the Outcome Domain

Generally speaking, the sensitivity of the outcomes to the value model will be found to be the greatest when the investments are well displaced from the period of significant revenues. Examples are nuclear plants, coal mines, oil shale, coal gasification plants, large commercial aircraft, hard wood timber, and the space shuttle. One can see why the industry would like the government to fund some of these investments. An upward shift in the prevailing interest rate is enough to make the strategies of investing in these projects look very unattractive.

THE MODEL AS A COMMUNICATION DEVICE

The existence and the availability of the strategic model or models will bring to the surface all the aspects of "freedom of information" within the corporation. Obviously, here we have strategic information that a competitor would love to have. The experimentation that Ms. Jones has just made may offer powerful clues about the thinking of management. (Ms. Jones was pretty pessimistic about capital authorizations in the period of tight budgets.) Thus, the security restrictions in the use of the model are likely to be quite tight and will probably extend to the private versions as well as to the official version. Yet, managers will need the model to communicate better about the aspects of strategy for which they are responsible and the effect of these strategies on the corporation as a whole.

As the model becomes a vehicle for communications about strategy, it is up to management to decide how much internal communications they wish to have. Perhaps only a few people would be allowed access to the corporate overlay part of the model, and only one or two local managers could use the SBU model. It is really too early to tell what the experience will be because most of the current models have not been designed to be interactive for managers, and the human interface has received very little attention.

REFERENCES

Ackoff, R. L. 1981. On the use of models in corporate planning. *Strategic Management Journal* 2: 353-59
Mazzolini, R. 1980. The limits of top management power. *The Journal of Business Strategy* 1, No. 2: 3-8
Naylor, T. H., ed. 1979. *Simulation models in corporate planning.* New York: Praeger.
Rubin, L. J., and Geraghty, D. M. 1981. Models in support of the electric utility corporate planning process. *Public Utility Fortnightly* June 18: 39-44.
Sage, A. P. 1981. Behavioral and organizational considerations in the design of information systems and processes for planning and decision support. *IEEE Transactions on Systems, Man, and Cybernetics* SMC-11, No. 9: 640-78.

CHAPTER 8
APPLICATIONS AND EXAMPLES

To this point, virtually all our attention has been directed to the methodology or mechanics of planning. We now turn to a description of some applications and examples that illustrate how the tools described may be used most effectively.

Our purpose is to address more directly the related questions of how much and what kind of planning are appropriate in a variety of situations. One way of answering such questions is to illustrate by example how our tools have actually been applied. Our point of departure will be the stages of planning first introduced in chapter 3.

PLANNING STAGES

In chapter 3, we introduced the principal stages of planning, moving from little or no formal strategic planning to scenario-driven planning. Clearly, no real corporation or business unit can be adequately categorized in such simplistic terms. On the other hand, the notion of a continuum of planning stages does provide a useful benchmark for selecting appropriate planning tools and for making useful organizational comparisons. Furthermore, an awareness of these planning stages highlights the requirements, benefits, and risks of moving from one stage to the next.

The characterization is best applied directly at the product or business unit level. For the corporation as a whole, one can imagine an averaging over all products or business units. In principle, each corporation then has associated with it a unique planning profile. The shape of that profile is dependent on a large number of factors, including business objectives, product/service life cycles, and management style.

The five principal stages (stages 0 to 4) introduced in chapter 3 are shown in extended form in table 8.1. The extensions reflect the planning dimensions and tools described in chapters 4, 5, and 6: scenarios, candidate strategies, and models. In terms of *scenarios* and *candidate strategies*, the five stages may now be very simply characterized as 0 x 0 (stage 1) — that is, no scenarios or candidate strategies — to n x 1 or n x n (stage 4), where n is greater than 1. Similarly, as we progress through each stage, the models used evolve basically from financial accounting to financial planning to full strategic (financial plus human and physical process) modeling.

A brief description of each planning stage will be provided before illustrating how our planning tools may be applied in making transitions between stages.

Little or No Formal Strategic Planning

The first stage in table 8.1 represents the baseline case. The focus is almost exclusively on short-term budgets and performance. Major decisions are made on the basis of current momentum and in response to day-to-day changes. Little or no attention is paid to long-term environmental shifts, nor is there any perceptible movement in accordance with a set of explicit or implicit objectives or in accordance with some grand design. It is almost strictly a "below-the-line" tactical operation represented diagrammatically as in figure 8.1. We estimate that as many as 10 to 15 percent of major (*Fortune* 1000) U.S. corporations still basically function in this way.

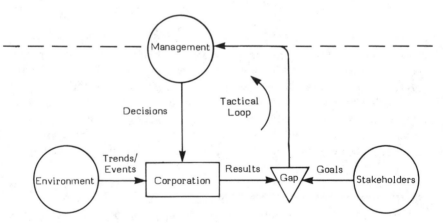

Fig. 8.1. Stage 0: Little or No Formal Strategic Planning

Table 8.1 Strategic Planning Stages

Stages	Scenarios	Options, Candidate Strategies	Formal Modeling	Comments
0-Little or no formal planning (0 x 0)	0	0	None (short-term budgets)	Essentially tactical day-to-day control
1-Objective-Driven (0 x 1)	0	Single strategy at a time	Usually standard financial accounting model capable of revising current plan and budget	Strategies are considered one at a time and evaluated vis-à-vis objectives
2-Financially-Driven (1 x 1)	Single (detailed) scenario, often basically a projection of current trends (no probability assigned)	Single strategy at a time	Financial planning model for fast exploration of the effect of changes in elements of the scenario	Present strategy is modified only when elements in current scenario change
3-Strategy-Driven (1 x *n)*	Single (simple) scenario (no probability assigned)	Multiple strategies	Financial planning model plus judgmental physical process models	Alternate strategies are examined systematically
4-Scenario-Driven *(n* x 1)	Multiple (simple) scenarios (probabilities assigned)	Single strategy at a time	Early strategic (physical plus financial process) model	Contingency planning by playing optional strategy against scenarios
(n x *n)*	Multiple scenarios with assigned probabilities	Multiple strategies	Full strategic (human, physical, financial) model	Full exploration of strategic alternatives

Objective-Driven Planning

Many (about 30%) major corporations are at least partially involved in objective-driven planning. In the past, this stage has represented some of corporate America's most widely recognized success stories — for example, IBM, 3M, Hewlett-Packard, Procter & Gamble. A distinguishing characteristic is the stress on a *key business value*, or *objective*, that largely shapes the organization and usually produces a distinctive and coherent

internal corporate culture. Options or candidate strategies are evaluated largely in terms of their "goodness" vis-à-vis a driving objective. External
developments (except for technology and customer needs) are not viewed as
paramount in shaping the corporation. Financial accounting models are used
that are not suitable for quickly evaluating strategic alternatives. Diagrammatically, this stage may be represented as the simplest extension "above the
line," as shown in figure 8.2.

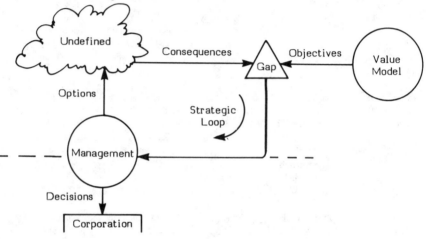

Fig. 8.2. Stage 1: Objective-Driven Planning

Financially-Driven Planning

About 30% of the major U.S. corporations would position themselves at
the financially-driven planning stage. Some attention is directed at the external environment, although closer examination usually reveals that the
dominant scenario is basically a projection of the most current trends. New
options or candidate strategies are generated and evaluated only when shifts
in some key elements of the dominant scenario are perceived. A simple financial planning model is available to do quick evaluations of new options or
candidate strategies. Diagrammatically, it is the simplest "single-thread"
stage − it contains the barest outlines of all the essential elements of a complete planning framework, as shown in figure 8.3.

Strategy-Driven Planning

The focus at the strategy-driven planning stage is in opening up the candidate
strategies or options to be explored and evaluated. The primary use of the
dominant scenario is to help stimulate the generation of new candidate
strategies. Thus, although the scenario used will contain fewer variables than

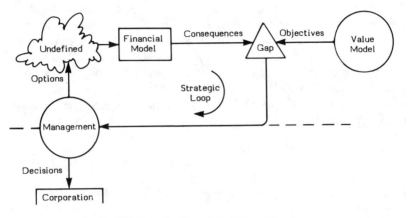

Fig. 8.3. Stage 2: Financially-Driven Planning

in stage 2, each dimension of the scenario will be developed at greater depth, focusing on industry, market, and competitive variables. The corporate model will include some early (judgmental) physical process modeling to generate costs and benefits that are aggregated by the financial planning model. It is estimated that about 20% of major U.S. corporations have approached this stage. Diagrammatically, it may be represented as in figure 8.4.

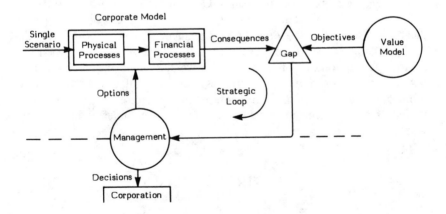

Fig. 8.4. Stage 3: Strategy-Driven Planning

Scenario-Driven Planning

The scenario-driven planning stage represents the highest level of the use of planning tools for the full interplay of multiple scenarios and multiple candidate strategies. The corporate model may contain elements of human resource processes (hiring, compensation, career paths, retirements), as well as representations of physical and financial processes. With such tools, an interactive search may be made for new candidate strategies, and a range of contingency options or strategies may be prepared. Few major U.S. corporations (GM, Shell, Hewlett-Packard) − perhaps less than 10 percent (Linneman and Klein 1979, pp. 83-90) − are, at this stage, represented diagrammatically as in figure 8.5.

Summary

In accordance with the planning stages described, we estimate the placement of major U.S. corporations (*Fortune* 1000) to be as shown in figure 8.6.

Our best judgment is that the center of gravity is somewhere between level 1 and level 2. As noted earlier, each individual corporation may be characterized by its unique organizational profile, but it should not be assumed that a shift to the right (or left) of the planning profile for a corporation is necessarily desirable or undesirable. In fact, one of the most important choices the management of any organization must make is to position itself along this continuum to best match its current needs.

A number of external and internal factors should influence the position and shape of the distribution − individually for a single organization and collectively for a group of companies. Generally, the more *stable* the external environment, or the more *distinctive or unique* the product or service niche, or the *less participative* the management style, the more likely that the best match will shift the curve to the left. Conversely, when the external environment becomes more *uncertain*, or when *competitive* forces intensify making product or service distinctiveness more difficult to achieve, or when more *open and participative* decision-making processes are needed or expected, then a movement toward the right (or more complex planning stages) would result.

ILLUSTRATIVE CASES

The five examples that follow have been selected to illustrate how the methods described have been used in the context of the principal planning stages. Either one or the other author has been directly involved in each study. In three of the examples, even though proprietary information places constraints on the specific details that can be discussed, such limitations have not distorted the descriptions of how the methods were applied or the nature of the results that were obtained.

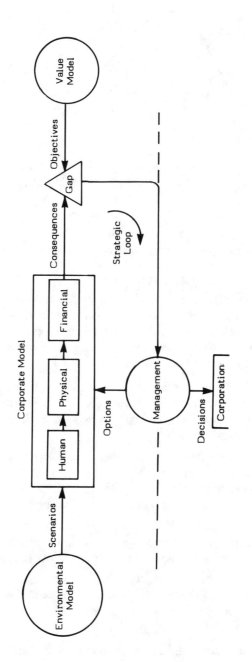

Fig. 8.5. Stage 4: Scenario-Driven Planning

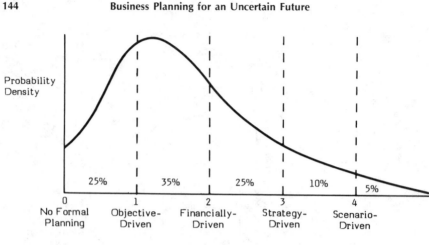

Fig. 8.6. Estimated Planning Profile of Major U.S. Corporations

A Transportation Company

How useful and effective are the tools introduced earlier to corporations or businesses predominantly at stage 0? Perhaps surprisingly, they can be very useful and effective. In fact, often some very large gains may be made at this stage with relatively small investments. Organizations at this stage may have any of the following characteristics:

- *Very stable businesses/products*: A market niche is being filled that attracts few competitors, or that is (perhaps inadvertently) protected by government regulation, or that is largely impervious to shifts in the external environment.

- *Founder/owner businesses*: Businesses developed and driven by the innovation, energy, and motivation of a single individual; a variant is a business headed by a dominant, intuitive CEO who may not have been the founder/owner, but who rules with an iron hand.

- *High-technology products/services*: Businesses dominated by rapid and dramatic changes in technology (e.g., computer/communications) making other environmental factors or constraints relatively unimportant.

- *Businesses led by tactical "superstars"*: Even fairly large organizations may be led by CEOs who have acquired the skills for orchestrating very successful "thinking and acting in their heads" without the need for formal planning systems.

Why then do such organizations eventually seek planning assistance? For any number of reasons. The environment changes unexpectedly, or an industry is deregulated, or new and strong competitors appear "out of nowhere," or the founder/owner disappears from the scene. Often, the response simply results from the accumulation of a long series of tactical choices (for maximizing short-term performance) that finally catches up with a company as production facilities become outmoded, or new ideas for product/service improvements dry up because of inadequate capital and R&D allocations in the past.

Example A. The following example is fairly typical of a number that have included organizations representing the chemical, insurance, banking, and oil industries.

In this instance, the company has the following principal characteristics: It is a medium-sized ($100 to $500 million in sales), partially diversified transportation company. It comprises several SBUs — dominated by trucking services, followed by truck manufacturing. Essentially no formal planning system nor clear sense of direction exists. Management style may be described as "day-to-day tactical"; performance over a long period has been unspectacular as measured by earnings and by return on assets.

During the 1970s, the company was confronted by two major shocks. The first was the rapid escalation of oil prices; the second — more gradual but equally important — was the continuing deregulation of the trucking industry. Both changes required a reassessment of long-term direction. The first shock was not foreseen, while the prospects for deregulation had been in view for some time.

The CEO was concerned because performance was at a plateau or perhaps even slowly degrading. The external environment had clearly become more uncertain and considerably less friendly. For perhaps the first time, he recognized that the absence of a clear sense of long-term direction was hurting company performance. Was the long-term future of the company to be found in providing traditional trucking services? Or, should he consider allocating large amounts of necessary capital to the truck manufacturing arm in order to position the business strongly against future competitors? Or, should he look entirely outside the transportation industry for diversification opportunities? What, indeed, were the basic strengths and weaknesses of the organization around which some long-term objectives might eventually be structured?

Basically, the CEO wanted access to a process that could be used to help him and his management team begin to think in strategic terms. He wanted an overall profile of management perceptions on long-term threats and opportunities, strengths and weaknesses, and strategic issues. In other words, he wanted an internal audit — so to speak — of management perceptions that addressed the following two questions: "Who are we?" and "What long-term directions can (or should) we take?"

The processes used here — and in a number of similar instances — are identical to those described in chapter 4 for identifying key factors affecting a business or corporation. Semistructured interviews were held in private with the top 50 executives. (The number may be as few as 15 or 20.) The interviews included the chairman, the CEO, and all corporate officers. In addition, the interviews also included a sample drawn from a younger staff group who were perceived to be "fast trackers." Interviews were private and not electronically recorded; all information was used strictly without attribution. Although a specific interview protocol was used — including interviews with a hypothetical "clairvoyant," the generation of desirable and undesirable scenarios, and the identification of key choices — sufficient time was allowed during the interviews for respondents to digress as they saw fit.

Most executives delighted in being challenged in circumspect but interesting ways to identify factors they normally did not take time to consider very deeply, if at all. Some executives prepared themselves for the interviews; most did not. Great variability existed among executives on the number, breadth, and depth of factors identified. However, at the end of each interview it was rare not to have identified between 10 and 20 distinctive factors bearing on the company's long-term future.

Of course, considerable overlap usually exists in the factors identified by each interviewee. When distilled and aggregated, the factors fall into several well-defined categories (unique for each organization) relating to the external and internal environment. We have used simple frequency counts to establish relative importance approximately by "number of mentions" (chapter 4). Such simple representations usually follow the "80-20 rule" — that is, the overwhelming majority of "mentions" account for some fraction (1/5 to 1/3) of all factors mentioned.

We also usually perform some simple content analysis. In this instance, the issues raised spanned a wide spectrum. To give an idea of this range, a sample will be drawn from the table of contents of the resulting 100-page report (Amara and Palmer 1979). The major division was between external and internal factors. External factors were in turn divided into economy, role of government, deregulation, role of the railroads, and international expansion — with a focus on specific vulnerabilities that included takeover threats, concentration in transportation, and fuel supply. Under internal factors, the following were identified as crucial: strategic planning, management depth, relationships between SBUs, compensation, computer needs, stock price, and public image.

Even more instructive may be a few excerpts from the final report. One of over 10 pages dealing with company strengths and weaknesses is shown as table 8.2. Also, one of the most critical factors dealing with the absence of any (strategic) planning within the company is outlined in table 8.3. In each case, distillations of actual comments made during interviews are included.

Table 8.2. Summary of Strengths and Weaknesses
(Excerpt on Management Characteristics)

Strengths	Weaknesses
Very strong top management	Lack of depth of management
Open-minded management	Thinness of management candidates to take over top operational
Lean management	positions (a "gap" exists between young "Turks" and present senior
Excellent management — honesty	management)
Management integrity	Middle management not that strong
Management organization — team — a lot of political infighting up to 1972, 1973. Now a strong team.	Inability to attract and groom junior management
Very little internal politicking	
Management policies and people are superior to competitors	
Good solid management in parent and subsidiaries with willingness to look at problems	
	Summary: Very strong at top but lacking in depth, particularly at middle levels.

Follow-up. What does an organization normally do with the kind of information that has been described? Of course, no simple answer is possible. In this instance, the absence of a tangible sense of direction was clearly creating considerable divisiveness within the company. On the other hand, neither organizations nor individuals can be expected to progress from stage 0 to stages 1 or 2 by virtue of the information made available by a single study — no matter how well done.

As might be expected, the follow-up responses by companies at this planning stage fall into several categories:

1. Some will simply ignore the information (for any number of reasons) and return to their old ways of doing business.

Table 8.3. Internal Factors: Strategic Planning

Need for a strategic plan. Uppermost is the need for ABC to set and provide explicit strategic direction regarding which businesses it wants to emphasize, which it wants to get out of, and how much growth is expected. The strategic plan should then become the primary basis for defining objectives, allocating capital, and measuring performance. A great deal of uncertainty exists regarding the overall direction of the company:

- The company really needs a plan for the future. In the past it hasn't been that necessary.

- There's too much emphasis on next year, not enough on anything beyond, and no measurement of long-range goals and achievements.

- ABC now has objectives but no hints as to how to get there (e.g., we have a 20 percent growth goal but no details on people, business mix decisions, or how to achieve the goal).

- Somebody has to put down on a piece of paper what ABC wants to be and where it's going. People would really like to see it, and then they would do anything to follow the plan.

- The biggest vulnerability is that there is no real strong sense of where the company is going. There is no defensive strategy. Also, we have to face the fact that if everything goes well, the company will be rolling in money, and this increases takeover possibilities.

- ABC should view itself as being in the distribution business (including assembly, point of sale, packaging, transportation, and storage). All strategic planning should start from here.

---

2. Some will embrace the information, but cannot find effective ways to take tangible steps to continue the processes set in motion or to tie them to operational activities.

3. Some set up specific machinery (task forces, groups, etc.) to identify a master set of critical issues, and initially focus on the first two or three in earnest.

Although no single study is — or should be — responsible for particular choices made by any organization, it is interesting to note that in this instance the CEO began a move away from diversification and toward consolidation of operations, sharpening considerably corporate objectives around the unique strengths of trucking services.

A Communications Company

The distinguishing feature of stage 1 organizations compared to stage 0 is the presence of a strong cohering "driving force" aimed toward a set of clearly defined objectives. Many other terms have been used to capture this notion: key business value, enduring theme, imagery, metaphor. Many astute observers of the corporate landscape identify this particular characteristic as the key to success, claiming, at the same time, that complex planning systems are neither necessary nor effective. As previously noted, the usual corporate examples cited include IBM, Texas Instruments, Hewlett-Packard, 3M, Digital Equipment Corporation, Dana, and Procter & Gamble — companies that span a broad range of industries and product lines. The roots for such views may be traceable to Peter Drucker (e.g., "Forecasting is not a respectable human activity"), but in recent years others (Peters 1980; Tregoe and Zimmerman 1980) have also championed the same ideas.

It is difficult to dispute the point that a clearly defined set of corporate objectives is the sine qua non of many, if not most, successful organizations. Without such objectives, it is almost impossible to make evaluations of alternative choices or strategies. As has often been noted: "Without a clearly defined destination, almost any route will get you there." But objective-driven planning has been elevated almost to a mystique by some since it often fashions — and then is driven by — a corresponding internal corporate culture. Such cultures are usually built around some core corporate characteristics that are neither easily changed nor discarded. Although it is difficult to generalize, the most important features of such organizations are:

- Action- rather than planning-oriented
- Ultrasensitivity to customer needs
- Concentration on unique strengths.

With some notable exceptions — namely, forecasting technological developments and customers' needs — knowledge of the external environment usually plays a secondary role in the management of such corporations.

The operational advantages of stage 1 organizations are clear. They generally know where they are going and how to behave. Heavy reliance is placed on personal hands-on management that provides a tight interplay of thought and action and that stresses practicality. Few resources are allocated to planning with two notable exceptions: product planning that exploits new technologies and market forecasting of customer needs.

Such practices are not, however, without their hazards. Eventually, some elements of the outside world that have been ignored (e.g., new competitors) do change markedly, and the corporation may be caught flat-footed and unprepared. When this happens, few, if any, internal mechanisms for responding adequately are normally in place. In such instances, the existence of a strong corporate "mono-culture" may work against the organization as it tries to adapt.

Example B. The example chosen to illustrate how an organization at stage 1 (0 x 1) begins to move to stage 2 (1 x 1) is a major study done for AT&T

in the early 1970s on the future of the telephone industry to the year 1985 (Baran and Lipinski 1971). The focus of this work was clearly to provide a comprehensive description of the *external* factors affecting the industry into the next decade. It thus was a first attempt to construct a comprehensive scenario of key developments in the telephone or, more appropriately, the communications industry. Quoting directly from the study's final report, the objective was "to examine the future of communications, both from the view of the public interest and that of the long-range corporate goals of the Bell System." Basically, the purpose was to provide AT&T with information that would help it make choices for transforming itself from essentially a single-minded, "objective-driven" utility to a more diversified corporation.

In principle, the study could have begun with a formal identification of key factors (as was done in Example A). In this case, most of the key factors had been previously identified by AT&T. It was necessary only to augment and distill the initial set to produce the following major groupings: changes in U.S. society; labor force characteristics; regulatory environment; existing networks and services; and future networks and services. Each of the major categories was subdivided into five to ten sectors. For example, changes in U.S. society included demography, future of cities, state of the economy, and public attitudes toward bigness.

At the time the study was done, it was perhaps the most ambitious effort to date using formal tools for systematically eliciting and aggregating expert judgment. Over 200 carefully chosen outside experts were matched to the five principal areas (i.e., panels) of inquiry. The processes used were forerunners of those described in chapter 4. The centerpiece was a carefully administered, two-round Delphi inquiry eliciting, via questionnaires, point estimates rather than full distributions for the variables under study. Probabilities of occurrence were estimated on a five-point scale. In addition, a five-point self-rating scale was used for the first time, permitting the weighting of responses by level of expertise. A sample of the two scales, together with the actual distribution of responses for a particular question, is shown in table 8.4.

Several features of the methods used may be noted. The respondent's single estimate was treated as the median of his or her probability distribution. In other words, it was assumed that it was equally likely that actual future values would be larger or smaller than estimated. By randomly subdividing panels, tests were made to establish that the results were repeatable. Also, interestingly, second-round responses produced shifts that were of the same order of magnitude as those produced by panel subdivision. This provided a good cross-check on the adequacy of using only two rounds of questionnaires.

The final report provided one of the first integrated overviews of the most important developments impacting the communications industry. Perhaps the most prescient forecasts were those made by the panel on future networks

Table 8.4. Sample of Summary Responses to Delphi Inquiry

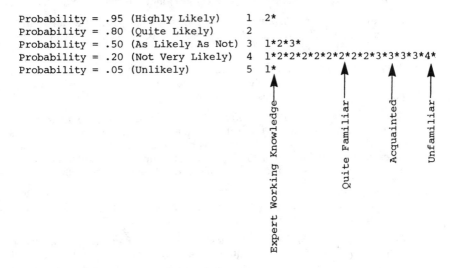

RAISING CAPITAL BY EQUITY
New capital for the telephone business will be raised
in the future by greater reliance on equity financing.

```
Probability = .95 (Highly Likely)     1  2*
Probability = .80 (Quite Likely)      2
Probability = .50 (As Likely As Not)  3  1*2*3*
Probability = .20 (Not Very Likely)   4  1*2*2*2*2*2*2*2*2*3*3*3*3*4*
Probability = .05 (Unlikely)          5  1*
```

and services and subsequently reported in greater detail (Baran 1971). In the first round, the panelists in this category were provided a list of 30 potentially new information services to the home (table 8.5). For each of the services, the respondents were asked to provide estimates of the following characteristics:

- Average dollar value of one transaction (low, median, and high estimates),

- Duration of one entire transaction from completion of dialing to disconnect,

- Percentage of actual transmission of data or message,

- Average number of transactions per month, per home,

- Percentage of service home subscribers could be expected to pay,

- Most likely year of mass introduction in the United States (earliest median, and latest estimates),

- Percentage penetration of households five years later,

- The most likely entrepreneur to offer this service.

In the second round, first-round responses were fed back, and panelists were given an opportunity to revise their estimates.

Table 8.5. Brief Descriptions of Potential Home Information Services

1. *Cashless-Society Transactions.* Recording of any financial transactions with a hard copy output to buyer and seller, a permanent record and updating of balance in computer memory.

2. *Dedicated Newspaper.* A set of pages with printed and graphic information, possibly including photographs, the organization of which has been predetermined by the user to suit his preferences.

3. *Computer-Aided School Instruction.* At the very minimum, the computer determines the day's assignment for each pupil and, at the end of the day, receives the day's progress report. At its most complex, such a service would use a real-time, interactive video color display with voice input and output and an appropriate program suited to each pupil's progress and temperament.

4. *Shopping Transactions (Store Catalogs).* Interactive programs, perhaps video-assisted, which describe or show goods at request of the buyer, advise him of the price, location, delivery time, etc.

5. *Person-to-Person (Paid Work at Home).* Switched video and facsimile service substituting for normal day's contacts of a middle-class managerial personnel where daily contacts are of mostly routine nature. May also apply to contacts with the public of the receptionist, doctor, or his assistant.

6. *Plays and Movies from a Video Library.* Selection of all plays and movies. Color and good sound are required.

7. *Computer Tutor.* From a library of self-help programs available, a computer, in an interactive mode, will coach the pupil (typically adult) in the chosen subject.

8. *Message Recording.* Probably of current available type but may include video memory (a patient showing doctor the rash he has developed).

9. *Secretarial Assistance.* Written or dictated letters can be typed by a remotely situated secretary.

10. *Household Mail and Messages.* Letters and notes transmitted directly to or from the house by means of home facsimile machines.

11. *Mass Mail and Direct Advertising Mail.* Higher output, larger-sized pages, color output may be necessary to attract the attention of the recipient — otherwise similar to item 10 above.

12. *Answering Services.* Stored incoming messages or notes whom to call — possibly computer logic recognizing emergency situation and diverting the call.

13. *Grocery Price List, Information, and Ordering.* Grocery price list is used as an example of up-to-the-minute, updated information about perishable foodstuffs. Video color display may be needed to examine selected merchandise. Ordering follows.

14. *Access to Company Files.* Information in files is coded for security; regularly updated files are available with cross-references indicating the code where more detailed information is stored. Synthesis may also be available.

15. *Fares and Ticket Reservation.* As provided by travel agencies now but more comprehensive and faster. Cheapest rates, information regarding the differences between carriers with respect to service, menus, etc., may be available.

16. *Past and Forthcoming Events.* Events, dates of events, and their brief description; short previews of future theater plays; and recordings of past events.

17. *Correspondence School.* Taped or live high school, university, and vocational courses available on request with an option to either audit or graduate. Course on TV, paper support on facsimile.

18. *Daily Calendar and Reminder about Appointments.* Prerecorded special appointments and regularly occurring appointments stored as a programmed reminder.

19. *Computer-Assisted Meetings.* The computer participates as a partner in a meeting, answering questions of fact, deriving correlations, and extrapolating trends.

20. *Newspaper, Electronic, General.* Daily newspaper, possibly printed during the night, available in time for breakfast. Special editions following major news breaks.

21. *Adult Evening Courses on TV.* Noninteractive, broadcast mode, live courses on TV — wider choice of subjects than at present.

22. *Banking Services.* Money orders, transfers, advice.

23. *Legal Information.* Directory of lawyers, computerized legal counseling giving precedents, rulings in similar cases, describing jurisdiction of various courts and changes of successful suits in a particular area of litigation.

24. *Special Sales Information.* Any sales within the distance specified by the user and for items specified by him will be "flashed" onto the home display unit.

25. *Consumers' Advisory Service.* Equivalent of *Consumer Reports*, giving best buy, products rated "acceptable", etc.

26. *Weather Bureau.* Country-wide, regional forecasts or special forecasts (farmers, fishermen), hurricane and tornado warnings similar to current special forecast services.

27. *Bus, Train, and Air Scheduling.* Centrally available information with one number to call.

28. *Restaurants.* Following a query for a type of restaurant (Japanese, for instance), reservations, menu, prices are shown. Displays of dishes, location of tables may be included.

29. *Library Access.* After an interactive "browsing" with a "librarian computer" and a quotation for the cost of hard copy facsimile or a slow-scan video transmission, a book or a magazine is transmitted to the home.

30. *Index, All Services Served by the Home Terminal.* Includes prices or charges of the above, or available communications services.

The results of the inquiry provided the general outlines of a new industry. Perhaps the most important message from the study was that virtually no revenue would be generated from such services before 1980 — ten years after the forecast was made. Table 8.6 shows the estimated growth in revenues year by year, based on the assumption that each service would experience exponential growth for the first five years after introduction, with a halving of the rate of growth for every subsequent year thereafter.

Although no one can ever be sure how much impact a single study may have on any organization, there is little doubt that the study provided some stimulus for AT&T to rethink its possible roles in a changing industry. Ultimately, such thinking set in motion organizational and staff changes that have since positioned AT&T favorably in this new market place.

A Business and Professional Services Firm

As previously noted, it is our judgment that the distribution of major U.S. corporations (*Fortune* 1000) along our planning continuum (see figure 8.6) probably peaks near stage 2 or, more precisely, between stages 1 and 2. None of the characteristics of companies at this stage is very distinctive. They might best be described as including a "little bit of each" of the elements of our planning framework. The members of the group typically have reasonably well-defined objectives. Each has a fairly coherent strategy, even though usually not nearly as sharply tuned to objectives as organizations in stage 1. On the other hand, many members of this group will have generated a "set of assumptions" or, using our terminology, a scenario describing the external environment. Although such a set of assumptions, or scenario, often may be no more than a projection of current trends, adequate processes for tracking the external environment are usually in place. Also, in such cases, simple financial planning models are either being developed or are available for evaluating easily options/strategies in response to possible or perceived environmental changes. In short, organizations at this stage have usually developed the outlines of a first-cut "single-thread" strategic planning system.

Table 8.6. Potential Revenues for New Home Information Services
(millions of 1970 $)

Service	1980	1981	1982	1983	1984	1985	1986	1987	1988	1989
Cashless Society	12.	29.	73.	182.	457.	1146.	1438.	1621.	724.	1810.
Dedicated Newspaper	5.	14.	34.	85.	214.	537.	674.	760.	808.	849.
Computer-Aided Instruction	0.	14.	34.	86.	216.	542.	1361.	1708.	1925.	2047.
Shopping Transactions	0.	0.	0.	5.	12.	29.	74.	186.	466.	584.
Paid Work at Home	0.	0.	0.	0.	0.	43.	108.	272.	683.	1713.
Video Library	18.	45.	113.	284.	714.	1791.	2247.	2533.	2694.	2829.
Computer Tutor	9.	23.	57.	142.	357.	895.	1123.	1266.	1347.	1414.
Message Recording	1.	2.	4.	11.	27.	67.	84.	95.	101.	106.
Secretarial Assistance	5.	11.	28.	71.	178.	448.	562.	633.	674.	707.
Mail and Messages	5.	11.	28.	71.	178.	448.	562.	633.	674.	707.
Mass Mail and Ad Mail	0.	0.	0.	0.	0.	0.	0.	0.	0.	0.
Answering Services	5.	12.	30.	75.	187.	470.	590.	665.	707.	743.
Groceries	4.	9.	23.	57.	143.	358.	449.	507.	539.	566.
File System	0.	0.	0.	0.	0.	1.	3.	7.	18.	46.
Fares and Tickets	1.	2.	5.	12.	31.	78.	98.	111.	118.	124.
Events Calendar	0.	0.	1.	2.	6.	15.	37.	92.	115.	130.
Correspondence School	0.	0.	0.	0.	9.	24.	60.	150.	376.	943.
Reminders	0.	0.	0.	2.	6.	15.	37.	93.	233.	292.
Computer-Assisted Meetings	5.	11.	28.	71.	178.	448.	562.	633.	674.	707.
Electronic Newspaper	0.	0.	0.	0.	0.	5.	13.	32.	80.	200.
Evening Courses	7.	18.	45.	114.	285.	716.	899.	1013.	1078.	1131.
Banking Services	4.	9.	23.	57.	143.	358.	449.	507.	539.	566.
Legal Information	0.	0.	0.	0.	0.	7.	18.	45.	114.	285.
Special Sales	2.	6.	14.	36.	89.	224.	281.	317.	337.	354.
Consumer Advisory Service	2.	6.	14.	36.	89.	224.	281.	317.	337.	354.
Weather Information	8.	21.	52.	131.	164.	185.	197.	206.	217.	228.
Bus, Train, and Air	7.	17.	43.	54.	61.	65.	68.	71.	75.	79.
Restaurants	0.	1.	1.	4.	9.	22.	28.	32.	34.	35.
Library Access	0.	0.	0.	0.	0.	2.	6.	15.	38.	95.
Index of Services	1.	2.	4.	11.	27.	67.	84.	95.	101.	106.
Total Market	99.	261.	656.	1598.	3781.	9231.	12391.	14613.	16822.	19749.

In terms of our abbreviated notation, we have described a (1 x 1) stage 2 planning organization. Such companies usually enjoy long periods of good but not spectacular performance. They tend to be reasonably adaptive to environmental shifts, and often such adaptability is enhanced by highly decentralized organizational structures. Generally, they are low-to-moderate risk takers who tend to run in the "middle of the pack."

What may sound like a very comfortable existence almost always eventually leads to feelings of management uneasiness. Although the organization is doing well, managers feel they are not doing nearly as well as they could be. Some may even sense that their performance vis-à-vis competitors may be degrading imperceptibly. But perhaps the most unsettling perception is that the CEO feels a gradual loss of control in achieving corporate objectives. That loss is often reflected in the paucity of choices or alternative strategies made available to him.

Thus, the planning "handle" that usually characterizes the transition of an organization from stage 2 (1 x 1) to stage 3 (1 x n) is the search, generation, and evaluation of a wide range of alternative directions or strategies. As noted briefly in chapter 1 and in greater detail in chapter 5, the processes for developing a rich menu of options or strategies are not well understood. A particularly attractive (but not commonly used) method involves the use of scenarios or, more precisely, a single dominant scenario to "open up" the range of options and, ultimately, candidate strategies composed of such options to be considered and evaluated. Our next example describes the processes in greater detail.

Example C. The example to be described is drawn from a firm engaged in providing business and professional services (BPS). Such services include: accounting/auditing/bookkeeping, advertising, computer services, engineering/architectural, equipment leasing, legal, management consulting, personnel, and research. The firm had most, if not all, of the characteristics previously noted for defining a stage 2 organization. The only notable exception was the absence of a well-defined financial planning model. The firm did use a single scenario — basically projecting historical trends three years into the future — that had served the organization reasonably well. Even so, neither the growth nor the profitability of the firm had kept up with its major competitors in recent years; and the prospect for new competitors entering the market was increasing significantly each year.

It was clear at the outset that a fresh look would have to be taken at the key factors impacting the business and the firm. Beyond that, the factors themselves needed to be more sharply and systematically defined. The starting point for the study was thus pushed back to that resembling a stage 0 organization.

In fact, the project was begun by conducting a set of in-depth interviews with the equivalent of 15 to 20 top corporate officers. The format for such interviews was precisely as described in the Stage 0 example. In this instance, however, since the objective was ultimately to use a scenario to generate a rich set of options, a group of 10 to 15 perceptive outsiders was also interviewed using essentially the same format. The only difference was that the focus of the questions for outsiders was on the factors affecting the future of the business rather than the firm.

The factors identified by both groups were combined into a single composite list. A categorization and frequency count within each category were made. In this instance, the key factors clustered into 15 major areas, including the economic environment, regulation and the role of government, client needs, characteristics of competition and competitors, and characteristics of professional recruits and staff. Each, in turn, was subdivided into a large number of subsectors. For example, the economic environment included inflation, growth of the U.S. and international economy, level of domestic capital formation, the form of financial markets, business starts and mergers, international capital flows, and growth of international trade. The full list and description of key factors were evaluated in depth by a task force working group from the firm: the list was distilled and regrouped into a final set of 12 categories. These formed the basis for the generation of a most likely scenario.

The time horizon for the scenario was 10 to 15 years. It should be reemphasized that its main objective was not to make a deterministic forecast or to force consensus of perceptions, but rather to identify those changes that were most relevant to the organization and that would stimulate the generation of option and choices. Inputs to the scenario were provided from several sources. The principal source was a set of 25 experts — again as in the stage 1 example — matched to the key factors identified. Here, the experts were drawn from government, universities, manufacturing companies, business system software design firms, research organizations, management consulting groups, and accounting firms.

Since our primary interest was in generating a single scenario, full distributions of key variables were not elicited. Instead, the focus was on specifying a set of factors for a most likely scenario. To do that, a probabilistic tree of the most "independent" key factors (e.g., economic environment, technology, role of government) was constructed with probability estimates for each branch elicited from the experts; as a result, the branch with the highest probability assignment was selected as the most likely scenario. This permitted defining a broad set of conditioning macrovariables on which forecasts of the dependent variables were based. For example, with "middling" assumptions on national economic growth rate, rate of new technology diffusion, role of government, and so forth, a number of characteristics of potential users of BPS were specified, such as those shown in tables 8.7, 8.8, and 8.9.

Table 8.7. Corporate Assets by Firm Size
(share of assets by firm size)

	Under $50M	$50-100M	$100-250M	Over $250M
1960	37.7	6.6	9.9	45.8
1970	28.0	5.5	8.4	58.1
1980	20.0	5.5	7.0	67.5
1990	14.5	7.0	6.5	72.0

Table 8.8. Total Number of Public Companies

1960	3,712
1970	9,030
1980	9,831
1990	13,500

Table 8.9. New Incorporations (annual average, in thousands)

1960-64	186
1965-69	223
1970-74	303
1975-79	428
1980-84	580
1985-89	630
1990-94	690

Similar details were developed about the expected competitive environment as well as the characteristics of the professional labor market. The full scenario comprised over 60 pages of text, tables, charts, and graphs, providing an integrated view of the environment for BPS in the 1980s and beyond.

The processes for option and choice generation were then started. Since the provision of BPS is essentially "client-needs" driven, a detailed review was first made of the characteristics of potential users as described in the scenario. In some instances, a particular characteristic — such as the growth in the number of public companies and new incorporations (see tables 8.8 and 8.9) — might suggest a corresponding candidate strategy (i.e., specialized services to emerging companies). In other instances, particular groups of scenario elements might be combined and used. In either event, using the scenario as a primary stimulus, the broad outlines of over a dozen *distinctive* candidate strategies were generated. At this point, each such candidate contained the description of a new BPS, including the characteristics and location of potential clients and the nature of the expected competition.

To develop the full dimensions of each strategy, the following process was used. The full set of "option knobs" was specified, similar to those first introduced in figure 3.7. These fall into three major categories: human, physical, and financial resources. In our example, such options or choices were dominated by the human resource dimension since the provision of BPS is a highly labor-intensive business. In fact, over 15 of the 20 choices defining resource allocations corresponding to each candidate strategy were human-resource related. Examples included staff skill mix, role and proportion of women, use of paraprofessionals, and flexibility of compensation. In each instance, a very specific, and usually quantitative, setting is required of each "choice or option knob" for each candidate strategy. A "0" setting means that the option is not relevant for this candidate; a "1" means that present practices would be continued unchanged for this candidate; and an "X" means that a different (than present) allocation of resources will be required. Schematically, if we designated Strategy 0 as the baseline (present strategy) case, then table 8.10 shows how the candidate strategy versus option matrix looks in summary form. Ultimately, fine tuning of "knob" settings was done for each candidate strategy.

Table 8.10. Candidate Strategies versus Options

		Options							
		A	B	C	.	.	.	.	.	T
	0	1	1	0	.	.	.	.	.	1
	1	X	X	0	.	.	.	.	.	1
	2	1	X	0	.	.	.	.	.	0
Candidate	3									
Strategies	.									
	.									
	.									
	.									
	12									

A simple financial planning model using simple profitability measures provided very important clues on the relative merits of a wide range of candidate strategies. In this instance, a model was constructed that was used to aggregate perceived costs and benefits — initially judgmentally determined — to yield approximate measures of profitability. Thus, for the first time, the firm was able to compare its present baseline case strategy directly with alternatives that would set quite different long-term directions.

An Investment Location

To this point, we have examined at most only "single-scenario" planning systems. This is because considerable progress normally needs to be made in improving the content of such scenarios. Furthermore, most executives find it difficult to arrive at decisions or strategies in the face of uncertainty implied by multiple scenarios — even when dealing with two or, at most, three. As a result, the transition to multiple scenarios should be made only when management is fully ready to use them.

What are the conditions that lead to or justify the use of multiple scenarios? The following three are most usually cited:

1. Probability distributions of key environmental variables are very wide, making it dangerous to suppress the full ranges of such variables in a single scenario.

2. A need exists to undertake contingency analysis or to explore simple choices based on the probable state of some key environmental variables.

3. The objective is to identify robust strategies that will perform reasonably well over a broad range of conditions instead of being sharply tuned to a single scenario.

It is our estimate that less than 10 percent of *Fortune* 1000 corporations currently use multiple scenarios to generate, evaluate, and help select strategies. Most such corporations use two or three scenarios, and many are initially motivated by the desire to evaluate simple, binary (go/no go) choices. However, for evaluations of the consequences of multiple scenarios, reasonably sophisticated corporate strategic models may have to be used, incorporating representations of both physical and financial characteristics. The following example illustrates how this may be done.

Example D. In this example (Lipinski and Loveridge 1982) in which the emphasis was on creating multiple scenarios rather than on constructing a strategic model, 16 major United States and United Kingdom corporations jointly underwrote a study of future characteristics of the United Kingdom in order to determine its attractiveness as a location for new investment. The strategic options were simple: to locate a new investment in the United Kingdom, France, or the United States.

The Scenarios

Identification of important issues. Questionnaires were prepared incorporating parallel approaches (see chapter 4) to elicit the relative importance of future issues. These were:

- Interrogation of a hypothetical clairvoyant,
- Description of a favorable future,
- Description of an unfavorable future,
- Information needed for current decisions,
- Intended use of the information.

Each of the sponsors was then asked to select and rank order by importance (on a scale of 1 to 5) the five issues that had surfaced most often during their deliberations. A weighted histogram of all the issues (16 sponsors) yielded the following list (total weight shown in parentheses):

- International trade (46);
- Politics and government (36);
- Productivity (27);
- Inflation (18);
- Industrial structure (18);
- Growth of GNP (17);
- Labor relations (16);
- Taxes (11);
- Social values (9);
- Energy policy (8);
- Economic climate (7);
- Unemployment (4);
- Regulation (4);
- Investment (4);
- Other responses (11).

Translation of issues into quantifiable variables. The above list of issues was translated into a list of quantifiable variables. The relationship between client concerns and the scenario variables does not lead directly to a one-to-one mapping. The relationship was divided into three categories:

- Variables that directly respond to or are a close proxy to client concerns;
- Variables that could be indirectly mapped through quantitative relationships to client concerns;
- Variables that could be inferred from client concerns.

These relationships are shown in table 8.11.

Table 8.11. Relation between Study Variables and Client Concerns

Study Variables	Direct Mapping	Indirect Mapping via Computations	Inference
1. Price of crude oil	Energy policy		
2. Growth of world trade	International trade		
3. Change in commodity prices		Change in GNP	Industrial structure
4. Value of Sterling (as trade weighted index)			
5. Personal direct taxation	Taxation		Social values
6. Government spending		Unemployment	
7. Gross fixed capital formation, private sector	Investment		Regulation
8. Savings		Inflation	
9. Growth/decline in productivity	Productivity		
10. Growth in wages and salaries			
11. Number of MPs not representing either major party	Politics and government		
12. Man-days lost through industrial disputes	Labor relations		
13. EEC budget as % European GNP			

The final list of variables was divided into input and output variables. Information on the input variables was obtained by elicitation of expert opinion and then fed to a specially constructed econometric model of the United Kingdom. The ten input variables selected as scenario components were:

1. Oil price,

2. Growth of world trade,

3. Commodity prices,

4. Value of the pound sterling,

5. Average annual increase in taxation,

6. Increase in governmental spending/GNP ratio,

7. Average annual growth of private investment,

8. Average saving rate during the period,

9. Average annual growth of productivity,

10. Average annual increase in earnings.

To elicit expert judgment in numerical form, each variable was sharply defined, as shown in table 8.12.

Table 8.12. Definitions and Dimensionality of Study Variables 1-10
for first-period 1978-85*

Variable No. 1	Crude oil price, dollars per barrel, in 1978 dollars.
Variable No. 2	Avererage annual growth of world trade in manufacturing goods in the period 1978-85, as a percent.
Variable No. 3	1985 dollar index of commodity prices, excluding crude oil with 1978 value of the index = 100.
Variable No. 4	1985 basket value of pound sterling − National Westminster basket. (May 1970 value = 100).
Variable No. 5	UK taxes on income plus National Insurance contribution as a percentage of personal income in 1985.
Variable No. 6	1985 public expenditure (White Paper basis) includes adjustment for public corporations, debt interest, and capital consumption as percentage of GNP. Respondents provided percent change from the current 1978 values.
Variable No. 7	Annual change in gross fixed capital formation, private sector, average in the 1978-85 period.
Variable No. 8	Personal savings as percent of personal disposable income in 1985.
Variable No. 9	1985 total productivity (actually in the period around 1985, in order to reduce the effect of short-term variation). Total output/man-days worked, annual increase in percent.
Variable No. 10	Annual increase in wages and salaries in percent, in or about 1985. The same, somewhat loose, definition as in Variable No. 9

*For the second period, substitute 1986-95 or 1995 as appropriate.

An econometric model was employed that used the preceding as input data to compute the following scenario variables:

- Annual rise in dollar index of world prices,
- UK inflation,
- The GNP and its growth rate,
- UK exports of goods,
- UK exports of services,
- North Sea contribution to trade balance,
- Trade balance without oil,
- Private consumption,
- Government consumption,
- Unemployment.

To capture the dynamics of the UK future, two time slices were examined: 1985 and 1995. Inputs were needed for each time slice, and the econometric model had to run twice, computing values for each time slice — thousands of times for the first time slice but, by using metascenarios, only a few times for the second.

Sequencing of input variables. After several attempts, the input variables were sequenced so that the information obtained on a preceding variable or variables would be most useful in forming a judgment on the next variable being considered. Thus, the process of elicitation started with the most exogenous variable. The problem of mutually interdependent variables was partially met later by "circling around" in the interviewing process and letting experts reexamine their judgments after they had seen the values derived from judgments on variables "above" as well as "below" theirs in the sequence ladder. In the final sequence, oil prices led as the most exogenous variable, and the first three variables served to describe the world environment of the United Kingdom as a trading country. When the key variables were identified, selected experts were matched to the variables.

Eliciting information. The core of the interviewing process was the elicitation of a nine-point mass function describing expert opinion. But each expert was also calibrated to record his or her substantive expertise and assessing ability. Typical interviews followed this sequence:

Step 1.   The respondents were asked to evaluate themselves as "experts" using the self-evaluation criteria of table 4.2.

Step 2.   The respondents were then asked to complete the first page of the assessing ability test: the 10 questions from the *Guiness Book of World Records.* The test of the assessing ability position at the start of the interview was essential, as the test administered a "jolt" to most respondents and alerted them to their imperfect treatments of uncertainty. Typically, respondents allocated limits that were far too narrow. While the test had the appearance of "fun" or "a party game," its intent was serious enough: to improve subsequent responses.

Step 3.   The respondents' judgments were elicited next. The respondents were given questionnaires consisting of three sets of assumptions relating to all or some of the preceding variables, and a form in which to frame their responses to the corresponding three sets of nine questions defining a nine-point mass function for each set of assumptions. Where necessary, probabilities were translated into their word equivalents.

Step 4.   A repetition of the assessing ability test completed the formal part of the interview. While similar in form to the first part, the questions were taken from the 1977 edition of the *U.S. Statistical Abstract*, or, for the United Kingdom respondents, from the 1977 edition of *Social Trends*, both of which the respondents considered more serious than the world records in the *Guiness Book of World Records*.

At the end of each interview (typically an interview lasted 1.5 to 2 hours), a second interview was arranged that would address the 1986-95 timeframe. At the latter interview, only steps 3 and 4 were necessary.

Derivation of the joint density function for each variable. To prepare data for the probability tree, all assessments on a given variable had to be placed on a scale that would encompass the entire range of values. The individual distributions were individually corrected for assessing ability *before* adding them according to a weighting that depended on the respondent's self-evaluation of expertise.

The joint distribution of several calibrated experts was made from their individual judgments by probabilistic weighted addition. The weights were as shown in table 4.3.

To provide inputs to the probabilistic tree, each density function was divided into equal probability segments. For the first level, we needed nine segments; thereafter, each judgment was divided into three equally likely segments. The values in the tree were the expected values of the respective segments.

Creating the tree. The first ten variables supplied the structure of the probabilistic tree. Their order of appearance defined the tree. Figure 8.7 illustrates half the tree. In the first round of interviewing, level 1 (crude oil price) was an exception to the general rule of having three sets of assumptions for each respondent: respondents on crude oil prices were not given any assumptions and, consequently, they made only *one* assessment (in the form of a nine-point mass function).

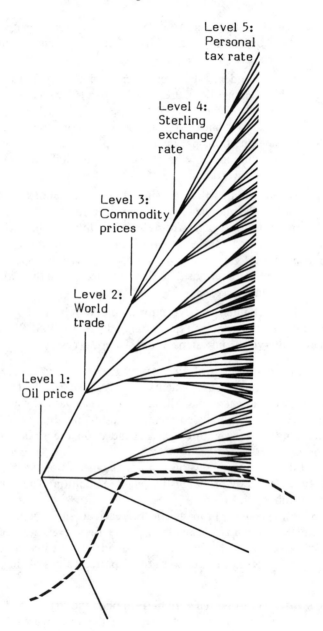

Fig. 8.7. Scenario Tree

The first level of the tree (oil price) yielded nine equally likely values of price. We used one dummy variable in order to split oil prices into nine segments, rather than three, so that at least one section of the tree would have oil price values agreeing with the then "conventional" forecast of oil price. In 1978, that forecast was a continuation of the then current oil price except for adjustment for inflation (approximately $12.40/barrel). The next set of assesments (world trade) should have been conditional on these nine oil prices, that is, nine separate judgments, one for each oil price. However, the assumptions given to each expert contributing to the higher levels had to be limited to three to avoid fatigue.

Therefore, the elicitation conducted at level 2 yielded three sets of expert judgments about the 1985 annual growth of world trade, each conditional on one of the three equally likely 1985 oil prices. Dividing each of the probability density functions into terciles, these three assessments yielded nine equally likely expected values of world trade. Here, a device was used to generate additional useful information from the three assessments provided by the experts.

It seemed reasonable to assume that the way assessments change across the tree is "well behaved," meaning that there are no sharp discontinuities anywhere within the spectrum of the individual scenarios, which ranged smoothly from very optimistic (low oil prices, high value of world trade, etc.) to very pessimistic (high oil prices, stagnant world trade, etc.). It became possible, therefore, to interpolate and extrapolate existing judgments to derive others. These were intended to approximate what the respondent *would have said* had the interviewing at level 3 been done exhaustively.

Using this approach, in addition to the three "real" judgments, six *synthetic* judgments were generated. The nine distributions (that is, three real and six inferred) were then split into terciles, yielding 27 values (Fig. 8.8).

Beyond level 2, the number of elicitations and inferred distributions were kept constant at three and six, respectively, yielding 27 different values at each level. Thus, beginning with level 3, a repetitive pattern began to emerge in which, to use an example, scenarios 1, 2, and 3 were composed of the same values of oil price and growth of world trade but differed in the value of the commodity price (table 8.13).

Table 8.13. Lowest Scenarios at Levels 2 and 3

At Level 1 (Oil Price) 9 Scenarios	At Level 2 (+ World Trade) 27 Scenarios	At Level 3 (+ Commodity Price Index) 81 Scenarios
	35.3,-0.9	35.3,-0.9,241.8
		35.3,-0.9,212.0
		35.3,-0.9,196.0
		35.3,-0.6,241.8
35.3	35.3,-0.6	35.3,-0.6,212.0
		35.3,-0.6,196.0
		35.3,-0.1,241.8
	35.3,-0.1	35.3,-0.1,212.0
		35.3,-0.1,196.0

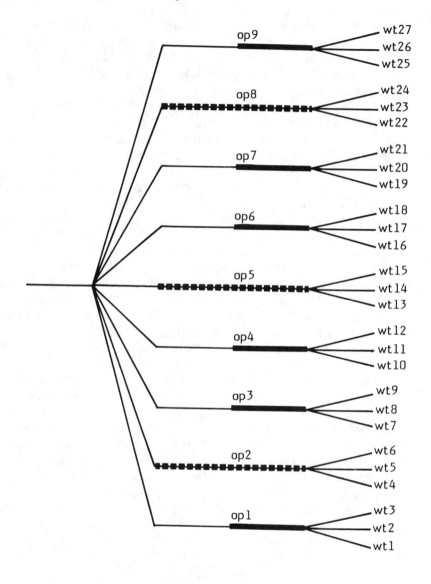

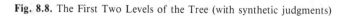

Inferred Distributions

Elicited Distriptions

op = Oil Price

wt = World Trade

Fig. 8.8. The First Two Levels of the Tree (with synthetic judgments)

This procedure continued down the tree until at level 10 (annual rise in earnings) there were 177,147 different individual scenarios, each consisting of a unique sequence of numbers describing the 1985 situation in the United Kingdom. The generation of the tree was, of course, computerized so that the only inputs required were the elicitation results. Each of the scenarios became an input to the simple econometric model that computed the additional 10 variables defined following table 8.12.

Averaging the scenarios. Scenarios served three purposes: (1) creating probability distributions of major indicators, (2) making a scenario "map" of the United Kingdom, and (3) deriving the metascenarios that would be presented to the sponsors. Depending on the purpose, the original large number of scenarios was reduced to a smaller set of scenarios, each of which was an average of a small bundle of scenarios. Finally, for the presentation to the sponsors, all the scenarios were reduced to three metascenarios, each consisting of 20 numbers (10 input and 10 output variables) covering the period 1978-85.

To evaluate the next period, 1986-95, the output values of the three 1985 metascenarios were used as input values to the econometric model. The model then extended the computations to the 1986-95 period, resulting in three metascenarios for the entire 1978-95 period.

These metascenarios were then slightly "hand" adjusted and qualitatively augmented by a group of "quantitatively oriented" generalists prior to being used as information given to the more qualitative and operationally experienced "generalists." Their principal assignment was to add to or "flesh out" further the bare quantitative skeleton of each metascenario. The end of the interviews with the generalists also marked the end of elicitations. Now all the information was in place: the quantitative metascenarios were enriched by the qualitative contributions of the generalists.

The next step was to present that information to the sponsors who wanted to use it in evaluating the relative merits of locating a new venture in the United Kingdom, France, or the United States. To make the comparison, information about France and the United States was presented in the same format as for the United Kingdom so that three metascenarios described the future of each country, principally characterized by high, medium, and low future costs of energy.

The actual modeling of the financial performance of a hypothetical company, were it to be located in the United Kingdom, France, or the United States, was made by the senior executives of the sponsoring companies during a workshop they attended. A hypothetical company, rather than an actual one, was structured because each of the sponsoring companies operated in a different line of business. Subsequently, to gauge the effect of the UK future on its particular operation, a sponsoring corporation could play the UK scenarios against the strategic model describing its new venture.

A New Consumer Product

The final planning stage is our *(n* x *n)* case in which we consider the full interplay of multiple scenarios and multiple strategies. Only a few major corporations have reached this stage of development. Such companies have examined only qualitative interactions (Naylor 1980), or have adopted a highly simplified shirtsleeve approach (Linneman and Kennell 1977), or have fully explored only the relative merits of narrower strategies such as new product development opportunities.

Example E. In this example, a large foreign corporation explored the profitability of introducing a new material to be substituted for the traditional material used in a popular consumer product sold in the United States. Because of the competitive sensitivity of the project, neither the name of the new material nor the type of consumer product can as yet be identified. The strategic options were perceived to be:

1. Produce and market the new material in the United States (i.e., build a new plant).
2. Produce and market the consumer product and the material in the United States (a new plant and a factory to produce the product).
3. Acquire a U.S. company familiar with the consumer product and make the new material in the United States.
4. Enter into a joint venture with a U.S. manufacturer who currently makes that consumer product but who uses the old, traditional material.
5. License U.S. companies to produce and market the new material.
6. Export the new material from the country of origin for sale to all U.S. manufacturers of that consumer product.

The scenarios

The introduction of the consumer product that would include the new material needed approval by the health authorities. They probably would demand a repetition of health tests already passed in the country of origin. The results of the new tests, the approval by the health authorities, and the consumer acceptance of the new synthetic material instead of the traditional, "natural" material were all uncertain. These became the principal elements of probabilistic scenarios. The final probabilistic elements of the scenarios were:

1. Success of the health test in the United States.
2. Success of the pilot study to test consumer acceptance.
3. Improvement (in order to increase acceptance) in one key attribute of the product.

4. Reaction of health authorities to a change in the key attribute.

5. Improvement in safety of the product.

6. Reaction of health authorities to the presumed improvement in safety.

7. Market penetration of the new product.

Successes or failures of the tests and the tactical decisions of management to omit or undertake some tests are shown in the probabilistic tree of figure 8.9.

Depending upon a string of successes and failures resulting from any combination of the states of the first six binary events, an appropriate probability was assigned to the three possible values of market penetration (Fig. 8.10).

Each of the six different strategies resulted in a different time stream of revenues and preliminary product introduction expenses for each scenario. The revenues depended on the market penetration and on the price charged for the product. The expenses depended on the number of tests conducted and the duration of the tests.

There were slightly more than 13,000 such scenarios. Future management decisions, such as whether to build a smaller or larger manufacturing plant after the pilot plant has been built, were treated probabilistically as one of the scenario elements. Depending on the strategy being explored, some elements were omitted.

A financial planning model of the operations required for the strategies was constructed. It computed the costs of building a manufacturing plant or plants, marketing development, acquiring a U.S. company, negotiating a joint venture, negotiating a license agreement, export fees, and shipping the material from the country of origin to the United States. The overall financial model consisted of:

- The cost and demand model. This model calculated the annual cost of material used in the product, the response of the prices charged by the makers of the traditional material to the change in demand caused by the introduction of the new material, and the impact of material substitution on the industry's inventory and production expenses.

- The financial model of the industry. The financial model of the industry producing the traditional material and the product was used to compute the industry's present worth, recognizing that the industry would be affected by a loss of demand for its old product and a need to substitute a new product at a different price. The price of the new product could then be adjusted in the model so that the industry's present worth would not be affected.

- The financial model of the manufacturer of the new material. This model, coupled to the industry model, computed the manufacturer's net pres-

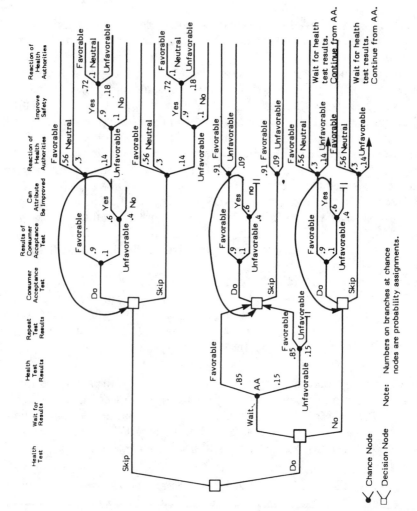

Fig. 8.9. Section of Tree Showing Health and Consumer Acceptance Tests

X Chance Node

Y Decision Node

Note: Numbers on branches at chance nodes are probability assignments.

172

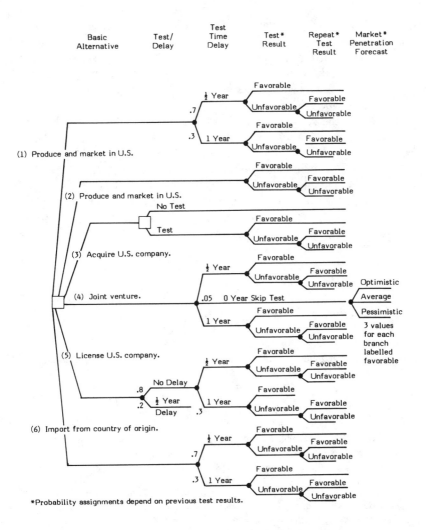

Fig. 8.10. Section of Tree Showing Basic Alternative and Market Tests

ent worth (after taxes) at a discount rate required by the decision maker. Depending on the strategy being considered, the financial model of the manufacturer was used to aggregate costs and revenues associated with new plants that were required to be built, acquisitions to be made, license fees to be collected, and so forth.

The measure of the goodness of a strategy was the "certain equivalent" (see chapter 9) — a risk-adjusted, expected value of the net present worth of cash flows (discounted at 15 percent annually) over a period of 25 years. The adjustment for risk aversion was made by computing the expected utility rather than the monetary value (present worth) of each scenario. To compute the utility, the analysts elicited the utility function of the senior executives in the U.S. company who would be in charge of and responsible for the success of U.S. operations.

To reduce the computational burden of running the model through the 13,000 distinct scenarios involved in each of the six strategies, a "surface" model was constructed. This surface model displayed the certain equivalent as a function of the crucial parameters, i.e., price, size of the initial plant, and a percentage substitution of the new material for the old material. Thus, the hundreds of equations of the three detailed models were reduced to one equation of the surface model, which was then evaluated for all strategies and all scenarios.

REFERENCES

Amara, R. C., and Palmer, M. 1979. *Strategic issues: A profile of top management concerns*. Menlo Park, CA: Institute for the Future.

Baran, P. 1979. *Potential market demand for two-way information services to the home, 1970-1990*, Report R-26. Menlo Park, CA: Institute for the Future.

Baran, P., and Lipinski, A. J. 1971. *The future of the telephone industry*, Report R-20. Menlo Park, CA: Institute for the Future.

Linneman, R. E., and Kennell, J. D. 1977. Shirt-sleeve approach to long-range plans. *Harvard Business Review* March-April: 141-50.

Linneman, R. E., and Klein, H. E. 1979. The use of multiple scenarios by U.S. industrial companies. *Long-Range Planning* 12: 83-90.

Lipinski, A., and Loveridge, D. 1982. IFTF's study of the UK, 1978-95. *Futures* 14, No. 3: 205-38.

Naylor, M. E. 1980. Planning for uncertainty — The scenario/strategy matrix. *Business Week Strategy Planning Conference*, September 22-23, New York.

Peters, T. J. 1980. Putting excellence into management. *Business Week* July 21: 196-205.

Tregoe, B. B., and Zimmerman, J. W. 1980. *Top management strategy: What it is and how to make it work*. New York: Simon and Shuster.

CHAPTER 9
VALUE MODELS

To this point we have assumed that objectives are given and that comparisons can be made between objectives and consequences (or outcomes) of a corporate model. Furthermore, we have specifically constructed a strategic loop (Fig. 1.9, chapter 1) to provide feedback to management to modify *options* or *candidate strategies* to find the "best match" between consequences and objectives.

In so doing, we have said very little about objectives. We have not provided any detailed description of how objectives may be generated or selected, how they may be compared to consequences, or when and how they may be modified. Such questions deal with the nature and structure of the value model, the most difficult and least understood part of the strategic planning framework. In fact, value models are treated superficially by most planners — much more so than either environmental or corporate models.

To dig more deeply into value models, we need to get back to basic definitions. We have previously defined objectives as "end points" or destinations to be achieved over time. Goals are intermediate milestones *actually* applied by stakeholders to the performance of a corporation. Some confusion continues to exist on the definition of objectives, goals, purposes, and missions. For our purposes, we will assume that objectives translate corporate purposes and missions into measurable and understandable "destinations" to be achieved year by year. As shown in figure 3.5 (chapter 3), objectives can also be subdivided into subobjectives indefinitely. Most important, any useful statement of objectives must be accompanied by a set of guidelines on how trade-offs among objectives are to be made. We shall return to this point later in this chapter. It is generally true that goals (intermediate milestones)

175

at one level of an organization may be translatable into objectives at a lower level.

A strong connection exists between objectives and options or candidate strategies. The search for and selection of options or candidate strategies may be viewed as a process of providing control signals (settings of option "knobs") to the corporate model that guides it in making "hits" (consequences) on "targets" (objectives) under the uncertainties of the external environment.

A value model should serve three important functions. First, it helps us to generate and select appropriate objectives. Second, it provides guidelines on how alternative sets of consequences (corresponding to alternative options or candidate strategies) may be evaluated. Third, it permits us to explore alternatives for modifying our objectives. In this chapter, we shall address the following three questions bearing on the functions of a value model:

1. How may objectives (or targets) be selected?

2. How do we compare consequences with objectives (to determine degree of "match" or closeness to target)?

3. How do we decide when to modify our objectives (independent of or in conjunction with the trial of options)?

SELECTING OBJECTIVES

Some would claim that there is only one legitimate corporate objective: to make a profit (Hussey 1976, p. 103). To be sure, without profit over a long period of time, no corporation will survive. However, the need to earn profit is not a sufficient statement of objectives. Many levels of profitability can be achieved over time; many paths can be used to reach the desired end point; and, along the way, many other things can be achieved — or not — many of which are not directly financial (e.g., quality of product or service). What is required, therefore, is a "map" of objectives or a representation of the desired route and conditions along the way to the end point, as well as how trade-offs are to be made along the way. Thus, corporate objectives are closely related to, and must be viewed in, the context of a larger set of values that underlie them.

As previously noted, "corporate culture" is a phrase that has acquired considerable currency in recent years as a shorthand for a set of traditions, values, and practices within a corporation. Thus, culture becomes a synonym for values from which objectives may be inferred that set a pattern for a company's actions. In fact, culture, values, objectives, and actions become so intertwined that it is often not clear where one ends and the others begin. What is clear, however, is that real changes in *one* dimension of this "ball of wax" imply change in each of the others. Accordingly, objectives based on deep-seated, long-standing traditions cannot be expected to respond quickly to pressures for change. Objectives may be set by the following nonexclusive generic methods.

Incremental Objective Setting

Objectives set the previous year are continued with only minor modifications. A classic example of a corporation that has operated with an essentially unchanging — or, at best, a slowly changing — set of objectives is J. C. Penney. The founder, James Cash Penney, laid down a set of guiding corporate principles in 1913 around which a remarkably stable "Penney culture" has been built. In summary form, "the Penney idea" is embodied in the following seven general objectives:

- To serve the public, as nearly as we can, to its complete satisfaction.

- To expect for the service we render a fair remuneration and not all the profit the traffic will bear.

- To do all in our power to pack the customer's dollar full of value, quality, and satisfaction.

- To continue to train ourselves and our associates so that the service we give will be more and more intelligently performed.

- To improve constantly the human factor in our business.

- To reward men and women in our organization through participation in what the business produces.

- To test our every policy, method, and act in this wise: "Does it square with what is right and just?"

Over the years, these objectives have served the company and its employees well. They have fostered an open, humanistic culture that inspires loyalty. Although J. C. Penney has recently come on hard times vis-à-vis its competitors, few within the organization feel it is because of any inadequacies of corporate objectives. Nevertheless, it is quite likely that over a period of time some adjustment may have to be made to thrive in a different competitive environment.

Several variants of incremental objective-setting exist. One such variant may be expressed as follows: doing at least as well as one's competitors (on the average) or doing better than one's competitors. Still another variant — particularly when objectives are largely stated in financial terms — revolves around the notion of "opportunity costs." Return on investment (ROI) must be at least equivalent to the cost of capital, or the prevailing long-term interest rate. Otherwise, in the long run, shareholders will elect to shift their investments or equity to more attractive options.

Other versions of basically incremental approaches may be used. However, generally, these methods share a set of common characteristics: they are passive; they display a "follow-the-leader" (the leader may be oneself) orientation; and they result in very slowly changing (or even unchanging) statements of purposes. Yet, the great majority of corporations — many large and successful — have used precisely variants of this approach over long periods of time.

Another outstanding and relatively young organization that has perhaps best exemplified an incremental approach to objective setting is Hewlett-Packard (Ouchi 1981, p. 225). Although a number of modifications have been made since 1957 when the first set of objectives was published, the basic thrust of corporate purpose has remained essentially unchanged. This is embodied in its objectives reflecting the strong personal philosophies of its founders, William Hewlett and David Packard:

1. Profit. To achieve sufficient profit to finance our company growth and to provide the resources we need to achieve our other corporate objectives.

2. Customers. To provide products and services of the greatest possible value to our customers, thereby gaining and holding their respect and loyalty.

3. Fields of Interest. To enter new fields only when the ideas we have, together with our technical, manufacturing, and marketing skills, assure that we can make a needed and profitable contribution to the field.

4. Growth. To let our growth be limited only by our profits and our ability to develop and produce technical products that satisfy real customer needs.

5. Our People. To help HP people share in the company's success, which they make possible; to provide job security based on their performance; to recognize their individual achievements; and to insure the personal satisfaction that comes from a sense of accomplishment in their work.

6. Management. To foster initiative and creativity by allowing the individual great freedom of action in attaining well-defined objectives.

7. Citizenship. To honor our obligations to society by being an economic, intellectual, and social asset to each nation and each community in which we operate.

It is unlikely that Hewlett-Packard's long tradition of funding growth from internally generated cash; of creating a strong, stable, participative management structure; and of focusing in market areas where strong leadership can be achieved will be changed in the near future. Usually, inadequacies in objectives appear only when the external environment changes abruptly, a new competitor appears on the scene, or when a new CEO is appointed.

Objective-Driven Planning

On occasion, objectives are set, or changed drastically, by an individual — usually the CEO. In chapter 3 (stage 1 planning), objective-driven planning was defined and illustrated by brief references to such organizations as United Airlines, IBM, and Bank of America — each led by a dominant CEO. Perhaps no better recent case illustrating this alternative in greater detail can be found than that represented by International Paper (IP).

When Edwin A. Gee became CEO in 1979, he laid down a set of corporate objectives that — although continuing a "culture shift" that had been set in motion by his predecessor — marked a fairly radical departure from the past. Basically, prior IP management had not kept pace with a drastically changing competitive environment in which a host of new contenders from the wood products industry had moved into the paper market. As they did, using the residual chips from wood products to make pulp, they achieved economies that permitted them to cut costs below those of International Paper which was a high-volume but high-cost producer. The inevitable result for IP was the continual loss of market share and a rapid decline in profitability. The new set of objectives promulgated by Gee may be summarized as follows:

- To become the lowest cost rather than the highest volume producer of paper.

- To diversify more heavily into lumber and wood products without losing dominance in paper.

- To increase long-term profitability even at the expense of short-term returns.

These objectives have set in motion a series of changes within IP, the outcome of which cannot be evaluated for a number of years. Assets not in line with the new objectives are being sold (e.g., oil exploration), and new ones are being acquired (e.g., prime timberland). The most antiquated and least efficient paper mills are being shut down, and all capital equipment expenditures are being scrutinized vis-à-vis their relevance to the new objectives. If successful, the IP of 1990 will look far different than the IP inherited by Gee in 1979.

The set of objectives laid down at IP are somewhat more multifaceted than those often used by others; also, the process may or may not involve a dominant CEO. In many instances, a single dimension of a corporation's makeup may be used successfully as the basis of the "driving force" (Tregoe and Zimmerman 1980) for providing long-term direction. Such driving forces have been defined as the primary determiners of the scope of future products and markets. Each can be based on one of the following basic categories: products/markets; capabilities (supply, technology, production, sales/distribution); or results (size/growth, return/profit). Primary examples of single-driving-force enterprises are: product-driven — Ford, MGM; supply-driven — Gulf, DeBeers; technology-driven — DuPont, Texas Instruments; and sales/distribution-driven — Avon, Spiegel.

In passing, it is interesting to note that objective-driven planning often becomes the basis for management by objective (MBO). In such instances, planning may be translated into action without elaborate environmental analyses, corporate models, or evaluations of candidate strategies. In a real sense, MBO becomes the *direct* linkage of corporate and division objectives to the level of individual managers by providing a consistent framework for action. Its principal advantages are simplicity and directness. Its shortcomings stem from the short-circuiting of analytical processes that provide a richer set of alternatives in a rapidly changing business environment.

Consensual Objective Setting

Whether done incrementally or episodically (as is often done in objective-driven planning), increasingly, the setting of corporate objectives is being, and will be, influenced by *group* action. Such groups may comprise only professional managers; or, more generally, such groups may include representatives of employee groups, activist organizations, or government agencies. In either case, objective-setting processes become more subtle and less direct, involving delicate bargaining and negotiation processes.

An interesting recent case illustrating consensual objective setting by a management group is the Chase Manhattan Bank (CMB). In the late 1970s, CMB's return on assets slipped appreciably as the banking environment rapidly became more competitive. The CMB "style" — smug, inbred, courtly — had grown increasingly at odds with the needs of the market place.

Recognizing that drastic action was called for, a group of top executives, including the chairman and the CEO, embarked on a program of "culture-change" and redefinition of objectives. One of the first steps taken by the group was the generation of a three-page mission statement that identified precisely the businesses in which CMB's greatest strengths lay. Also spelled out were specific targets for key financial measures: return on assets, return on equity, and debt-to-capital ratio. Most important, the consensual process gradually involved larger and larger internal groups, reversing the long-standing tradition of a strictly hierarchical management style and creating a new *esprit de corps*. This process change was considered by most to be the key to making lasting changes. The ultimate substantive results included a host of major reforms: drastic revamping of reward structures to stress the value of high performance; the infusion of aggressive outsiders; and the phasing out of unprofitable businesses.

It may be that the most advanced form of consensual objective setting is represented by the Japanese style of management. Again, only one class of stakeholders is involved — professional managers, and the process is not very explicit. What we do know is that, through a long series of person-to-person and person-to-group interactions, a sense of common values and purpose emerges that gradually becomes an explicit or implicit set of objectives. The terms "participative," "consensual," and "egalitarian" have been used to describe the characteristics of such groups. Perhaps the essential processes can work only when a fairly dominant corporate culture already exists. This may result, as in Japan, from the influence of a highly homogeneous society with a long history and tradition of common values. Or, in the United States, it may be the product of what has recently been described as Type Z organizations (Ouchi 1981). In the future, the primary candidates for consensual objective setting may be declining industries (e.g., automobiles), corporations in the public eye (e.g., natural resources), corporations subject to intense foreign competition (e.g., steel), or organizations dealing with critical services (e.g., health). The result may be a greater focus on nonfinancial objectives, inclusion of a broader range of objectives, and more explicit statements of trade-offs among objectives.

The methods used for consensual objective setting with broad groups of stakeholders are least well defined; usually the rubric "coalition building" is used. One of the most widely publicized examples of corporate coalition building aimed at influencing industry-wide, if not corporate, objectives is the National Coal Policy Project (Murray 1978). This was an ambitious attempt in the late 1970s to reconcile environmental and industrial interests in the anticipated shift in the United States from oil and natural gas to coal. The nonadversarial principles adopted by the project as guidelines are the "Rules of Reason," articulated by Milton Wessell (1976). These simple rules (e.g., data should not be withheld, delaying tactics should not be used, motives should not be lightly impugned, dogmatism should be avoided) are intended to focus efforts on a search for a mutually agreeable outcome rather than presenting a case solely to "win" a favorable decision. Participants took part as individuals, not as representatives of their organizations. They came from a broad variety of organizations: big companies like Allied Chemical, Amax, Consolidated Coal, and Monsanto; universities like Pennsylvania, California (Berkeley), Princeton, and Montana; utilities like PG&E, Gulf States, and Texas Utilities; and environmental groups like the Environmental Defense Fund, the Environmental Law Institute, the National Wildlife Federation, and the Sierra Club. Participants were divided among five task forces covering the full range of coal-related energy and environmental issues. The tangible result: a set of approximately 200 agreed-upon recommendations for guiding the expansion of coal-producing capacity in the future. Thus, the primary focus was on identifying and working on issues that could be resolved and that could provide guidance on setting industry-wide objectives (though the study was just as explicit in listing unresolved issues).

COMPARING CONSEQUENCES WITH OBJECTIVES

Objectives are by nature multidimensional. As illustrated in chapter 3 in generic form (Fig. 3.5) and in the previous section by specific example, objectives include both financial and nonfinancial performance measures, as shown in figure 9.1.

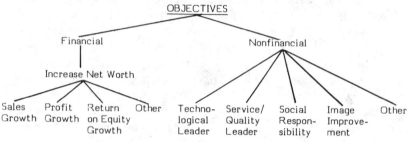

Fig. 9.1. Generic Representation of Corporate Objectives

We will assume that profit or, preferably, net cash flow will always be included as one dimension of corporate objectives or corporate performance. And this is the dimension that will be used as the common medium (expressed as equivalent cash) for equating other objectives. Net cash flow is simply the difference between a year-by-year stream of revenues (or cash in-flow) and disbursements (or cash outflow). Revenues are defined as income from all sources: proceeds from product or service sales, tax refunds, compensation from sale of a subsidiary, proceeds from patent licenses, a favorable court judgment resulting in a cash award, money received from a bank loan — in effect, all positive cash flows. Similarly, disbursements are all negative cash flows: salaries, payments to subcontractors, taxes of all kinds, license fees, interest fees, dividend payments, and so forth.

The consequences of a candidate strategy might be expressed as three time streams — one of revenues, the second of disbursements, and the third of the resulting net cash flow, as shown in table 9.1. For simplicity, only five years are shown.

Defining Objectives

In order to compare consequences with objectives (and with each other), we need to develop some ground rules for the form in which objectives must

Table 9.1. Hypothetical Streams of Revenues and Disbursements
(in thousands)

	Year 1	Year 2	Year 3	Year 4	Year 5
Revenues	100	120	150	180	250
Disbursements	150	130	120	145	180
Net Cash Flow	(50)	(10)	30	35	70

be framed. Each objective must be measurable on some scale — even if the scale is relative and judgmental rather than objective and quantitative. For example, again using only the first three objectives (emphasis added) contained in the Hewlett-Packard statement previously introduced:

Objective 1. To achieve *sufficient* profit to finance our company growth and to provide the resources we need to achieve our other corporate objectives.

Objective 2. To provide products and services of the greatest possible value to our customers, thereby gaining and holding their *respect and loyalty*.

Objective 3. To enter new fields only when the ideas we have, together with our technical, manufacturing, and marketing skills, assure that we can make a needed and profitable *contribution* to the field.

Unless the terms "sufficient," "respect and loyalty," and "contribution" are defined in measurable terms using some appropriate indicators, little can be said about how well any set of consequences matches the set of objectives. Possible indicators for the three Hewlett-Packard objectives might be:

Profit: X percent of sales (to be converted to an equivalent net cash flow measure) (Objective 1)

Customers: Number of repeat sales divided by number of complaints (Objective 2)

Field: Profit in each product line divided by number of competitors (Objective 3)

These objectives may be considered "end points" or destinations to be reached after a number of years, say 5 or 10. What is also necessary are the intermediate, year-by-year milestones that lead to the desired end points. For example, over an n-year period, the milestones may be represented as O_{ij}, where i = objective and j = year as indicated in table 9.2.

Since we will be making comparisons between objectives and consequences later, we shall represent the time-sequenced set shown in table 9.2 structurally in figure 9.2.

Table 9.2. Intermediate Objectives

Objective	Year 1	2	3. . . . . .n
1. Net Cash Flow	O_{11}	O_{12}	O_{13}. . . . . .O_{1n}
2. Customers	O_{21}	O_{22}	O_{23}. . . . . .O_{2n}
3. Field	O_{31}	O_{32}	O_{33}. . . . . .O_{3n}

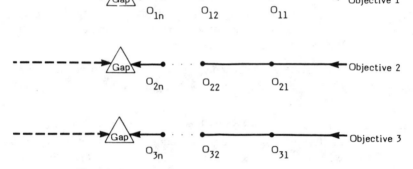

Fig. 9.2. Structural Representation of Intermediate Objectives

Equivalence Preference

We are now ready to determine equivalence or trade-off relationships among objectives. The equivalences will be obtained in terms of the profit or net cash flow objective using equivalent cash (EC). With intermediate objectives provided (as in the previous section), such trade-off relationships will be specified year by year.

The proposed method for determining equivalences is Saaty's pair-wise comparison method (Saaty 1977) introduced in chapter 4. Working with a group, judgment can be aggregated cell by cell, indicating how much more or less important each objective O_{ij} is than each of the others for each year. After processing, the final weights for the set of three objectives introduced earlier may be expressed relative to objective 1 (net cash flow) as in table 9.3.

These may be considered *weighting* factors to be applied to consequences C^{kl}_{ij} resulting from a particular option, $k,$ and a particular scenario, $l,$ being evaluated. For example, for year $j,$ the equivalent cash EC^{kl}_{j} for the set of consequences corresponding to the set of three objectives may be expressed as follows:

$$EC_j^{kl} = \left\{ \frac{C_{1j}^{kl}}{O_{1j}} (1.00) + \frac{C_{2j}^{kl}}{O_{2j}} (a_{2j}) + \frac{C_{3j}^{kl}}{O_{3j}} (a_{3j}) \right\} O_{1j}.$$

Table 9.3. Intermediate Objectives

Objective	1	2	3	. . . . n
1. Net Cash Flow	1.00	1.00	1.00.	. . 1.00
2. Customers	a_{21}	a_{22}	a_{23}.	. . a_{2n}
3. Field	a_{31}	a_{32}	a_{33}	. . a_{3n}

Expanding figure 9.2 further, we can now present the equivalences as shown in figure 9.3.

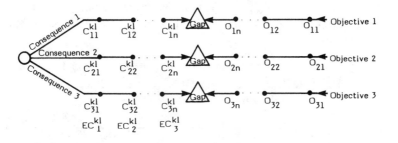

Fig. 9.3. Consequences vs. Objectives: Equivalent Cash

In principle, then, for any set of consequences over time resulting from the selection of an option and a scenario, we can represent that set as a time sequence of equivalent cash.

Before proceeding further, a number of important caveats and problems ought to be noted. First, we have assumed that a set of objectives can be prespecified year by year. Valid objections can be raised about the justification for so doing, particularly when multiple stakeholders are involved. How reasonable is it to assume that we can define precisely what future stakeholders may want from an enterprise? Not very. We have done so primarily for analytical convenience. We shall return to this point later.

Second, we have assumed that trade-off relationships among objectives can be readily established and monetary (cash) equivalences imputed. Even if this can be done, it is not reasonable to assume that such relationships will apply over the full range of each objective pair, nor is it reasonable to assume that trade-offs between any pair of variables are independent of the values of other variables. At the cost of greater complexity, such nonlinearities can and should be accommodated when they are important.

Perhaps the most important caveat is that the processes for setting objectives are poorly understood. Accordingly, the kind of successive iteration that has become accepted practice in generating and evaluating options (and candidate strategies) might profitably be extended to generation and evaluation of objectives. This may suggest some kind of progression from the most general specification of objectives to successively detailed sets as we iterate through the other parts of the planning process.

Time Preference

Since a dollar tomorrow is worth less than a dollar today — not because of inflation, but because of the delay in having access to it — some discount rate must be applied in "rolling back" the EC^{k}s (equivalent cash year by year) to determine a present equivalent (PE). To compute PE, let's assume that future cash flows are discounted at a 10 percent annual rate (the derivation of the appropriate discount rate will be given later). Table 9.4 shows the computation.

Table 9.4. Illustrative Computation of Present Equivalent for Discount Rate of 10 Percent

	Year 1	Year 2	Year 3	Year 4	Year 5	
		(in thousands)				
Net Cash Flow	(50)	(10)	30	35	40	
Discount Rate (=10%)	1	0.909	0.826	0.751	0.683	
Discounted Net Cash Flow	(50)	(9.09)	24.78	26.28	27.32	
Present Equivalent	(-50) +(-9.09)	+24.78	+26.28	+27.32		= 19.29

If the assumed discount rate of 10 percent correctly represents the decision maker's time preference *and* if no risk is involved, he or she would be indifferent to receiving $19,290 now or engaging in a risk-free business producing the net cash flow shown.

In principle, the discount rate reflects the time preference for money or its equivalent (Rappaport 1981, p. 139). The basic concept of time preference is that of deferred gratification. In an experiment with small children in Trinidad (Mischel 1958, p. 57), the psychologists offered the youngsters a choice: "You can have a chocolate now, or I can bring you two chocolates tomorrow. Which would you rather have?" Invariably, small children would take one right away, while older children preferred to have two chocolates the next day. If we express the time discount per period as $1/(1+r)$, where

r is the discount rate, the choice of the young child barely able to choose between one chocolate today or two tomorrow is:

1 (chocolate) $1/(1+r)^0 = 2$ (chocolates)$1/(1+r)^1$.

Solving for r, we get: $r = 1$, or a time discount of 100 percent per day.

To the senior executive, the equivalent of a chocolate today is good financial performance in this year's bottom line. Instead of a day, the period over which time preference is measured is, typically, one year. But the principle is the same: the executive is indifferent to a gain (or a loss) separated by several time periods when the coefficient r accurately simulates his or her time preference. The considerations for assigning a particular value to r (the time discount rate) are many, and the final determination can make use of any of the following:

1. *Internal Rate of Return (IROR)*. What is the next best profitable alternative (i.e., best candidate strategy) and what is its IROR? IROR determines the discount rate at which the present equivalent is equal to zero or the discount rate at which the present equivalent of revenues is equal to the present equivalent of disbursements. Obviously, in the example given in table 9.4, it must be higher than 10 percent. The computation is done by trial and error. For example, a 40 percent discount rate produces a string of discounted net cash flows shown in table 9.5.

Table 9.5. Illustrative Computation of Present Equivalent for Discount Rate of 40 Percent

(in thousands)

	Year 1	Year 2	Year 3	Year 4	Year 5
Net Cash Flow	(50)	(10)	30	35	40
Discounted Net Cash Flow	(50)	(7.14)	15.30	12.7	10.4
Present Equivalent	(-50)	+(-7.14)	+15.30	+12.7	+10.4= -18.74

These two points (19.29 and -18.74) are enough to provide a rough clue of the IROR. By using a simple linear interpolation shown in figure 9.4, the true IROR is approximately 25 percent. Typically, IROR is used for the individual projects, while the Present Equivalent can be and is used for the corporation as a whole.

2. *Opportunity Cost or the Cost of Money*. Lending money to others may be very attractive, and the cost of money (say, that of the Aaa corporate bond rate) may be a good approximation of the opportunity cost — that is, if lending is the best apparent alternative. Lending money to government by purchasing government securities is an almost no-risk option. Alternatively, at a minimum, the required discount rate should be equal

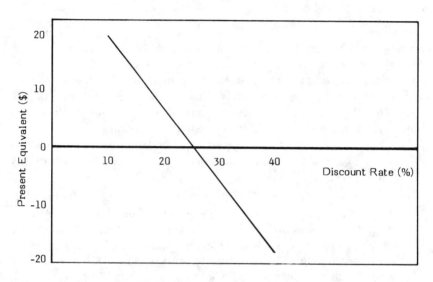

Fig. 9.4. Present Equivalent vs. Discount Rate

to the real cost of money — that is, the bank rate (short or long term) minus the expected inflation rate.

3. *Perceptual Costs.* The child's greed is replaced by the executive's possible realization that the board may not tolerate another year of losses, and someone else might be the new CEO. Or, from another standpoint, the executive retires in two years' time and, try as she might, she does not feel unduly excited about the oil shale revenues in the year 2005.

To elicit the discount rate, one poses a series of questions, offering trade-offs between gains (and/or losses) spaced one or several time periods apart. The gains (or losses) should be significant in relation to the unit's performance; for example, a windfall tax rebate of, say, $100 million, which might be 10 percent of the after-tax profit. The executive might have to decide whether he would rather have the $100 million this year or $300 million (adjusted for inflation) three years hence. If he would, what about $250 million? If that offer is still more attractive than $100 million now, what about $200 million? Let us say that the point of indifference is reached at $175 million. Then the implied discount rate r is given by:

$$(1+r)^3 = 175/100; \ 1 + r = 1.205; \ r = 0.205 \text{ or } 20.5\%.$$

Continuing in this manner, one obtains a series of discount rates for several time spans. Typical results are shown in figure 9.5.

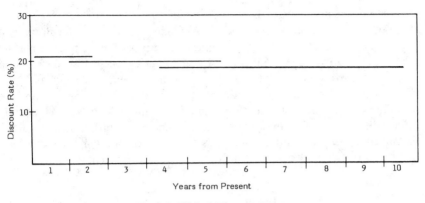

Fig. 9.5. Elicited Discount Rates

If the results suggest fairly uniform discount rates over time, then, for simplicity, a constant one can be assumed — in the example illustrated, it would be 19 percent. Under these circumstances, the PE would be expressed simply as:

$$PE^{kl} = \frac{EC_1^{kl}}{1+r} + \frac{EC_2^{kl}}{(1+r)^2} + \cdots \frac{EC_n^{kl}}{(1+r)^n}.$$

It is possible — and should not be too surprising — to find that an executive's perception of discount rates may reflect his or her expected tenure in a particular position. For example, figure 9.6 might represent the effective discount rate of a chairman who plans to retire after four years.

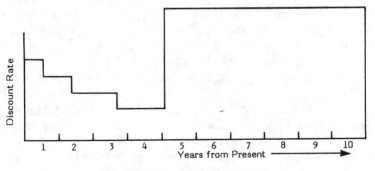

Fig. 9.6. Hypothetical Discount Rate

In such cases, the present equivalent, PE^{kl}, is computed by applying a variable r_j corresponding to the year j for each EC_j.

It should be noted that PE^{kl} is the present equivalent for a *single* option, k, played against a *single* scenario, l. To make this clearer, we will have to construct the complete planning framework. For our present example, let us assume that we are working with three scenarios (or metascenarios) and that we are evaluating a total of three options. Then, extension of figure 9.3 "backward" to show structurally the interplay of scenarios and options provides the complete picture of our familiar planning framework. The only minor difference in figure 9.7 from previous representations of the framework is that the "scenario" and "option" inputs to the corporate model have been rotated clockwise 90 degrees for convenience of representation.

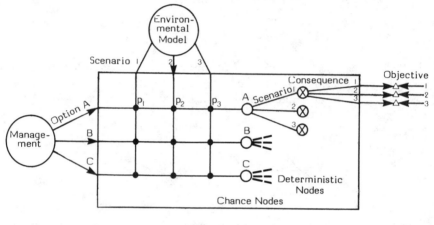

Fig. 9.7. Structural Representation for Evaluating Consequences vis-à-vis Objectives

We can see that PE^{A1} can be assigned to the uppermost deterministic node, which "generates" consequences (deterministically) from the interplay of option A and scenario 1. Exactly the same processes that have been described to generate PE^{A1} to this point may be used to generate PE^{A2} and PE^{A3}, corresponding to present equivalents for option A and scenarios 2 and 3, respectively. These would be assigned to the bottom two deterministic nodes in figure 9.7.

So far, the analysis has been strictly deterministic: a particular option (option A) played against a particular scenario (scenarios 1, 2, or 3) to yield three sets of consequences. We are now ready to "roll back" one more stage to evaluate an option against a *range* of scenarios. With assigned probabilities of p_1, p_2, p_3 for scenarios 1, 2, and 3, respectively, we can visualize a present equivalent lottery at each chance node A, B, or C in figure 9.7. For example, at chance node A, we have for the expected value EV^A:

$$EV^A = p_1 \, (PE^{A1}) + p_2 \, (PE^{A3}) + p_3 \, (PE^{A3}).$$

But how does EV^A compare with EV^B and EV^C, the corresponding expected values for chance nodes B and C, corresponding to options B and C? If EV^A is greater than EV^B and EV^C *and* each component present equivalent — PE^{A1}, PE^{A2}, PE^{A3} — is greater than its corresponding component of EV^B and EV^C, then EV^A *stochastically dominates* EV^B and EV^C. All this means is that option A performs better than options B or C in *each* of the three scenarios. No further analysis is necessary, for then option A will clearly be preferred to options B and C.

However, normally stochastic dominance does not hold. Most often, the probability of high gains for an option is accompanied by the probability of high losses for that option. In such instances, expected value is not a satisfactory measure for making a choice. Recourse must be made to another component of values — namely, risk preference.

Risk Preference

Risk preference of an individual may be determined by assigning a subjective value to any monetary gain or loss. The subjective value is defined as a "utility" expressed in an arbitrary scale (Von Neumann and Morgenstern 1947). Utility curves for individuals generally illustrate curvatures that characterize risk aversion for potentially large gains and risk seeking for potentially large losses (Kahneman and Tversky 1982, p. 160). Put differently, a risk-averse individual opts for a sure gain in preference to a gamble with higher monetary expectation and, conversely, a risk-seeking individual opts for a gamble in preference to a sure loss that has a higher monetary expectation. Diagrammatically, for individuals confronted with choices involving relatively small monetary amounts, the general shape of the curve may be represented as in figure 9.8.

Considerable understanding has been acquired in recent years about utility functions of individuals and some of the departures from objectivity that arise in their use (Schoemaker 1980; Tversky and Kahneman 1981, p. 453).

The processes for inferring individual utility functions are fairly straightforward. Each individual is offered a choice between a sure gain (or loss) and some gamble — say, a 50 percent chance of winning (or losing) a specified, known amount. The individual is asked to indicate a sure value X, which makes the sure amount equally as attractive (or unattractive) as the gamble. This may be represented as in figure 9.9.

For example, a typical value for X for a specified gain of $1,000 is about $350. In other words, the utility of $350 is equated to half the utility of $1,000 ($0.5 \times$ utility of $1,000). Similarly, a typical value X for a specified loss of $1,000 is -$400, making the utility of -$400 half the utility of -$1,000. And so forth. In order to develop a common utility scale for gains *and* losses, it is also necessary to include a gamble involving *both* gains and losses. A

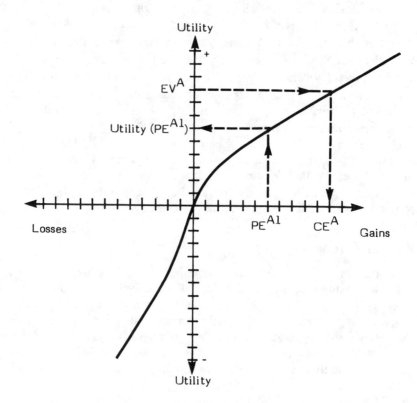

Fig. 9.8. General Shape of Utility Function

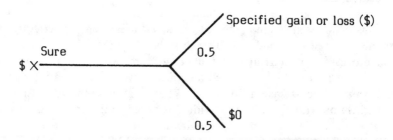

Fig. 9.9. Inferring Utility Function: Gains or Losses

convenient way to pose such a choice is a gamble in which there is a 50 percent chance of losing, say, $1,000 and an equal chance of winning an amount X. The choice is the *smallest amount X* that will make the gamble attractive or acceptable. This may be presented by figure 9.10.

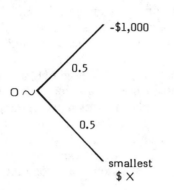

Fig. 9.10. Inferring Utility Function: Gains and Losses

A typical response would be about $2,000, since most individuals will enter a gamble with even odds only when the potential gain is much greater than the potential loss. Thus, the slope of the utility curve for losses is about twice as great as for gains, as shown in figure 9.8.

The potential gains or losses that would be used to elicit utility functions of corporate stakeholders — primarily those of senior management — would be several orders of magnitude greater, in the millions or hundreds of millions. But the general shape of the functions will likely be the same. Returning to our example as shown in figure 9.7, if we have elicited an overall management utility function, the utility of options A, B, and C may now be determined. For example, for option A, the utilities of PE^{A1}, PE^{A2}, and PE^{A3} are read off directly from the utility curve. Thus, the expected utility EV^A for option A is simply:

$EV^A = p_1$ (Utility of PE^{A1}) + p_2 (Utility of PE^{A2}) + p_3 (Utility of PE^{A3}). The question that can now be answered directly is the following: What is the amount that management would be willing to accept for *certain* as a substitute for the gamble or lottery among the three PEs? The answer is obtained directly from the utility curve by entering the curve on the "utility" axis at the value of EV^A and reading from the curve the value on the abscissa, which is designated the "certain equivalent" (CE^A). Thus, instead of comparing expected values (EVs) when stochastic dominance prevails, we now compare certain equivalents (CEs). That option is preferred that has the highest CE.

Recapitulation

We have tried to incorporate three dimensions of stakeholder values in the evaluation of consequences. The first, equivalence preference, is intended to capture perceptions on how trade-offs among objectives and their associated consequences are to be applied. The second, time preference, reflects the relative valuation placed on more distant gains and losses as compared to more immediate gains and losses. And the third, risk preference, is intended to portray the subjective valuation or utility of gains and losses of different magnitudes.

The methods described should be viewed only as crude first approximations for evaluating consequences vis-à-vis objectives. Many complex issues have not been raised, let alone addressed. For example, nonlinearities of various kinds have been overlooked. Interaction effects among equivalence, time, and risk preferences have not been considered. And, perhaps most important, the problems of aggregating *individual* perceptions to produce *group* or corporate trade-off matrices, discount rates, or utility curves have not been treated.

Even so, notwithstanding the many issues that remain to be resolved, the tools described do represent a beginning for the more systematic and explicit treatment of stakeholder values.

MODIFYING OBJECTIVES

The differences between setting objectives and modifying objectives result largely from differences in perspective. In describing objective-setting approaches earlier in this chapter (incremental, objective-driven, consensual) our focus was on *process*. Here, we would like to shift the emphasis from process to *conditions* and *timing* for objective modification.

We are not primarily interested in the resetting of objectives spurred by the threat of imminent catastrophe. Instead, we would like to examine less extreme cases to illustrate how objectives may be reset in *anticipation* of forthcoming change rather than in desperate response to it. We do not know how many successful case histories exist illustrating *proactive* objective resetting. We suspect that most of these may involve small, young, high-technology companies led by owner/founders. In any event, the search for more desirable objectives adds another important degree of freedom to the strategic planning process — one that is seldom explored. Clearly, the additional degree of freedom adds further complexity to an already overcomplex process. Three particular dimensions of proactive objective modification will be described.

Changed Ground Rules: American Telephone and Telegraph

Perhaps no corporation has worked as long or as hard at preparing itself for modifying its basic objectives than AT&T. The process — which has culminated in an agreement for AT&T to shed its operating companies in the next few years — began in the late 1950s or early 1960s. Even then, it was becoming clearer that the nature and pace of technological change would ultimately result in a new set of ground rules for AT&T and its potential competitors. In a sense, the Consent Decree of 1956 to limit AT&T's entry into the data processing business was only a stop-gap for a period in which distinctions between computer and communication businesses would become increasingly academic.

To prepare itself for the new environment in which it must learn to operate, AT&T embarked on a concerted internal effort to give as much weight to its marketing functions as to its traditional service functions. Culturally, it set to transform itself from the world of utilities, public interest, and fair return on assets to a competitive industrial environment where a primary objective is large profit for its shareholders.

This kind of transformation is far more easily described than done. AT&T's folklore and tradition had been built around its noncustomized services. It properly prided itself in providing the most efficient and dependable telephone service in the world. It excelled in speed of response, in standard operating procedures, and in following set policies hammered out over long years of experience. But, as the FCC provided increasing freedom to competitors to sell products in AT&T's once-captive markets, the handwriting was clearly on the wall. And AT&T management did not ignore it even though the changes to be tackled involved reorienting an organization of almost one million strong. This is not to suggest that all employees would be involved in the transition, but a whole new culture had to be created.

The progression was not an unbroken series of successes. Some early attempts did not take, for example, trying to educate marketing managers to concentrate on noncustomized sales without changing the old reward structure at the same time. Nevertheless, a great deal of productive effort was spent internally analyzing the requirements for change; acknowledging its weaknesses (marketing and cost control); and methodologically setting out to acquire key staff, change organizational structures, revamp reward systems, and stimulate marketing innovation to meet new forms of competition.

One of the new role models acquired in the early 1970s was Archie J. McGill, a former IBM marketing executive. McGill was not cast in the typical mold of the AT&T executive; far from it − this is why he was acquired. McGill in turn attracted a large number of key outsiders − all heavily marketing oriented. Among his pivotal moves was the transforming of all national account coverage from local telephone companies to AT&T Long Lines.

And the transition begun about 20 years ago is far from complete. Best estimates are that it will take three to five more years. Again, this is because changing basic objectives means changing internal culture and basic values. However, AT&T is now in an excellent position to exploit its new orientation. Divesting itself of local telephone companies will accelerate the transition and reinforce the culture shift. With Bell Laboratories, Western Electric, and Long Lines, the new AT&T will be able to go after a host of new markets including electronic mail, conferencing, and communication services to the home. In the longer run, AT&T will be a formidable competitor in computers, broadcasting, cable TV, and electronic parts and equipment — internationally as well as domestically. There is perhaps no better example involving a very large organization of proactive *positioning* for the future by resetting objectives.

Limited Growth Options: Dow Chemical

Another corporation that is attempting to position itself for the future by a major revision of its objectives is Dow Chemical. In this case, the stimulus has come from a desire to continue to grow at past rates. In the past, Dow has almost single-mindedly concentrated on becoming the biggest volume producer of commodity chemicals. However, as the growth of traditional big tonnage commodities — chlorine, caustic soda, polystyrene, and low-density polyethylene — has been perceived to slow, some of Dow's objectives have been reappraised, even though its primary objective of continued growth remains intact.

Dow's CEO, Paul Oreffice, has embarked on a program that represents a fundamental change for the company. Its new objectives may be summarized as follows:

- To diversify toward high value-added products,

- To move downstream toward the customer,

- To increase the role of high value-added products from 25 percent to 35 percent of total sales by 1985,

- To overtake DuPont in rate of growth of sales.

The revised set of objectives is riskier for two reasons: Dow could find itself in competition with some of its customers; and, Dow will be facing a host of new competitors firmly established in the specialty sector.

Nevertheless, here again, the handwriting was clearly on the wall, and management has tried to respond proactively. The "handwriting" in this case came from several sources. First, commodity chemicals were rapidly approaching a state of market saturation. Few new geographic markets remained to be tapped. Second, new competitors were likely to appear in force in the established markets, for example, major oil companies and foreign suppliers who have enormous financial resources to expand downstream. And, third, the continued expansion of commodity chemicals could make overly severe demands of Dow's capital spending for new plants and equipment.

For these primary reasons, Dow elected to diversify its product mix by pushing very hard for new product innovation. As a result, the new set of objectives has spurred the generation of new options, such as possible expansion into agricultural chemicals, ethical pharmaceuticals, hollow-fiber technology, polycarbonates, and genetic engineering.

The basic objective-shift at Dow has also initiated a number of cultural and organizational changes. Among these have been the establishment of a new Innovation Department to speed the development of new products; the setting up of the equivalent of small venture-capital companies to stimulate entrepreneurship; and the development of a range of new marketing and technical service approaches matched uniquely to new products.

Dow is in the fortunate position of being able to finance its downstream efforts with cash generated by its more mature commodity products. Thus, by a shift in traditional objectives, Dow has taken a gamble that aims to position it more advantageously for the long pull. This has not only required a revision of objectives but also a change in attitude toward risk.

Extending the Strategic Loop: The Objective Modification Loop

In chapter 1, the "strategic loop" was described as a process for modifying options in response to comparisons between consequences and objectives. And, indeed, generally we assume that objectives are relatively fixed and unchanging. But this assumption needs to be reexamined.

We have emphasized a number of times that objectives reflect underlying corporate values and organizational cultures — neither easily changed. Nevertheless, in some instances, the strategic loop may be "extended" to use it as much to educate ourselves on objective-setting or modification as on option or candidate strategy selection.

The illustration in the previous section may be a good case in point. In fact, one could argue that Dow has made a shift in *strategies* rather than in *objectives*. Diversifying product mix (by focusing on high value-added products or by moving downstream toward the customer) is simply a new way to continue achieving high rates of growth. On the other hand, one can also claim that the desire to increase sales of high value-added products from 25 percent to 35 percent or to overtake Du Pont in sales growth rates are changes in basic objectives (desired end points) that can be achieved by any number of candidate strategies. Here, the distinction between a shift in strategies (or options) and a shift in goals (or objectives) becomes increasingly obscure and perhaps is not worth pursuing beyond a point. However, a useful clue is contained: an iterative process analogous to the strategic loop might be used to consider objective-modification in parallel with option or strategy selection. In other words, both "ends" of the consequences vs. objective comparison would be candidates for change or selection. Figure 9.11, derived from figure 3.1, includes the objective-setting iterative loop first introduced without elaboration in chapter 3.

Not many students of management have suggested how this might best be done. Objective modification almost certainly involves trial and error ex-

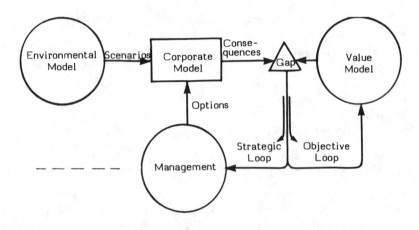

Fig. 9.11. The Objective Loop

perimentation or simulation. James March (1976) of Stanford University is one of the few who has focused his attention on the shortcomings of our value model. He has unequivocally identified one of the glaring weaknesses of what he refers to as the "technology of rationality" — systematic and organized processes for generating and evaluating options or candidate strategies to meet specified objectives. *The weakness is the almost total disregard of how objectives are selected and modified.* Traditional planning and decision-making theories regard option selection and objective setting as if they were completely independent processes. March makes a strong case for using some form of experimentation in the real world — or, to extend his notion, perhaps even a representation, such as a model — to conduct an active search for new objectives. He puts the case very convincingly:

> As a result decisions should not be seen as flowing directly or strictly from a pre-existent set of objectives. Managers who make decisions might well view the function somewhat less as a process of deduction or a process of political negotiation, and somewhat more as a process of gently upsetting preconceptions of what the organization is doing. [P.69]

The notion that underlying assumptions about which an organization should strive for, or that dictate values from which objectives are derived, should periodically be reexamined is not new. What is new is the suggestion that the search for new objectives should be considered an integral part of the planning process. Few, if any, organizations have consciously adopted such a comprehensive view of objective setting. Yet, if planning is to grow beyond the arbitrary limits of strict rationality under which it is now commonly practiced, considerable effort in the future needs to be directed toward the ways value models are created and modified.

REFERENCES

Bell, D. 1979. Multiattribute utility functions. *Management Science* 25: 749-53.

Fishburn, P. 1970. *Utility theory for decision making.* New York: Wiley.

Hammond, P. J. 1976. Changing tasks and coherent dynamic choice. *Review of Economic Studies* 43: 159-73.

Hussey, D. E. 1976. *Corporate planning theory and practice.* Oxford: Pergamon Press.

Kahneman, D., and Tversky, A. 1982. The psychology of preferences. *Scientific American* January: 160-73.

Keeney, R. L., and Raiffa, H. 1976. *Decisions with multiple objectives: Preferences and value tradeoffs.* New York: Wiley.

Lewis, A. A. 1980. *The use of utility in multiattribute utility analysis.* Santa Monica, CA: Rand Corporation, p. 639.

MacGimmon, K. R. 1968. *Decision making among multiple-attribute alternatives: A survey and consolidated approach* (Memorandum RM-4823-ARPA). Santa Monica, CA: Rand Corporation.

March, J. G. 1976. The technology of foolishness. *Ambiguity and choice in organizations.* Norway: Universitets forlaget.

Mischel, W. 1958. Preferences for delayed and immediate reinforcement: An experimental study of cultural observations. *Journal of Abnormal and Social Psychology* 56: 57-61.

Murray, P. X., ed. 1978. *Where we agree.* Boulder, CO: Westview Press.

Ouchi, W. 1981. *Theory Z: How American business can meet the Japanese challenge.* Reading, MA: Addison-Wesley.

Raiffa, H. 1967. *Preferences for multi-attributed alternatives* (RM-5868-DOT/RC). Santa Monica, CA: Rand Corporation.

Rappaport, A. 1981. Selecting strategies that create shareholder value. *Harvard Business Review* May-June: 139-49.

Rivett, P. 1980. *Model building for decision analysis.* New York: Wiley.

Saaty, T. L. 1977. A scaling method for priorities in hierarchical structures. *Journal of Mathematical Psychology* 15: 234-81.

Sage, A. P. 1981. Behavioral and organizational considerations in the design of information systems and processes for planning and decision support. *IEEE Transactions on Systems, Man, and Cybernetics* SMC-11, No.9: 640-78.

Schoemaker, P. J. 1980. *Experiments on decisions under risk: The expected utility hypothesis.* Boston, MA: Martinus Nijhoff.

Tregoe, B. B., and Zimmerman, J. W. 1980. *Top management strategy: What it is and how to make it work.* New York: Simon and Shuster.

Tversky, A., and Kahneman, D. 1981. The framing of decisions and the psychology of choice. *Science* 211: 453-58.

Von Neumann, J., and Morgenstern, O., *Theory of games and economic behavior.* Princeton, NJ: Princeton University Press.

Wessell, M. R. 1976. *The rule of reason: A new approach to corporate litigation.* Reading, MA: Addison-Wesley.

CHAPTER 10
THE POLITICS OF PLANNING

In this chapter we will put methodology aside and focus, instead, on the human aspects of planning. Our primary target is the manager who has been assigned the task of planning in an organization that has not done any strategic planning before, or that pays lip service to strategic planning as the chief executive flies essentially by the "seat of his pants."

The first recommendation we would make to the strategic planner is not to be discouraged because planning — or at least strategic planning — is a very unsettling and unnatural human activity (Morrison and Lee 1978, p. 44). Planning by nature is unsettling because it often introduces information that forces consideration of alternatives that are likely to upset the status quo. Planning may even force reconsideration of the objectives of the organization or at least the unspoken premises on which managers rely for security and guidance. Planners are paid to think and to encourage thinking but, as Sir Joshua Reynolds has said, "Man is the animal who will spare no energy, effort, to avoid the problem of thinking." Planning is unnatural because it tries to inject a longer-term perspective in an environment of short-term rewards. Planning tries to cope with uncertainty when certainty is what managers crave. Planning is unlike most of the other corporate activities necessary for the organization to run at all. It is basically a *discretionary* activity that can be jettisoned at any time without the results becoming apparent for a long time, if ever.

The planning manager is at the mercy of the CEO or the executive team. Without power to influence results directly, planners can only improve decisions that others make. By the very nature of the process, planning can bring into question decisions that have been taken in the past and can throw doubt on the quality of the decisions being taken today. Therefore, planning can be viewed as a threat by some decision makers who would rather not explain why they have taken a particular course of action or how they have evaluated the effectiveness of an option they have selected. According to one's viewpoint, planning is perceived by different individuals and at different times as a necessity, a useful but discretionary activity to be tolerated in times of plenty, a fad, or an unmitigated waste of resources.

As we noted in chapter 1, no one can offer convincing proof that good planning always leads to good outcomes. And, given the uncertainties of external events and the uncertainties in managing a corporation of unpredictable human beings, it is quite conceivable that a good decision, or a string of good decisions (or strategies) will, in retrospect, lead to poor performance — or worse.

Thus, in the final analysis, planning is an act of faith. In essence, planners are the sect of true believers who, with their prescribed liturgy, are trying to convert the unbelievers. Occasionally, the unconverted revolt and get rid of those who try to convert them. To avoid the martyr's fate, we should look carefully at the politics of planning, some aspects of which are universally applicable whatever the nature of the corporation.

UNDERSTANDING THE CULTURE

Planning is unfortunately often considered a staff function; therefore, planners are usually relegated to a section of the tribe whom Anthony Jay (1971) calls "women round the fireplace" — the warriors being the operational managers who bring game to the cave. Lucky is the planner who has been the warrior once and who can show the young warriors the scars of battle. One of the problems young planners experience is that they have no battle scars to show. Battle-scarred operational managers find it hard to be lectured by young business school graduates on the principles of planning: "Those guys have never met a payroll in their life and wouldn't know how!"

The point we are trying to make is that brains and techniques are not enough. They might have been enough if the results of strategic planning were readily evident, providing quick validation by experience for all to see (Hobbs and Heany 1977). But, as we have already indicated, planning is to some extent based on faith, whereas planning methodology derives largely from logic and rationality. Yet, corporate life is only partly rational, and the surface signals can sometimes be very misleading. Understanding the corporate culture is crucial here. Imagine writing a manual for the young trainee who has just joined the corporation. The title of the manual might be "How Does XYZ Really Work?" or "The Art of Survival." This is the task of the much needed corporate anthropologist: to describe the tribal dances (meetings and decision making), the tribal smoke signals (corporate communications), and the tribal power structure. Where in that structure does planning fit?

Are planners the witch doctors, the juju men, praying on the dark fears of the receding economy and proposing a sacrifice of fair maidens to propitiate the gods? Or are planners the court jesters who manage to disguise the unwanted truth in the joviality of court banquets? The manual might describe the career of a young warrior: How is his puberty recognized and celebrated? What sacrifices must he make to gain admission to the Council of the Elders? Is there a Bar or a Bat Mitzvah? Or a Confirmation? How do the smoke signals work? In one very large corporation where promotions came almost always from the inside, the new planning manager was brought from the outside and (horrors!) from another industry. He was appalled by the antiquity of the planning methods used and called a meeting of the operational managers to give them a lecture on how to do it. At the end of the meeting, every one of the managers attending approached the speaker and warmly thanked him for an outstanding contribution to their perceptions of planning. The newcomer was delighted because no one told him that, in the culture of that particular corporation, such profuse reactions were the kiss of death, saying, in effect, "You really made an ass of yourself, didn't you?" Instead, the proper accolade would have been a wink, a nod, or a remark such as, "You really would like us to swallow all that drivel?"

Turning to the corporate power structure, the questions that the manual might address are: Who are the senior elders that count? How do the power alliances work? What are the profiles of interest and attention of the senior people? How did they arrive at the position they hold today? What successes (and disasters) might have been responsible for their current power standing? What career prospects lie in front of them? Where would they move if blocked? And, increasingly, what might be their second career upon retirement?

A very important part of the corporate culture for the planner is the degree of formal support required for any statement made to senior executives. This corporate characteristic bears directly on the problem of establishing validation and credibility of any information sources or models that may be used. Before a planner can be truly effective (that is, get beyond the paper shuffling stage), he or she must spend time on the analysis of the corporate culture. This is because he or she, of all people, may have to modify that culture by helping executives to extend their time horizons or to deal explicitly with the uncertainties of the external environment. Only then can one feel confident of understanding the layout of the "jungle" well enough to plot one's own strategy. The long-term objective of that strategy should be to build the strategic planning competence of operational managers.

PLANNING BY MANAGERS

The commanders on the corporate battlefield are the operational managers. They are the decision makers, and they receive credit or blame for operational results. If the unit is truly a strategic business unit, they are responsible for the results of the strategy they choose to adopt. In that sense they are the real planners, considering alternative courses of action in the light of alternative perceptions of the external environment and the consequences of candidate strategies. The task of the planner is to assist managers in making better decisions. Managers can choose whether to take advice or even whether to listen to it.

An interesting difference exists in the treatment of intelligence (or, more generally, information about the external environment) by the German army vis-à-vis the U.S. army. In the organization and doctrine of the German army, the general staff has exceptional influence and prestige. General staff officers are the planners par excellence, bred and weaned on planning which constitutes their whole career. At each major unit level, whether it is the division or the army corps, the operational commander and the general staff officer work as twins. If the commander is disabled, his general staff alter ego takes over. Promotions and careers of general staff officers proceed on parallel yet distinct channels from the rest of the army. In the U.S. army, the operations staff reports to the operational commander. He is in full control, determining the staff officer's promotions and prospects. Given that difference in handling, one would assume that the German commander would be expected to give more weight to information provided by the general staff officers than his U.S. counterpart. That's where the surprise occurs — the German commander does not have to. He can disregard it. He does not even have to listen to it, and he can make his own estimates on what the enemy is up to. In contrast, the U.S. army doctrine prescribes that the U.S. commander listen and pay attention to the appraisal of his G.2 intelligence expert.

The German practice stems from the principle that the commander is responsible for both the decision *and* the information on which the decision has been based. He cannot blame bad advice for a lack of success. Perhaps the German principle of undivided responsibility is to be preferred — it avoids the "headquarters ought to get the planners off my back" complaints. But it is a humiliating experience for the planner not to be consulted in the process of decision making. We know of a corporation where the planners may find out about the next major strategic move by encountering, in the elevator, the pilot of the CEO. "Where are you flying, Joe?" they ask. "Oh, Peru," is the answer. Then the planners have a meeting. "Why the hell would the old man want to fly to Peru? What's he up to this time?" They do this because, when he comes back, they often have a lot of mopping up to do, trying to figure out how to meet the commitments made by the CEO while he was in Peru.

The irony of the story is that the CEO who does not consult his planners may represent the nearly perfect situation — the CEO is both the planner and the chief executor of the plans. The situation could be even better if the

CEO made better use of the planners. But if he is comfortable in the mode of operation just described, so be it. The goose is his. Perhaps, in his judgment, the planners cannot contribute much to the quality of the decision making. Therefore, one of the tasks the planner might set is to improve the quality of decisions being made through consultation. That should be a part of his or her strategy.

NEED FOR A STRATEGY OF PLANNING

Well before helping managers evaluate alternative strategies for a corporation, the planner should set his or her own planning strategy (Amara and Lipinski 1974; Kotter and Schlesinger 1979; Naylor and Neva 1979; Rothschild 1980). The strategic knobs of the planner are:

- Scope of the proposed planning,
- Degree of sophistication to be used in the planning process,
- Development of a favorable climate,
- Development of the network of planners within the corporation,
- Development of contacts outside the corporation.

The scenarios that the planner will use should contain:

- An appraisal of the budgetary allowance for planning,
- Manpower that might be available,
- Current and future support for planning,
- Expected shifts in senior management positions,
- Expected corporate organizational changes.

We will now try to connect strategy components to the scenarios.

Scope

It is best to start small. The planner should look for an operation that, in a reasonably short time, might benefit from a systematic application of planning. Very likely, it will not be a situation calling for strategic planning. No matter. The planner should try to help the managers involved in the solution of a current problem. Hopefully, the result will be operationally convincing proof that the planner is (1) not an egghead but can actually contribute to the bottom line, and (2) a potential ally (as long as most of the credit accrues to the manager responsible for the operation). As part of the planning strategy, a sequence of such assistance programs should be established, relying as much as possible on each manager's word of mouth in advertising the planner's usefulness.

Sophistication

Sophistication frightens people. Even if the concept employed is sophisticated, it must be presented as very simple. The notion of "a common sense approach" goes well with managers. And when the adjective "common sense" is combined with "systematic," most managers will become believers. If someone with a good reputation within the corporation has previously used some of the techniques the planner proposes to employ, ample credit should be given to his or her missionary work.

Uncertainty must be introduced slowly and in small doses. Movement should be from a central forecast, to the central forecast plus a deviation on either side, and then an outline of the effect of these deviations on operational results. Here, it may be best to talk to the financial people to use their opinion about the extent of deviations. Sometime later, the concept of an alternative strategy should be introduced.

In the next stage (probably at the next annual planning exercise), one can replace deviations from the central forecast with two side scenarios and arrange for them to have nontrivial probabilities, for example, each 20 percent. This is a preliminary step so that, at the next opportunity — perhaps a year later — one might structure three scenarios that are equally probable.

At a much later stage of advanced planning, it might become possible to start modeling the corporation by assembling operational managers and having them attempt to model their operation verbally. The planner might even get to the point when the managers themselves will begin to perceive that some of their descriptions can be translated into relations that might later lead to the development of a model.

Favorable Climate

We assume that a corporate planner already has a "guardian angel" who is sympathetic to his or her efforts. One should use such an individual to gauge the probable reception of whatever is the next step in planning strategy. The planner should not be satisfied with one sponsor but try to enlarge the receptive circle to two or more senior managers, eventually aiming at creating a strategic planning committee of which he or she might be the secretary. To preserve the climate of support, one should be very careful not to "bomb" senior executives with memoranda, however pertinent these may seem. It is much better to pass along the document to one carefully selected executive and let him or her pass it on judiciously to those who might read it.

Network of Planners

Corporate planners rely on divisional planners to: (1) prepare scenario components that are relevant to the divisions but not to the corporation as a whole; (2) outline the appropriate candidate strategies (main and alternate) for their operation; and (3) help develop answers to the questions so often posed by senior management. In addition, divisional planners can be the advance listening posts warning of problems that might need corporate attention and that they themselves feel unable to mention or address. It is obvious that the corporate planner must treat many such signals with the utmost confidentiality, and that an experienced planner always knows much more about divisional operations and politics than he or she is ever able to communicate to corporate management. Deciding what to communicate and what to suppress is a skill that comes with experience.

Outside Contacts

Corporations, particularly those having a strong internal culture, are in danger of mentally isolating themselves from the world outside. Senior managers begin to think alike, talk alike, and see the outside world through the same dark (rarely rose-tinted) glasses. "The government is out to get us, the unions are impossible, the competitors' latest prices are downright irresponsible!" Also, the procedures of some corporations have become so sanctified by long usage that strategic planning is identified with the ritual of budget reviews: departmental, divisional, group — each review taking a large amount of time to prepare and, if bounced back, to resubmit.

A strategic planner in a corporation is often thrust into a position of questioning the perceptions of senior executives and the process by which the budgets are set. Because of his or her position within planning, the planner might appear to an outsider (for example, to a staff member in a regulatory agency) to be almost "human" and capable of listening to the regulator's gripes. If the planner is careful (by limiting discussions to the future) and skillful in human relations, he or she will have contacts in several government bodies: the young staffers on the Hill, lawyers in Justice, engineers in the Energy Department. If he or she is an exceptionally able communicator, his or her acquaintances will include individuals in public interest groups whom senior executives might classify as the Devil's own kinfolk.

In talking to other planners, particularly in different industries, the planner will encounter a new set of perceptions about the world at large. He or she might not be able to communicate the changed perceptions immediately to senior executives, but, recognizing the dangerous gap between the newly acquired understanding and the "reality" as viewed internally, the planner might begin to close the gap.

From contacts with other planners and from attending professional meetings, he or she will learn about planning practices of other corporations. As a result, the planner might be able to slowly divert the corporation away from using the budgeting process as a substitute for planning. As we have seen in chapter 5, budgeting is only the last step in translating a candidate strategy into an actual strategy. The sequence should be: (1) candidate strategy, (2) operational plan, (3) the budget. Instead, very often, the preparation of the budget consumes 99 percent of the manager's time because emphasis is placed on careful aggregation of departmental operations (sales, sales expenses, production, etc.), while the strategic part of planning is given short shrift — often embodied in a few-sentence preamble to the entire document.

FITTING STRATEGIC PLANNING INTO THE CORPORATE ORGANIZATIONAL STRUCTURE

There is perhaps no more controversial set of questions about the strategic planning function than that concerning its position within the corporate organization. Should it exist as a separate entity? If so, should it report to the CEO, a committee, or a line or staff officer? And what should be the relationship of corporate planning to the planning function at the business unit level?

No simple answers can be given. In practice, virtually every possible arrangement and combination have been tried with little or no consensus about which is best. This is because each arrangement has its own share of advantages and disadvantages reflecting the following basic dilemma: If planning is (as ideally it should be) part of each line organization, then enormous pressures build to focus attention on primarily short-term or operational issues that subordinate its principal function. On the other hand, if planning is split off as a separate staff activity, then it stands a high risk of being emasculated by losing its credibility with line managers.

At the corporate level, the three principal organizational choices boil down to the following: attaching planning to the CEO, to the Chief Financial Officer, or to a planning committee. Of these, attaching strategic planning to the office of the CEO is perhaps the preferred choice. It clearly provides planning the requisite stature and visibility, particularly if the CEO in fact embraces it as a major tool for shaping the future of the corporation. Success, however, depends critically on the nature of the "chemistry" between the CEO and the chief planning officer. Ironically, if and when that relationship sours, there is no greater "fall from grace" or isolation than when strategic planning has been attached to the CEO.

Second best is the chief financial officer. Here, the strategic planning activity can have direct influence on the life blood of any corporate enterprise, i.e., budgeting, particularly capital budgeting. And, in some instances, it works that way. Too often, however, the understandably narrow and usually short-term financial view of the chief financial officer reduces the strategic planning activity to no more than a "number-grinding" or "bean-counting" budget preparation exercise.

Perhaps the least desirable arrangement is attaching the planning activity to a planning committee. Such committees generally include several staff and all major line officers and is chaired by the CEO. Like any committee, it suffers from a lack of continuing effort; a separation of operational and planning issues; and, unless the CEO plays an unusually dominant role, a diffusion of responsibility that undercuts the taking of any strong initiatives.

Another set of organizational choices concerns the relationship between planning at corporate and planning at business unit levels. Almost everyone agrees that planning must have both a "bottom-up" and "top-down" component. But what about the relative strengths of these components? Should "corporate" be essentially a collector, assembler, or facilitator of plans generated by the business units, or should it be more?

Although many corporations still have rather perfunctory corporate planning functions, as the economy and the competitive environment have tightened, the trend for "corporate" to intervene very strongly in the flow of information up from the line has grown considerably. This may first take the form of providing the business units a set of guideline forecasts on key macrovariables likely to impact all business units. Or, at the next stage, it may take the form of "limits" on capital expenditure. Or, "corporate" might require the evaluation of any strategic option by a business unit against a set of scenarios rather than the presentation of a single, "expected-case" analysis. In other words, the role of "corporate" as an assembler, or even as a facilitator, appears to be giving way to its role as a strong initiator — developing an overall framework within which plans by individual business units are generated and evaluated.

RELATING STRATEGIC PLANNING TO OTHER STAFF FUNCTIONS

When strategic planning is finally nested in the organizational structure, to be effective, it should also develop information linkages to a wide variety of other staff functions. To date, very little effort has been directed by most corporations toward streamlining staff activities that should rely on a comprehensive and uniform base of strategic environmental information. The most important corporate activities that have "long tails" into the future are capital budgeting, diversification and acquisition, issues management, human resources, research and development, and product planning.

The capital budgeting activity is usually the spur for initiating the systematic collection and analysis of corporate-wide environmental information. A principal early user of such information has been the diversification and acquisition function — partly because the corporate planning manager and the diversification and acquisitions manager normally report to the same senior staff officer. In recent years, "issues management" has come into vogue, usually as an extension of the public affairs or government relations function. Although dealing with information almost identical to that collected for the generation of environmental scenarios, few corporations have found effective ways to integrate these activities. And the same errors are likely to be repeated as the human resource function tools up to play a far more prominent role in the strategic planning process. But perhaps the biggest strategic information gap exists in R&D and product planning, where information about long-range shifts in consumer expenditure patterns is seldom factored into resource allocation choices.

Enormous payoffs are possible and will likely be realized in the future as corporations learn how to "cross link" now disparate functions sharing a common information base.

OCCUPATIONAL HAZARDS FOR THE PLANNER

Every human activity has its unique set of hazards, and planning is no exception (Hussey 1976, p. 301; Steiner 1979, p. 287). Prudence demands that such hazards be clearly acknowledged and, since most can be fatal to the planner, studiously avoided. We believe that the most common are:

1. Promising too much. The basic difficulty is that the "bottom line" for planning is always off in the future, and it is not usually crisply defined. Promising too little can also be fatal.

2. Getting "hung up" on paper. Paper often becomes the planner's "security blanket." Generally, however, the planner's effectiveness is inversely correlated with the amount of paper generated or flowing through his or her office.

3. Getting "hung up" on methodology. Methodology can be effective in developing credibility for such questions as: Does it add up? Is it sound? It cannot provide answers to the critical question: Does it feel right?

4. Losing touch with the CEO. Having the backing of the CEO has almost become the planner's cliché. The trouble is that it is still true.

5. Losing touch with the line. Even though a planner may survive for a while without the support of line managers, ultimately the loss of such support will lead to loss of touch with the CEO.

6. Not answering the "so what" questions. Using a vacuum-cleaner approach to information acquisition will only serve the planner well the first year. The second year, he or she will be asked: So what? What relevance does the information have to choices that I am now considering?

7. Bringing back the conventional wisdom. The CEO and line have a right to expect considerable "value added" to the information they already have. If this expectation is not met, the planner's value is correspondingly perceived.

8. Using the planning office as a stepping stone. It is not unusual for promising staff to be assigned to the planning office for a specified period. If the office is viewed as a resting place or a launching pad for other, more important activities, its role is doomed from the outset.

9. Perpetuating a planning facade. Many corporations retain all the output trappings of a planning activity without the substance, dedication, and resources to have it exercise any perceptible influence on corporate choices. In such instances, planning, to paraphrase and extend Peter Drucker, is "not a respectable human activity."

10. "Crossing up" related staff functions. The planning activity is an equal among equals. If its sister activities begin to view it as "more equal than themselves," its effectiveness with the CEO and line will be seriously impaired.

REFERENCES

Amara, R., and Lipinski, A. 1974. *Strategic planning: Penetrating the corporate barriers.* Menlo Park, CA: Institute for the Future.

Bower, M., and Walton, C. L. 1973. Gearing a business to the future. *Challenge to Leadership.* New York: Conference Board.

Drucker, P. F. 1954. *The practice of management.* New York: Harper and Row.

Hobbs, J. M., and Heany, D. F. 1977. Coupling strategy to operating plans. *Harvard Business Review* May-June: 119-26.

Hussey, D. E. 1976. *Corporate planning theory and practice.* Oxford: Pergamon Press.

Jay, A. 1971. *The corporation man.* New York: Random House.

Kotter, J. P., and Schlesinger, L. A. 1979. Choosing strategies for change. *Harvard Business Review* March-April: 106-14.

Morrison, J. R., and Lee, J. G. 1978. Barriers to strategic thinking. *Strategic leadership: The challenge to chairmen.* London: McKinsey and Company.

Naylor, T. H., and Neva, K. 1979. The planning audit. *Managerial Planning* September/October: 31-37.

Rothschild, W. E. 1980. How to ensure the continued growth of strategic planning. *Journal of Business Strategy* Summer: 11-18.

Steiner, G. A. 1979. *Strategic planning: What every manager must know.* New York: Free Press.

CHAPTER 11
THE FUTURE OF MANAGEMENT:
TEN SHAPERS OF MANAGEMENT
IN THE 1980s

The remaining element of our strategic planning framework, which we have not examined in detail, is "management" (see either figure 1.12 or figure 3.12). It is the keystone, the only element straddling the horizontal line between the upper and lower "thinking" and "acting" halves of our framework. Management is the central element at the intersection of our strategic and tactical feedback loops.

It is not our intent to review in detail the considerable body of literature and understandings on the function of modern management that have been accumulated over the past 50 years (Cyert and March 1963; Drucker 1954; McGregor 1960). Instead, we would like to provide some clues on how the management function may be changing in the next decade due to the influence of a number of social, economic, and technological developments. More specifically, we want to explore how changes in the management function may influence the practice of strategic planning in the 1980s.

Just what does a manager do? And how precisely do we distinguish between good or excellent managers and poor or marginal ones? These are simple enough questions on the surface; it is only when one attempts to answer such questions in depth that doubts arise about the accuracy and validity of any general response. Fortunately, such questions have been posed many times before. Among those seeking answers or, rather, improved understanding have been a number of very able students of management (Braybooke and Lindblom 1963; Sayles 1969; Simon 1957). Unfortunately, surprising though it may seem, we still appear to be a long way from being able to specify clearly "what constitutes the job of management" (Mintzberg 1973). And, as has been pointed out many times, if we cannot define the essential elements of a manager's job in terms of what he or she *really* does that makes for success or failure, how can we possibly train managers, improve management decision making, design management information systems, or make organizations more effective? To this list of questions must also be added another: under the circumstances, how can we speculate intelligently about the future of management?

The only sensible way to approach the problem is much in the way an airborne reconnaissance mission would approach the mapping of unfamiliar terrain: look for patterns and distinctive features from a variety of altitudes and directions. And this is what we will try to do here.

DIFFERENT WAYS OF PORTRAYING WHAT A MANAGER DOES

A wide number of ways have been developed to get at the essentials of what a manager does. We will briefly examine three, deliberately omitting much detail.

The classical textbook approach used in one form or another for decades might be labeled the "top-down" method. Generally, this method pictures the manager as a planner, organizer, coordinator, and decision maker. It derives in part from the "great man" or the "captain of industry" anecdotal school that probably had its greatest currency in the earlier part of this century, with its strong emphasis on leadership qualities and style (and perhaps we are coming back to these notions, at least in the public sector). It is not a bad "model" of management *functions*. It simply is terribly narrow in conveying much understanding of the limitations of the power wielded, of how a real world manager operates, and how such a manager views his or her job. For example, it would be almost impossible for any manager to allocate time in accordance with the categorization provided. Management issues simply do not present themselves in such neatly distinct packages, requiring just "planning" or "coordinating" skills. What is more, the functions smack more of how a manager is perceived by others to operate, or how a manager thinks he or she should operate. In other words, it draws a fairly idealized picture of the manager that seems diminishingly useful and increasingly at odds with the practical world. A very senior vice president describes his function as that of trying to stir the olive at the bottom of a martini glass with the aid of several straws stuck together. Most of his effort results only in the bending of the chain of straws, but nothing at all happens to the olive.

Somewhat at the other end of the scale in characterizing management's job is the so-called "work activity" school or, as we prefer to label it, the "bottom-up" approach. A sensible and direct way of getting at the question "what does a manager really do?" is to make direct observations of management *activity*, to collect information recorded in diaries, or to analyze work records and documents. And, in the last decade or two, a moderate number of laudable efforts have been made in the United States and elsewhere to measure empirically the allocation of selected managers' time during "typical" work days or work weeks (Mintzberg 1973). The results of such efforts are not purported to be based on statistical measures of activity but, rather, resemble more the empirical way in which an anthropologist might proceed to characterize and describe activities of an unfamiliar group or foreign culture. Among the most useful insights is, for example, the very large portion of time (50 to 70 percent) that managers typically devote to face-to-face meetings with individuals or groups for whatever purpose. Here again, however, such particular "cuts" of management can provide only a limited glimpse of what a manager does.

Somewhere between the extremes outlined is the picture of the manager in various *roles* (Mintzberg 1975, p. 54). Perhaps one of the more useful categorizations is the manager portrayed in an informational role — collecting, analyzing, and disseminating information of all kinds; the manager in a decisional role — allocating organizational resources to achieve desired goals; and in an interpersonal role — acting as employer, colleague, representative, role model, motivator, and so forth. Again, such roles yield another set of perspectives on management, overlapping to some extent the classical functions (e.g., decision maker) and work activity categories (e.g., "meets with others") described earlier. At the same time, each approach adds a somewhat unique component to the management mosaic that emerges.

A DYNAMIC VIEW OF MANAGEMENT

Any attempt at the general portrayal of the "management mosaic" is fraught with dangers of misrepresentation. Often what has been done by some investigators is to portray the "myth" vs. "reality" or the "theory" vs. "practice" of management. Such representations have called attention to long-existing inconsistencies in our views of management. However, the basic shortcoming in so doing is the portrayal of the results of empirical observations, with all their inherent limitations, as "fact," with complementary behavior labeled as "theory" or "myth." A more accurate representation may be one that emphasizes the dynamic tension in which management necessarily operates. Loosely, this may be the "yin and yang" or the "left and right" hemisphere manifestations of management behavior. Thus, for example, managers may on some occasions (and perhaps as circumstances dictate) be fairly reflective and systematic in approaching an issue (this is a precondition of strategic planning), even though the normal tendency is to respond to the inevitable pressures of the environment and to operate in an interrupt-driven, action-oriented mode (the tactical lower half in figure 1.3). It seems more accurate to recognize the necessity for managers to alternate between these opposing styles of operation and behavior than to characterize one as "fact" and the other as "myth" — almost in the same sense as "right" and "wrong." Similar observations may be made about the kind of information that managers seek (aggregated vs. collecting odds and ends), the type of data that managers prefer to work with (hard vs. soft), and the dominant view that managers hold of their profession (science vs. art form).

MANAGEMENT SHAPERS

To begin overflying our symbolic region "U.S. Management in the 1980s," we will start at fairly high altitudes to try to discern the macro ("big picture") features first. Four, in particular, stand out that frame the region of interest (Amara 1978): *limits* dictated by slower economic (2 to 3 percent per year), energy (1 to 2 percent per year), and personal consumption (2 to 3 percent per year) growth; *participation* by individuals and groups "wanting in" on decisions affecting their lives; *complexity* from the greater interactions of everything bumping up against everything else; and *change* accelerating to make history a less useful guide to the present and future. On both the philosophical and pragmatic levels, the implications for U.S. management (as well as for society generally) in the 1980s can be profound. The general slowing down of growth (including growth of many traditional markets) means that "not all boats will rise with the rising tide." Thus, management competence will be a more critical factor in making more difficult choices to get an edge on the competition. Growing participation by various groups and individuals will be reflected in the demand to share power that, in some instances in the past, has been considered the exclusive prerogative of management. As complexity multiplies faster than our ability to comprehend it, meaningful information feedback loops must be tighter for closer monitoring of essentials and quicker response to real problems. But, at the same time as the pace of change quickens, explicit consideration and evaluation of the options and consequences (e.g., planning) become crucial.

Coming down to a more micro level, we can focus on ten major shapers of management and their implications to strategic planning. The first set of five are basically demographic, labor force, and economic in nature; the second set of five can be characterized as perceptual, life-style, and social.

Demographic, Labor Force, Economic

Middle management "crunch." By 1990, competition for middle-level nontechnical positions will rise dramatically. In the 1960s approximately ten workers vied for each middle management supervisory position. But in the late 1980s, the ratio will be about 20 to 1, and wage rates will rise much more slowly for this group than for professional technical positions.

The reasons for the crunch are not difficult to identify: movement of the baby bulge group, born between 1945 and 1965, in unprecedented numbers into candidacy for management positions; delayed retirement of present management incumbents, largely in response to persistent inflation; generally slower economic growth, limiting the development of new management opportunities; and the downward shifting of responsibility, ultimately perhaps to self-managed worker teams.

Such circumstances cry out for new management structures that can accommodate unprecedented numbers of potential managers without overburdening productivity. Flattening of organizational pyramids, creation of smaller, autonomous work groups, and development of "working" manager positions through job redesign and restructuring are some of the ways to ease the expected crunch.

Shrinking supply of entry-level workers. The bottom of the organizational pyramid will suffer from shrinking labor force growth. Such growth during the late 1980s is expected to be about half that of the 1970s. One reason is the rapid decline in fertility rates since 1965. Another is the slowdown in the growth of labor force participation rates for women, owing to the drop-off in the number of women in their early twenties (traditionally the group with the highest participation rates), and the restrictive effects of the "echo" baby boom expected during the next few years. We do not know whether high unemployment will ease the shortage — probably not, because many entry-level jobs are not attractive to the bulk of the unemployed.

Because wages will inevitably rise faster for such entry-level positions and turnover rates can be expected to be higher than normal, there will be strong incentives for substitution of capital for expensive or poorly qualified labor. Such capital investments will clearly reshape the structure and organization of jobs, as well as of management functions associated with them. This substitution is likely to have the greatest impact on employees and management in commerce, banking, public administration, and office work in general.

Stress on productivity. A primary incentive for capital substitution for labor is productivity growth. At lower levels and routine jobs, this applies equally to managers. Little question remains that the resumption of productivity gains will become a major management focus of the 1980s since the United States has fallen to the bottom of the list in productivity gains among developed countries.

Considerable premium will be placed on two aspects of productivity vis-à-vis management. The first is management as a catalyst — indeed, as an innovator — in spurring productivity gains, particularly in the growing service and information-handling sectors of the economy. The second is management in its own right in developing new management structures, roles, and practices that enhance appreciably the productivity of management itself. Central here may be the redesign of the entire information environment of the manager, for which a deeper understanding of "what constitutes management" could yield large payoffs.

Shifting economies of scale. What makes productivity gains so elusive in part is the rapidly changing work environment in which management operates. In addition to the changing physical environment, impacted by technological innovation, the regulatory and information environments are changing just as rapidly. The result is that, often, a dramatic shift will take place in economies of scale for particular businesses.

In many if not most cases, such shifts will be toward providing greater competitive advantage to the smaller, more decentralized, more flexible organizational management unit. This may be particularly true where energy may be generated and utilized locally (e.g., cogeneration), where prior restrictions on entry to particular markets are being lifted (e.g., communication services), or where differential access to information and human resources of larger organizations compared to smaller organizations may be diminished (e.g., research and development). Also, new industries will grow to provide specialized services (such as strategic planning models, etc.) to small companies. Indeed, in such instances, "smaller may be more efficient as well as more beautiful," particularly if a small company pattern of communications proves to be more efficient. Another driving force here may be the desire to achieve more understanding and manageability, translatable into more effective decision making and control in the long run.

International competition. Another important factor governing the substitution of capital for labor is the changing competitive position of the United States with respect to other countries on a range of products. Such shifts are due, of course, to long-term differences in productivity growth and unit labor costs, modulated by specific trade and government policy measures.

Though protectionism may delay the inevitable in the early 1980s, the basic vulnerability of our labor-intensive and low-technology industries must be addressed. There are three courses of action: protectionism for national security or political purposes; aggressive redesign of production processes through large capital investments; or gradual phase-out of vulnerable industries through operation of the marketplace. If the latter two courses of action are followed, management of human resources will emerge as the crucial factor.

Perceptual, Life-style, Social

Redefining "place of work." With the rapid introduction of computer communications capabilities into the office and work environment of the 1980s, coupled with the continued growth of the information sector, our notions of what constitutes the "place of work" need to be reexamined. Fellow workers need not be co-located, the home/office boundary need no longer remain sacrosanct, and a variety of work styles — part-time, consultants, "in and outers" into the workplace — can be accommodated.

The implications for management are many: the need for new coordinating mechanisms, the need for more explicit measures of work performance, and the need to set up overlapping communication networks. But perhaps the most important consequence stems from the requirement both to orchestrate more consciously face-to-face contacts that would not otherwise occur and to develop substitutes for face-to-face contacts (video, slow-scan, audio, computer conferencing) that are at least as good as, if not better than, personal contact.

New communication patterns. The revolution in the communication environment will permeate nearly all management roles. In particular, managers will find themselves in more direct contact with members of boards (as directors involve themselves more intimately in corporate affairs), will have to learn to deal with "neutral" parties (e.g., ombudsmen) overseeing employee relationships, and will be contacted by a variety of external groups (including representatives of the various media).

This new "fishbowl" communication environment can have a number of desirable consequences. We have seen how the development of strategic models can operate to expand the number of participants in strategy generation, evaluation, and selection. High priority will be placed on explicitness in decision making. The existence of multiplicity of networks — horizontal, level jumping, up as well as down — can make for improved organizational stability. Moreover, employee motivation may be more readily aroused because of the opportunities for greater organizational environment.

Evolving participation needs. The changing employee information and communication environment is part of the larger, changing "participatory" environment. Continued skepticism about the responsiveness of large institutions, the desire for a return to human scale in personal relations, and the continuing search for new mediating structures by an activist generation provide a backdrop for increasing participation by individuals in decisions that affect their (work) lives.

Inevitably, the result is a changing role for the manager, one in which identification of options and eventual decision making are more shared without, at the same time, abdicating responsibility for outcomes. Some have used the phrase "steering rather than driving" (Cleveland 1972) to convey a sense of the changed relationship of the manager to his or her group. Others have used the term "orchestrating." The changes go to the heart of our redefinition of leadership vis-à-vis the evolving needs and perceptions of employees in the 1980s.

Diversity of values and life-styles. The focus on human resources does not, however, end with new communication patterns and shared decision making. Management must also deal with an enormous variety of values and life-styles.

The particularly notable characteristics of the work force that are most relevant here are that a majority of all households will be two-wage-earner households, the desire for meaningful work will become even more pronounced, and increasing premium will be placed on individual competence and self-reliance. Managing human resources in this kind of environment must necessarily focus attention sharply on employee motivation, recognize the growing importance of nonecomonic rewards, and must be sensitively tuned to individual differences and needs.

Subjective judgments. The quality and use of judgment have always been a critical determinant of management peformance. Little doubt exists that the quality of judgment will become an even more crucial factor in determining success or failure of management.

The reasons, again, are not difficult to identify. As the capability for collecting, analyzing, and processing hard data becomes more widespread, differences in the quality of choices will depend more critically on the evaluation of soft information. The information level at which the manager operates is raised, and achievement of a competitive edge depends more heavily on the nonquantifiable skills and capabilities. Choosing objectives well, questioning assumptions, and extending the range of alternatives for evaluation (i.e., long- and short-term planning) become the most valuable coins of the management realm.

OTHER CONSIDERATIONS AFFECTING THE MANAGEMENT ENVIRONMENT

Although the factors identified will be among the most important shapers of management in the next decade, other factors may also play roles that have not yet been considered. We would like now to introduce several of these — some highly speculative — by examining briefly the management environment suggested by the primary roles introduced earlier: informational, decisional, and interpersonal.

Informational

Few changes surrounding the management function will match those occurring in the information environment. Some of these are fairly apparent even now, while the groundwork for others is just being laid. Described below are a few initial "beachheads" that may eventually be joined into truly integrated information networks serving management.

Perhaps the most imminent are the changes in our notion of "the office" — its structure, practices, and workflows. The principal driving forces here are the "push" of powerful technologies at attractive costs and the "pull" of increasing labor force expectations for job upgrading and enrichment. The automated office will almost certainly become a reality in many parts of U.S. business in the 1980s as a host of recordkeeping, accounting, report writing, and reporting tasks is performed by integrating networks of intelligent terminals, word processors, fax machines, copiers, and electronic mail systems.

The revolution in the information environment will not, however, be restricted to the office. Other beachheads for change may appear in activities related to the research and development function. Here, the driving forces stem from the need to stay abreast, to create an environment of high creativity and innovation, and to manage complex projects more efficiently. The information may be generally described as technical, "hard," and quantitative. And the implementing tools are likely to be in the form of data-base access, model building, and computer conferencing systems.

Potentially, the highest payoffs for management, however, exist in changes that may be made in the information environment of top management itself. The principal driving forces here are the high demand on top management stemming from verbal face-to-face contacts and the necessity to rely heavily on personal, "soft," and qualitative inputs. Not only is face-to-face communication time-consuming and expensive, but in many instances it may not be the most effective and efficient mode of interaction. Here, a variety of interpersonal and group conferencing systems will almost surely be used that orchestrate unique features of video, slow-scan, audio, and even computer conferencing systems to best match management needs.

Decisional

Earlier in this chapter was presented a "yin/yang" or "left/right" dynamic representation of opposing tendencies of management functions. We would like now to dwell on similar characteristics of the manager's decisional environment.

One of the errors we have made in the past — and that we may make periodically — is to view management functions in too strictly rationalistic or reductionist terms: collecting information, processing it in accordance with well-specified decision rules, evaluating alternatives, and making decisions that maximize benefits at lowest cost. There is no doubt that we will have increasingly powerful tools at our disposal — decision analysis, risk analysis, interactive modeling, and simulation. And there is no doubt that, at lower management levels, cadres of "business marines" will know very well how to apply these techniques to achieve a stated objective in the shortest, straightest, most direct line.

But overseeing these activities will be ships' captains and their associates scanning the horizon, monitoring for clues, fitting bits and pieces of information, and making judgments on which strategic objectives to pursue based on very incomplete information. The term "satisficing" has been used to acknowledge explicitly that all knowledge is partial, alternatives restricted in scope, and consequences of options poorly understood (Simon 1957). Under the circumstances, the best we can do is select alternatives that are "good enough" or that satisfice. For example, looking for diversification opportunities is different from designing an efficient inventory control system. In the former case, it may be that behavioral characteristics and limitations of the decision maker are more important than the characteristics of the environment in which the decision is made.

Closely related to decision-making style are role and value of information. Since the acquisition of additional information always entails costs of some kind, it is important to know the marginal value of such information in terms of its expected contribution to the "goodness" of a decision. This is easy to say but difficult to do. Measures of the so-called "productivity of information" are key in deciding when to stop collecting or stop analyzing or stop modeling. And, since such measures go to the very heart of the "information vs. understanding" question, they are important determinants of the information support systems that eventually evolve around management.

Interpersonal

Finally, we want to raise some questions about contextual or cultural aspects of management. In the next ten years, we are likely to witness a very large increase in the proportion of female managers, not only in specialist roles such as public affairs, legal, financial, human resources, and planning functions, but increasingly in line positions. What influence is likely to be exerted on the general management function? Are there dominant sex-linked characteristics that will match one sex to the likely environment of the 1980s better than the other? If so, what are these? Or, will the impact be almost negligible?

Another aspect of management is related to differences (and similarities) in public vs. private sector management. Are reputed differences likely to intensify? The usual observation is that public managers operate in organizations where goals and structures are set by others, where time horizons are very short and dominated by political considerations, and where no crisp connections exist to bottom-line measurements of performance (Bower 1977; Neustadt 1960). How significant will such differences be with increasing private sector involvement in public sector issues, with greater public pressure for explicit measures of accountability for government organizations, and with increasing sensitivity of private sector organizations to "public interest" consequences of choices? We suspect distinctions are becoming fuzzier and that management roles and functions in both sectors are becoming more alike.

And, lastly, we want to dwell briefly on one of the more interesting impacts on U.S. management philosophy that derives from differences in national cultures. Here, we would look carefully at the Japanese (or, more generally, Eastern) influence (Ohmae 1982; Pascale and Athos 1981). It is not suggested that U.S. management style will or should slowly gravitate toward the Japanese model of decision making. Cultural differences are too great for any kind of direct transplant. But too much evidence exists that Japanese management style is a key ingredient in sharp productivity and quality control gains made in recent years. And it is not necessarily true, as many of us would like to believe, that such dramatic differences stem primarily from the relative homogeneity of Japanese society and from their associated "workaholic" work ethic. The fact is that the same quantity and quality gains are realized by Japanese companies that manufacture in the United States and the United Kingdom. This suggests that the solution depends more on management than on the labor force. We are not sure about the precise forms in which management changes may evolve. Whatever the directions, we believe that U.S. management and planning practices will reflect far more widespread adoption of strategic planning and strategic management processes using the approaches and tools introduced in earlier chapters.

REFERENCES

Amara, R. 1978. *Five emergent features of U.S. society and their impact on management*, Paper P-60. Menlo Park, CA: Institute for the Future.

Bower, J. L. 1977. Effective public management. *Harvard Business Review* March-April: 131-37.

Braybooke, D., and Lindblom C. E. 1963. *A strategy of decision*. New York: Free Press.

Cleveland, H. 1972. *The future executive*. New York: Harper and Row.

Cyert, R. M., and March, J. G. 1963. *A behavioral theory of the firm*. Englewood Cliffs, NJ: Prentice-Hall.

Drucker, P. F. 1954. *The practice of management*. New York: Harper and Row.

McGregor, D. 1960. *The human side of enterprise*. New York: McGraw-Hill.

Mintzberg, H. 1973. *The nature of managerial work*. New York: Harper and Row.

————. 1975. The manager's job: Folklore and fact. *Harvard Business Review* July-August: 49-61.

————. 1976. Planning on the left side and managing on the right. *Harvard Business Review* July-August: 49-58.

————. 1979. *The structuring of organizations*. Englewood Cliffs, NJ: Prentice-Hall.

Neustadt, R. E. 1960. *Presidential power: The politics of leadership*. New York: Wiley.

Ohmae, K. 1982. The long and short of Japanese planning. *The Wall Street Journal* January 18.

Pascale, R. T., and Athos, A. G. 1981. *The art of Japanese management: Applications for American executives*. New York: Simon and Shuster.

Sayles, L. R. 1969. *Managerial behavior: Administration in complex organizations*. New York: McGraw-Hill.

Simon, H. A. 1957. *Administrative behavior*. New York: Macmillan.

AUTHOR INDEX

SUBJECT INDEX

ABOUT THE AUTHORS

Roy Amara's career spans 30 years of direct experience in business planning. Since 1971, as president and senior research fellow at the Institute for the Future, his work with over one hundred Fortune 500 companies has focused on business forecasting, strategic planning, and corporate decision making. While at SRI International from 1952 to 1970, he was manager, systems engineering laboratory, specializing in the planning and design of information systems for companies drawn from banking, airline, and wholesale/retail trade sectors; executive director, systems sciences division, during which time he organized and shaped one of the first groups applying decision analysis to corporate planning; and vice president of institute programs, responsible for planning and development of all major interdisciplinary research programs including communications, transportation, health, and education. Dr. Amara has published over 50 articles on corporate planning, long-range forecasting, communication and computer networks, and the role of management. He received his B.S. and M.A. degrees from Massachusetts Institute of Technology and Harvard University, respectively, and his Ph.D. in engineering from Stanford University.

Andrew Lipinski began his career 35 years ago in England as a research engineer with Standard Telecommunications Laboratories, an ITT subsidiary. After eight years, he joined Canadian Westinghouse for an eight-year period of line experience where he became a departmental manager. From Canada he emigrated to California to join the planning staff of Lenkurt Electric, which later became a subsidiary of GTE. After six years of corporate planning, he went back to research, joining first the economics division of SRI International and, when the Institute for the Future was formed, the Institute where he concentrates on improving methods of corporate planning. Mr.

Lipinski received B.Sc. and D.I.C. degrees from the City and Guilds College in London. He has published numerous papers on electrical communications, modeling, corporate planning, and futures research. He holds nine patents in the United Kingdom, Canada, and the United States and is listed in the *American Men of Science*.